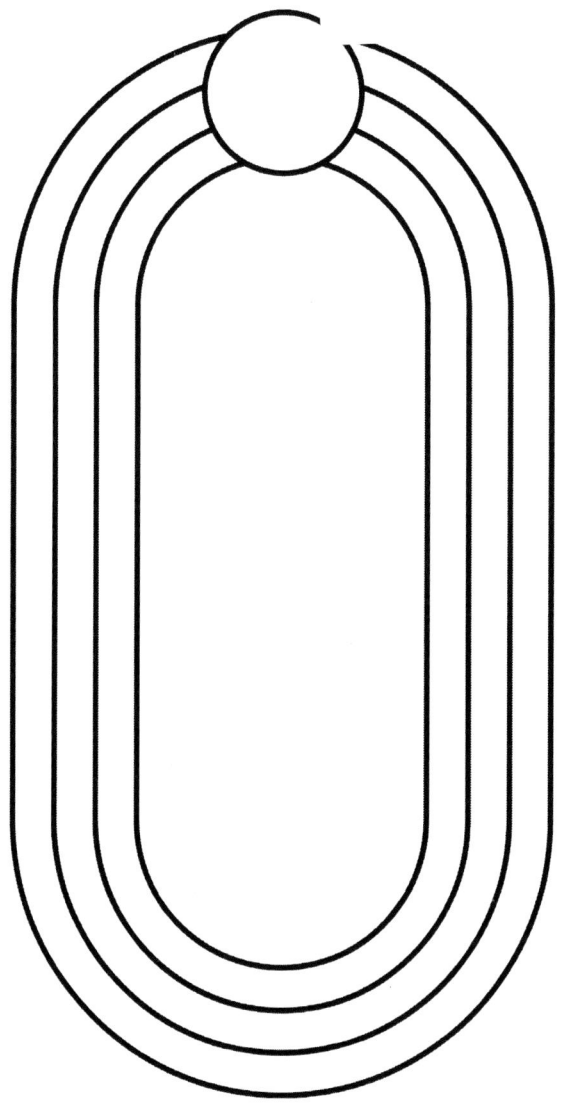

PORTAL

THE ART OF
**CHOOSING
ORGASMIC
PAIN-FREE
BLISSFUL
BIRTH**

YOLANDE NORRIS-CLARK

Copyright @ 2023 Yolande Norris-Clark.

All rights reserved. No part of this publication may be reproduced, distributed, or transmitted in any form or by any means, including photocopying, recording, or other electronic or mechanical methods, without the prior written permission of the copyright owner, except in the case of brief quotations embodied in critical reviews and certain other noncommercial uses permitted by copyright law. For permission requests, write to the publisher, addressed "Attention: Permissions Coordinator."

PAPERBACK: 979-8-9906072-0-0
HARDCOVER: 979-8-9906072-1-7
EBOOK: 979-8-9906072-2-4

Edited by Sophia Zaferes, Alicen Grey, and Olivia Seline.
Front cover image by Yolande Norris-Clark.

Printed in the United States of America.

First printing edition 2023.

Maieutic Books.

For my daughters, Treva, Xanthe, and Margaret (who grew in my womb while I edited the final manuscript),

For my sons, Cedar, Kristjan, Horus, Felix, Cosmo, Ignatius, and Helio,

For the child in my womb,

For every mother.

May you all choose well and wisely.

CONTENTS

Disclaimer 3

Preface 5

Introduction 9
    Allowing Bliss   9
    The Whole Truth   10
    A Personal Introduction   14
    Love Letter   17

Part One: Groundwater

    Chapter One: Renaissance   23
        The Tombs   23
        Migration   25
        The Invitation   28
        Interlude   31
        Integration Questions   36

    Chapter Two: Birthing the Cosmos   37
        Renegade   37
        Quantum Entanglement   42
        The Myth of Pain-Free Birth   47
        Ignatius   49
        The Wrong Kind of Birth   56
        Power and Pain   59
        Why is Birth Painful?   60
        The Structure of Surrender   75
        The Ultimate Edict   76
        Integration Questions   77

    Chapter Three: The Social Engineering of Birth   79
        Breaking Birth   79

    Vestiges of Violence   82
    The Obstetric Dilemma   85
    Embracing the Matrix   91
    Ancestral Medical Dependency   93
    Navigating Trauma   94
    Realming   102
    Curating the Vibration   106
    Integration Questions   107

Chapter Four: Choice and Victim Consciousness   109
    Choose Your Own Adventure   109
    The Drama Triangle   113
    Theatrics and Self-Ownership   119
    The Thrill of Victimhood   123
    Integration Questions   128

Chapter Five: The Proof of True Desire   131
    Found Wanting   131
    Ego and Sacrifice   136
    Arguing for Our Limitations   137
    Exceptional Circumstances   141
    Deservingness and Orgasm   145
    Managing Our Expectations   148
    Integration Questions   150

Chapter Six: Consent and the Architected Universe   151
    The Vortex of Industrial Birth   151
    Spirit and Birth-Place   156
    The Energetics of Birth   159
    Self-Sabotage   162
    Eyes Wide Open   167
    Anything You Desire   170
    Integration Questions   171

Chapter Seven: Birth as Spiritual Technology   173
    The Grace of God   173

Singularity	178
Infinite Choice	181
Religion and Reality Creation	183
Abundance and Virtue	187
Relinquishing Significance	190
The Eye of the Soul	194
Integration Questions	195

Part Two: Wellspring

Chapter Eight: The Ultimate Entheogen	**199**
Kambô	199
Bufo	211
Xanthe	216
Ego Elegy	219
The Spiritual Politics of DMT	223
Feast of Love	227
Integration Questions	229
Chapter Nine: Pilgrimage	**231**
Mother, Nature	231
Annunciation	235
Livestock Management	237
Wild Pregnancy	239
Keys to Freedom	242
Practice	246
Sexual Awakening	250
Nourishment	253
The Seat of the Soul	256
The Shape of Water	261
Energy in Motion	267
Inspiration	272
Earthing	274
Benediction	281
Integration Questions	283

Chapter Ten: Transfiguration — 285

- Simply Birth — 285
- How Birth Works — 286
- Limitations of The Hormonal Blueprint — 288
- Dissociation, Embodiment, and Transcendence — 292
- There is Nothing to Fix — 297
- The Discipline of Surrender — 298
- Riding the Wave — 299
- Eternal Repose — 300
- The Shimmering Now — 301
- Atomic Choice — 306
- Giving Up — 308
- Heaven On Earth — 310
- Integration Questions — 313

Chapter Eleven: Fear and Intuition — 315

- Fear Programming — 315
- Fear, Faith, and Death — 317
- Feeling Fear, Being Brave — 322
- The Tiger — 324
- Fear Dissolution — 327
- What If — 336
- Emergency — 342
- The Relationship Between Fear and Pain — 347
- Suffering is Optional — 350
- Integration Questions — 351

Chapter Twelve: Transmutation — 353

- Fracture — 353
- Healing Pain — 355
- The Science of Suffering — 356
- Descent — 360
- The Function of Dis-Ease — 362
- Heaven on Earth — 365
- Becoming Alive — 368

The Gift of Pain	372
Integration Questions	376
Chapter Thirteen: Integration	377
Helio	377
Continuum	388
Aftermath	390
Denouement	393
Postpartum	396
Sex After Birth	398
Coda	403
Integration Questions	404
Acknowledgements	405
Additional Resources	411
About The Author	413

Hello Dear One,

I am so glad you're here, and I am beyond grateful for your enthusiastic support of the publication of this book, an expression of my divine life purpose: to dispel the myth that childbirth is an ordeal from which we must be "delivered," and to guide women to remembering birth as the catalyst that it is for insight, self-love, healing, and spiritual evolution.

The following link will give you exclusive access to my Wild Mothering Masterclass Series, a seven-part set of powerful transmissions on wild pregnancy, freebirth, obstetric surveillance, and the spirituality of motherhood–my gift to you, in thanks.

With love,

Yolande

Simply scan the QR code below, for instant access.

http://www.yolandenorris-clark.com/portal-podcast-free-gift

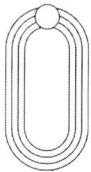

DISCLAIMER

I am not a medical practitioner of any kind. I have no formal medical training, credentials, or qualifications whatsoever. I am most certainly not a regulated or licensed midwife. The various academic credits and certifications I have accrued over the years in coaching, natural health, and movement are secondary to my lived experience as a mother, consultant, and independent birth-witness in service to mothers and babies and the world I love. None of the information shared in this book constitutes medical advice or should be taken as such.

Within these pages I have blatantly cherry-picked various bits and pieces of so-called scientific studies that I find interesting or relevant, adding my own commentary and interpretation but in general, I have no respect for "The Science" or statistics. In fact, I think it's all corrupt, fictionalized sophistry of the highest order.

This book is intended for entertainment purposes only, and constitutes a collection of my highly biased personal opinions, developed over the course of my own lifetime, rooted in my individual, embodied experience, and occasionally inspired by the ideas and philosophies of others, which I have sincerely endeavoured to honour with proper attribution.

Please take what resonates from this work and leave what doesn't. Only you are responsible for your actions and choices. I cannot promise a particular outcome as a result of reading this book, but I can promise that you *will* make choices one way or another, and that your choices will shape your life.

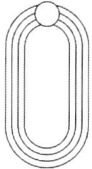

PREFACE

Part memoir, part practical guide, part philosophical treatise, and part poetic transmission, this book is the fruit of joy and ecstasy, but also pain and struggle, alchemized through the intensity of visceral phenomena into what I now know to be the truth about birth, life, suffering, and God.

Portal is not a "childbirth education book," nor is it merely a guide to planning your birth. It includes elements of both genres, but at its core, it is primarily an energetic transfer: a communication channelled from the imaginal cells of my direct experience and ancestral knowing, for those who feel the call to birth themselves into a new framework of being.

Portal is an atlas of embodiment. It is a mystical map, and a mythic playbook for shifting your awareness while pulling at the threads that have stitched up your beliefs about what birth allows, to give you an inlet for decoding and disentangling the old stories. This is the guide to unravelling your heart, body, and consciousness, and releasing everything that came before.

The journey to *Portal* spans the entirety of my life (and all the lives that may have preceded this one), yet the pages that follow came to me at the perfect time, following the cataclysm of 2020, a year of shocking change that brought (among other things) all that I had experienced up to that point into focus and coherence. For so many of us, 2020 represented an overturning of timelines, contracts, visions, trajectories, identities, and beliefs, and like so many people, I moved through what felt like a metamorphosis, and a reclamation of faith.

PORTAL

At the behest of the titanic shift ushered in on the slipstream of a manufactured pandemic, I, like countless others, was gifted insight into the purpose of my existence. Even amid so much displacement and seeming chaos, the work I had been doing all along in the realm of birth started to make sense in a way it hadn't before. Everything was being distilled.

In October of 2020, I answered the call from a magnificent mother to support the homebirth of her twins in Costa Rica. This invitation coincided with what, at the time, seemed like a staggeringly swift descent into totalitarianism in Canada, the country of my birth, where my husband Lee and I had raised our children and spent our entire lives up to that point. The invitation to practice birth-work elsewhere was a sign, and within a week, Lee and I had packed up our house, closed our pottery studio and business for good, and headed with our then-six kids to Central America.

In the rainforest, we were stripped bare, humbled, and reacquainted with the essence of who we were and are. We took all the medicine the jungle had to offer, and I received the message: *You're not done here.* Despite having heard the clear appeal from God, nature, and the soul of our new baby waiting to come through (and mustering up the courage to surrender to the summoning), when I discovered I was pregnant again in March of 2021, I was thrilled, but also terrified.

My ninth pregnancy, following the firewalk of my eighth birth—the birth of our little fire, Ignatius—was very challenging. It wasn't peaceful, or graceful. I had panic attacks and breakdowns throughout, specifically related to the fear I had of giving birth again. In the midst of it all, we left Costa Rica, and moved our family across the border into Nicaragua on foot, dragging our belongings across the tarmac in bins and suitcases.

Given my background in birthwork, I understand that stress during pregnancy is a significant factor in how a birth will play out, and I was genuinely scared of the birth process for that reason too. Despite my vast experience as a birthing mother, I felt tender and innocent and petrified (which perhaps you can relate to, as you begin this book).

I was also forty years old—a "geriatric mother" according to the medical community—not to mention tired and very out of shape (in all the ways). Beyond the obvious fearmongering and the talk of safety and risk, however, the deeper dread I felt about myself and my capacity was rooted in the thought that *friction and tension is all I know.*

Much of my pregnancy felt like a negotiation. *Please God, just let it not be terrible.* As you will discover in the coming pages, it was *not* terrible. It was, as it turns out, the most expansive, beautiful, divine, and blissful experience of my life thus far.

We are here for a reason—each of us. You and I have been called to this planet now for a profound spiritual purpose, and our children are the healers, warriors, and torchbearers. There is so much more available to us in birth, and life, than we have been led to believe, and the possibility to choose it all, is what I present to you, here, now, in *Portal.* Welcome.

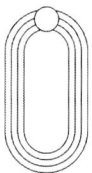

INTRODUCTION

ALLOWING BLISS

My water broke unexpectedly one evening before Christmas, and over the next four days, I danced myself into the vortex.

While floating in the land of the in-between, circling in a sea of worship and devotion, I received the broadcast, streaming in on a sunbeam. It was molten lava, and it dissolved me completely.

Birth is *the* technology.

Birth is an experience, yes. It is also an activation point.

Birth is The Portal.

Beyond the arrival itself, birth is the gateway to both consciousness and cosmos, a reflection of our inherent capacity for self-healing, and an example of our infinite aptitude for transformation.

Birth is the aperture through which we see what we are most deeply committed to.

And as my birth-dance began, I committed.

I committed to the knowing that birth is The Portal to true oneness, and to inseparability through self-responsibility, agency, integrity, and choice. Birth in power and pleasure is The gateway to individuation, the key to deep connection with the totality of existence, and God.

PORTAL

Birth according to this new (to me) blueprint was entirely devoid of pain, struggle, or effort. There was no more resistance.

The ceremony was wholly architected for my being to step into. The ritual created itself, and I experienced a massive expansion into the next tier of my capacity for embodiment, heartfulness, and love via ecstatic bliss.

In the crucible of my ninth birth, I learned that birth is not (and never was) supposed to hurt. I also learned that the fact that it *does* hurt for some of us—and that it did for me—is not wrong, or an indication that we are flawed.

Learning this lesson in no way diminished the adoration that I had (and have) for my previous excruciating births. But what I came to know in a flash of insight, through initiation, is that pain is not a part of the original schema.

Birth is not a punishment wrought by God or man. We as women (adult human females) have the innate capacity to give birth spontaneously, easily, and joyfully, according to the divine design of biological virtuosity.

Birth is a gift; it was never created to be agonizing. Pain in birth is nothing more than an entity that most of us pick up along the way, and its timeline has come to an end.

THE WHOLE TRUTH

Are you pregnant right now, or considering the prospect of welcoming a baby into the world? If so, you're probably thinking deeply about the birth process, especially if this is your first baby, or if your previous births fell short in some way of what you were hoping for.

You may be wondering:

- *What will it be like to give birth?*

- *Will I make it through?*
- *Can I handle the intensity?*
- *What about pain?*

These questions are universal.

For every woman, birth is a journey into an exotic, unknown landscape. If you are a new mother, you're in the enigma. If you have been seasoned by birth already, you might be wondering what else is available to you. And if you're a someday-mother or a birth professional, you are likely continuously seeking knowledge and a variety of perspectives to share with your clients and your future self.

This book is for every woman contending with the possibility of bearing life within her womb, and for any person interested in exploring what it means to give birth, to be born, or to choose in any context.

In our current reality, we are surrounded by a proliferation of conflicting opinions about birth and birth choices, yet one thing that is *rarely* debated is that birth is an incredible challenge, and that pain is intrinsic to the territory.

Birth is the hardest thing you'll ever do, they say, *and you can do it anyway.*

That's true, but it's not the whole truth.

My own truth is that I was blindsided by the raw, shocking pain of my first birth. I was twenty years old, and when my baby finally came—after fifty hours of blood, sweat, and wailing—I felt both elated and destroyed.

I loved it all, but the intensity was overwhelming. I never wanted to acknowledge birth as "painful," exactly, because it was so much *more* than pain, so I used the word *excruciating* instead.

PORTAL

Birth will obliterate you; that's one of its gifts, I have stated in the past. And again, this is a portion of the truth; one facet of the gem that is the story of *us* and our creation.

Through birth, I staked my claim to courage. Birth, to me, was part conquest and part spiritual self-immolation.

You're probably feeling some tension in your body as you read this right now, so before we continue...

Breathe in.

Then let it go.

What I now know, and what I am so delighted to share with you in this book, is that birth doesn't have to be that way at all.

Birth, for every woman, can be a journey through Arcadia.

For each one of us, birth can be a form of intimate communion with divine Source energy.

Birth is designed to be the supreme psychedelic journey.

Birth is the ultimate entheogen.

Birth is pure delight.

Birth is the Garden of Eden.

The ecstasy of birth is already here, within you, for you to receive, tap into, attune to, and become.

All of this is yours for the choosing, if you simply allow it to be so.

I know that some readers may be rolling their eyes—or already setting this book aside. You might even feel angry, triggered, or betrayed, especially if you have had a previous birth experience during which you thought you had "done everything right," or prepared yourself in all the "correct" ways for a peaceful, even orgasmic, experience, but felt pain anyway.

Maybe you believe that your body just isn't made for an ecstatic, pain-free birth. Perhaps you were told that your baby's position, or something about the shape of your pelvis, or some other aspect of your physiology or morphology is to blame, and that therefore blissful birth simply isn't accessible to you.

You may also feel tender, and even defensive of the births you have already had. The premise that I am presenting—that you can choose your birth experience, and that pain-free birth is an option for you—might strike you as suggestive that it is somehow *better* not to experience pain during birth, or that your outrageously ferocious, turbulent, wild, and possibly painful birth is, or was, *lesser than* a birth that is placid, euphoric, pleasurable, and without pain.

Rest assured that this kind of comparison is not something I believe in. The notion that birth can ever rightfully be ranked according to an arbitrary hierarchical classification is contrary to all I am hoping to impart to you through this book.

But especially if you feel somehow excluded from this seemingly idyllic or idealistic portrayal of what birth can be, stay with me, because I am determined to show you that:

- you are not uniquely flawed, in body or mind
- you are not forbidden or disqualified from the option of claiming bliss
- there is nothing special about how broken you may think you are

- you have far more power than you have even come close to perceiving,
- you are only exclusive in your magnificence, and
- blissful, effortless, pain-free birth is an experience that is possible to choose, if you want to.

A PERSONAL INTRODUCTION

My name is Yolande Norris-Clark.

I have been working in the field of childbirth education, birth-witnessing, and birth-freedom activism for over twenty years. I am, as I complete this book, the mother of nine children, all of whom were born at home. Telling my own stories has always been a core element of my life's work in service to women, babies, and families, and it is the greatest honour to have an opportunity to share this chapter of my evolution.

I have never shied away from speaking the unspeakable aloud, especially about birth, health, and healing, and I have always openly questioned and stood up to false authority. Not everyone appreciates my perspective or my candour, and that's fine with me. My role is that of a spell-breaker, a way-shower, and a trail-guide, in service to the rebirth of humanity, which I believe we are fully in the midst of at this time.

As a leader in the area of natural, undisturbed, radical birth, I have coached, supported, and witnessed thousands of women as they have traversed the landscape of pregnancy and birth.

But while a handful of the births I have had the privilege of attending were painless and euphoric, most were beautifully strenuous. Perfect, yes, because there is perfection in every aspect of the unfolding of life, but also full of exertion and so much *effort*.

Even within the so-called "natural birth" world, birth is often, at best, compared to running a marathon—a feat of endurance; an experience we must train for and steel ourselves to cope with. (While long-distance running probably incorporates certain forms of euphoria and transcendence, I think, in most regards, it is a fairly poor analogy for birth.)

Birth is hard. This is what I knew, and this is what I shared with my clients as The Truth. I saw in other women (and lived the reality myself) that birth is tough. It's work. *It's labour.* Until very recently, I believed birth to intrinsically be an endeavour, a battle. And so, I experienced it that way. I saw birth as something that I could *withstand,* wrestle with, and ultimately overcome.

To be clear—I have loved all of my babies' births. They were each exactly what I and the child coming through me needed at the time, in order to gain the perspective that allowed me (and them) to scale to the next level of awareness. This upleveling touched all areas of my life, including my understanding of motherhood, God, marriage and relationship, my body, and myself.

But…*ouch.*

Looking back now, I can say that I knew, when I found out that I was pregnant at nineteen, that birth and mothering would become my life's work. I knew that within the scope of birth—in the intersection of its visceral potency, its holiness, and its mysticism—was *something*, a piece of information, a kind of program, which held the key to my understanding of not only myself, but of the world and my place within it.

I spent that first pregnancy obsessively immersed in study, analysis, contemplation, and discovery. I was utterly preoccupied with birth, and I could hardly wait to experience it. My research consisted of watching hundreds of birth videos and reading every single birth-related book I could get my hands on, not to mention every scientific study on birth that I could find, and all of the "mainstream" birth books, which I relentlessly parsed and critiqued.

I also read all of the so-called "alternative" books, scrutinising them with the same intensity, and I began to notice disturbing similarities between both the purportedly "natural" approach and the institutional model. I became increasingly aware of what I now see as the false dichotomy between "homebirth" or "natural birth" (and even "physiological" birth) and the industrial, medicalized cognitive frame.

When I finally entered the birth-process with my first baby, at nearly forty-four weeks' gestation, I was stunned by the challenge and difficulty of it. With the unerring support of my beloved midwives, Gloria and Wendy, I endured three days of anguish, and I pushed, screaming, for seven hours.

I felt most of the sensations in my lower back, and I remember feeling as though my pelvis was actually being ripped apart. When my son was finally born, I was thrilled, yet totally depleted. I had almost entirely lost my voice from my howling and shrieking, and my eyes were bloodshot.

In the immediate, astonishing aftershock of postpartum, I lay on the sofa next to the muddy, bloodied birth pool with my newborn on my breast, in a state of dazed elation. My beloved friend at the time, Sarah, came over to meet my son, and I will never forget looking up at her through a veil of tears saying, *That was the most pain I've ever felt in my life.*

I loved that birth—and my beautiful son—so very much.

I was twenty years old at the time—a girl, still, in all ways—and I was so proud of myself for surviving, as I had every right to be. The birth of my first baby initiated me into the Knowing that birth is a spiritual passage, an act of devotion, an experience of transcendence and transformation, and a source of immense power.

Prompted in part by my investigation and questioning, an intuitive recognition began to germinate within me: a sense that it might be possible that our most fundamental collective and societal conceptualizations of birth—and my personal beliefs and assumptions about it at the time—were far more distorted than I had previously thought.

Looking back, this instinctive hypothesis was entirely correct, but it has taken me over twenty years to follow that thread back to the well of my own consciousness, back to the genius of my body, and to finally allow myself to know the radical truth that is offered to us through the holy sacrament[1] of birth. This truth—the truth about birth, power, and choice, is what this book explores, along with providing what I hope is something of a roadmap for how to access and claim your true desire.

LOVE LETTER

Wise woman and birthkeeper Jeannine Parvati Baker[2] famously proclaimed, "Peace on earth begins with birth,"[3] and she was right…and it's also not always that simple.

---

[1] My dear editor, friend, colleague, and theological consultant Sophia Zaferes explained to me that in the Orthodox Christian tradition, events through which divine presence is made manifest are referred to as "Mysteries," but that the term "Sacrament" is also used in the same context. Within the Orthodox tradition, these mysteries/sacraments are where "God discloses Himself through the prayers and actions of His people...[and] they serve to make us receptive to God." These disclosures are a revelation and a uniting point between the divine and the earthly, and are usually accompanied by a transformation from one thing or state to another.

[2] Jeannine Parvati Baker also coined the terms "birthkeeper" and "freebirth," and was one of the first modern midwives to publicly champion freebirth as a legitimate option, suggesting that all women could be their own midwives.

[3] I don't recall where Jeannine Parvati Baker first published this saying, but I read most of her wonderful books in my early twenties, and I especially loved "Prenatal Yoga and Natural Childbirth."

You too may know women who have had powerful, beautiful freebirths or homebirths, yet still struggle with things like postpartum recovery, mothering challenges, financial scarcity, boundary deficits, victim consciousness, self-sabotage, and other expressions of subconscious resistance to their own expansion. You may even be such a woman, which is nothing to be ashamed of.

What I share within this book is, at its heart, a set of practical guidelines for collapsing the perception of lack as an inevitable reality, while creating instantaneously in its place the capacity to invoke a resonant state of flow from your own internal psychic reserves, which I now understand to be our birthright as the magnetic, electrical beings that we are. We all have the gift of shifting the resonance of who and what we step into being and to harness the internal capacity to resource that resonance from our own psyches.

One of the most moving and poignant aspects of the realization that I experienced in choosing the birth I desired, is that each and every one of us can tap into our innate power to transcend and transform pain and suffering, and even to be unavailable for it—not only in birth (although birth is my particular focus) but also in our relationships, in our abundance or lack signature, and essentially in every area of life.

Birth is designed to be a channel that gives us access to this power, and in claiming it we can open ourselves to perspectives and ways of being that we never thought possible. But aside from the question of whether or not we choose travail or tenderness in birth, I firmly believe that the process of simply investigating our experiences of birth, facing our commitments, and exploring every available angle of how we approach birth and what we believe about it, will always enrich and expand our understanding of ourselves, in service to the future of humanity.

I want to reiterate that I cannot promise anyone a specific outcome from reading this book. No amount of information can change you. It is only through consciously implementing the teachings herein (specifically the teachings that pertain to the nuances, idiosyncrasies, and exactitudes of *choice*—what choice means, how we choose, and how we unconsciously thwart and sabotage our choices) that you will have the tools to then decide if you truly desire to birth yourself as the woman who disavows pain while embracing bliss and pleasure through the experience.

Ultimately, whether or not you actually end up having an orgasmic birth isn't really important. What I hope to underline throughout this text, is that blissful birth is *possible* for every woman, and that anything you truly desire in birth (and in any other aspect of life) is yours for the choosing. But I also want to encourage you to soften your beliefs, and to ready yourself to dive into the deeply messy, mucky, murky primordial recesses of your essential, and ever-changing state of being. The choice to step across the threshold into another way of seeing and being is yours to make.

Helio—the sun, our son—the child whose entry into the world was the catalyst for my awakening, is now, at the time of writing, almost five months old. His is the frequency of peace. All nine of my babies have been exceedingly happy and content, but Helio is a little cherub to the maximum.

His birth cracked me open, such that I received access to a kind of beatitude that has permeated my experience of motherhood like no other. When I placed my palm on his warm wet crown still inside my body at the culmination of his landing, I was made an initiate. At that moment of eruption, I conceived this offering for you, the sisterhood of mothers waiting in the wings to bring your babies forth in the utmost faith and adoration.

PART ONE

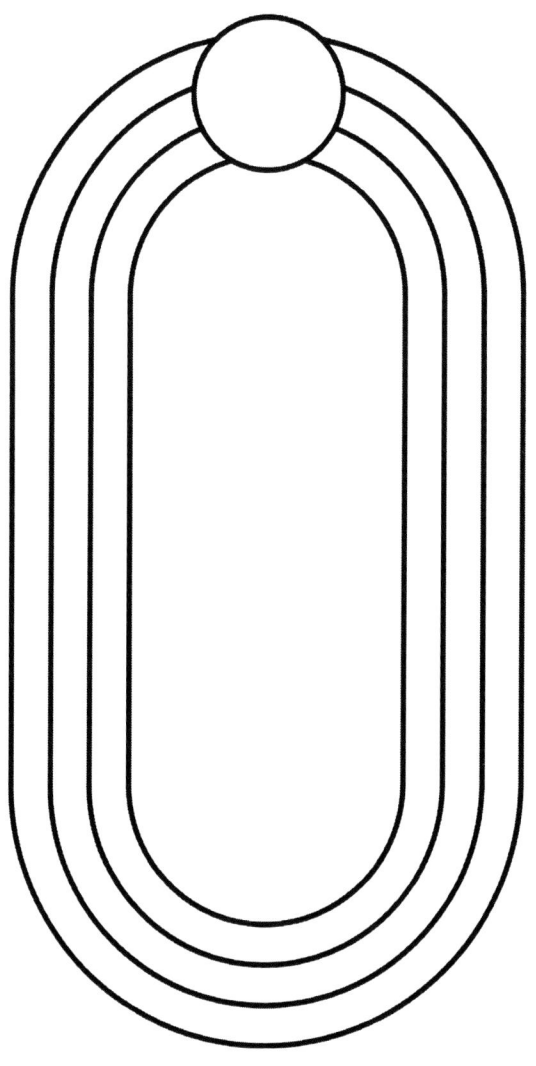

GROUNDWATER

CHAPTER ONE

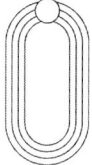

RENAISSANCE

THE TOMBS

Like so many people on an accidental spiritual quest, I find myself in the mountain valley of Las Tumbas, Costa Rica, exemplifying the ultimate cliché, as I am reborn (yet again) after one of the most humbling and harrowing experiences of disintegration I have ever weathered.

My eyes open onto the emerald gorgeousness of the Diamante waterfall, mist rising from the field as serene as a painting. The wind moves over the grass, and an egret swoops into view (the symbol of harmony, concentration, longevity, wisdom, love, and piety, I am later told). I close my eyes again, and in that moment, a point of light flickers into my field of vision. Little Sun. I know this is my baby's soul-presence, his auric resonance entering my consciousness.

My husband Lee and I drive home in awed silence—he too has received a visitation from our child, and we both *know*. That evening, we merge as one, welcoming creation, and I am pregnant.

Everything in our lives is unsettled. We're living in a half-finished, dilapidated shack in the southern Pacific Zone. It's paradise, and I hate it.

I hate the wet, thick, heavy jungle air, the stifling humidity, the rat that keeps returning to the kitchen for scraps. I hate that the entire back wall of our home is a tarp. I hate the gloss and the veneer, the social performance, the vegan propaganda, the political posturing, and the culture of seeking and pretense that is Costa Rica.

The landscape is stunningly beautiful here, but the heat and intensity are relentless. My body is endlessly ravaged by the flora and fauna, and she rebels. My bug bites ooze and fester, and despite trying every potion and technique to eradicate them, a lice infestation persists. I am under attack. Sharing my umbra, Lee and the kids have similar symptoms. We feel besieged.

Then, as the first season of my pregnancy unfolds, I begin to experience a daily episode of tormenting pain in my abdomen, lingering for three to six hours of agony at a time. This goes on for three months, every day, sometimes more than once a day.

My life becomes dedicated to pain—to knowing it, nurturing it, feeling it, loathing it. I also happen to be enormous. My belly is far larger than it ever was at this same stage with any of my previous pregnancies. Is it twins, or the inflammation of my internal organs? I'm not sure, but I also know there is no real information to be gleaned from any of the technological forms of assessment, testing, or analysis that have come to replace instinct, and so I submit to the mystery.

As my odyssey through the contours of pain continues, I have little doubt that this is what is commonly understood as "kidney stones" or a "kidney infection." Week after week, I come to understand this as one of the most intimate and terrible, but ultimately liberating, relationships with sensation I have ever known.

Kidney stones are far more painful than childbirth, unquestionably. But neither are what they seem, as I come to discover. With every cycle of horrific stabbing convulsions, I consider going to the hospital. I consider asking for morphine. I consider demanding to be saved. But I don't.

Eventually, instead of dying, I learn how to work with pain as a messenger, and when I decipher the message, my body finds the denouement and the resolution, and the pain abates, almost immediately. Throughout this extended episode which spans the middle season of my pregnancy, I learn that nothing can ever really harm me. I also realise that I don't belong here—we don't belong here—and we decide to leave the land of Pura Vida.

MIGRATION

I am almost six months pregnant when we cross the border at Liberia into Nicaragua on foot: six kids, four dogs, one cat, and twenty or so suitcases and boxes that contain our most beloved possessions—mostly books, but also clothes, the cast iron frying pan, stainless steel pots, rock collections that can't be parted with, and again, we start over.

We settle in San Juan del Sur, a little beach town on the Pacific Coast full of stray dogs, backpackers, and a growing community of foreigners looking for a home where our children can roam. We commit.

Our kids take up skateboarding and surfing, and we use our life savings to buy a scruffy little house charmingly named Casa Santa Rosa (most houses are personified here) made up of two simple Spanish style structures, built around an open palapa-covered courtyard, on a lot just under an acre in size. We plant papayas and bananas, we acquire a flock of chickens, and eventually, like local families, a pig.

We get down to the business of living. I work too much, but I also find myself drawn to the sun, and the sea. I swim in the ocean as often as possible, and I take in the sun's nourishment (abundant in our tropical environs) at every opportunity, letting it stream its energy into the core of my being through my pores, my eyes, my heart, my skin, my belly.

Despite the stress, anxiety, and desperation of the early part of my pregnancy, my baby grows, kicking and flipping joyfully in my rounding womb, and I know he is alive and well. Looking back, I see this pregnancy and its series of trials as an invitation to renew my faith in my own discernment, my capacity to tap into my intuition, and my trust in God. But in the midst of it, life seems fairly mundane. Nicaragua suits us. Our children lose their shoes for good, and no one minds.

I tend to gestate my babies for an unusually long time, considering that most mothers will have their babies "delivered" (evicted or extracted) if they are deemed "late"—according to the distorted assumptions and constructs of industrial obstetrics, that is. But I learned long ago to trust the organic timeline of my body (and my babies' bodies), and all eight of my older children were born at the perfect time, at nearly forty-four weeks.

At the thirty-nine-week mark of this pregnancy, I complete my semester of teaching midwifery,[†] safe in the knowledge that I will remain pregnant for at least another month and a half, during which I'll be free to finally focus on the personal tasks I'm planning to do before this baby arrives sometime around Christmas or even New Year's—not that I'm *really* planning anything based on the fickle predictions of biology, but I'm also not yet fully capable of releasing all of the instilled preoccupations with linear time, and in my mind, I am just now entering the season of "officially" waiting for the arrival of our new child.

On this day, however, I'm absorbed in office work, and picking up all the loose ends before I can really dig into editing my ongoing writing project (a book, but not this one), so I spend a few hours responding to as many messages as I can, dealing with the dangling residency issues, the business

---

[†] The Radical Birth Keeper School is the authentic midwifery program I co-created and teach alongside my colleague Emilee Saldaya.

with the lawyers, liaising with the contractor who is organising the building of our palapa studio, and the solar energy guy. In a blink, it's well after dark and I've missed dinner again. I message Lee, apologetic, and I manage to leave my office by nine, with the sense at least of having accomplished something.

The kids are asleep when I get home, but I resolve to stay in bed late the following morning to properly rest, and then to spend a good part of the day with the family. I attend to my rituals in the dark, including setting up the now-elaborate infrastructure required for the tenuous, highly interrupted form of sleep to which I have had to resign myself for the past several months. Lee brings a glass of lemon water and places it on the bedside table and arranges several pillows to be stacked between my folded knees and under my belly. The fan is on, inches from my body to diffuse the heat, and my music is cued.

I do crave the luxury of sleeping on my stomach or back—the simple pleasures—but I've chosen to forget what it's like to have a body to myself. Whereas, a month or two ago, the remainder of my pregnancy loomed, and the despair and exhaustion and neverendingness of my physical state was overwhelming, these days I actually feel quite cheerful, and grateful for the remaining weeks that inevitably await.

I wake up for the fourth or fifth time to pee, haul myself upright, stumble to the bathroom, sit down on the toilet, and as I release, I feel a subtle scratching; a rending sensation under my ribs where my enormous belly starts to swell. The perception is uncanny, and I register it, but the irritation passes quickly, and I dismiss it as yet another vagary of late pregnancy, and waddle back to bed. Just as I successfully hoist myself up onto the mattress, there is a soft detonation from the innermost reaches of my distended abdomen—the completion of the tearing sensation from a moment ago—and a warm, voluptuous gush of liquid seeps from between my legs, onto the sheets.

PORTAL

My waters have broken.

THE INVITATION

I shake Lee awake, and breathlessly express my shock. *What is happening? Why is this happening?* The prospect of twins crosses my mind again. I rationalize: twins generally gestate for less time than singletons, and I've made so many wry, exasperated quips about twins in response to the exclamations of strangers over the sheer magnitude of my belly, which at this stage really is enormous (*Are you sure there's only one in there? Nope, I'm not at all sure!*), that I've almost managed to convince myself that it's a real possibility.

Amid the commotion, Xanthe (five) and Ignatius (two) — whose beds are in our room — wake up. As soon as they realise what's happening, they run next door to wake the older kids, Treva, Felix, and Cosmo, who, in turn, run upstairs to alert our teenager, Horus, who has his own room above the kitchen. This is my ninth baby, and she or he (or they) could be here within the hour (four of my babies have, after all, been born within less than two hours from the first sign that birth was imminent), and I suddenly realise that nothing in our immediate environment is up to my stringent standards of tidiness and cleanliness. So I put everyone to work, folding clothes, organising books, scrubbing sinks, and the kids are so excited that everyone rallies with somewhat less opposition than usual.

With every twinge, I expect the waves will start to crash, but instead, despite the liquid pouring continuously down my legs, all is steady and slow and heavy, and after a couple of hours of hanging out and tidying up, the momentum wanes, and the kids start to ask if the baby is really coming or not. Finally, I come to terms with the fact that we all just need to settle down and go back to sleep. So we redo bedtime, and I lie down again too, my hands resting on my abdomen, comforted by the soft kicks my baby makes in response to my gentle prodding. Sleep descends once more.

I am awake at the first hint of morning sun. There is a cacophony of birds in the mango trees, and I hear the insistent huffing growls from the family of howler monkeys that often hang out right outside our window. The monkeys are loud and glorious, and I remember that I'm having a baby today.

My room is clean, the sun is streaming in. I loll and luxuriate and wait for the surges. The kids appear, and the energy heightens. Then I want space, so I banish them while I move through a few tightenings, heavy and low, but the energy is still slow. I check my email and remember that I have some tasks to do, so I mess around on my phone, still leaking constantly.

Our room starts to feel stifling. I venture outside with a little head wedged quite noticeably between my legs. Walking is unwieldy, but I roam around our walled garden and courtyard nonetheless, searching for opportunities to put people to work, blessing the tiles and flagstones and the ground beneath me with the benediction of my holy water.

I come upon the garage, and in my state of zealous birthy exactitude, the piles of boxes, suitcases, and pieces of luggage still partly packed from our flight across the border are deemed highly unsatisfactory. I immediately begin hauling boxes out and commandeering a full excavation. Our emergency food stores are organised, the Christmas gifts I've been collecting and have hidden in there are ordered, and my need for a sense of control is channelled fruitfully.

It's late afternoon by the time the project is complete. I'm energized and avid, and I realise I need to be in the sea. I ask Lee to load my paddleboard onto the roof of the truck, and I prompt the kids to get ready. Everyone (except our eldest, thirteen-year-old Horus, who elects to stay home and read instead) piles into the truck, and we trundle down our dirt road towards town.

There are only a handful of other people out at the playa tonight. The light is golden, and I sit on the smooth pebble beach while the kids take their places in the world in accordance with exactly who they are. Little two-year old Iggy wanders, exploring. Xanthe, five, sits down next to me, asking how I am and how the baby is. Seven-year-old Cosmo sets off immediately and begins the task of collecting rocks and meticulously stacking them up, creating a sculpture garden near the shore. Treva, our pre-teen, has her headphones on and is listening to music by herself, sketchpad in hand. Felix, nine, helps Lee get the paddle board ready, eager to venture out.

The water is cool and calm, and as I descend into it, I submit to a wave of love and grief and a terrible wild knowing that this is the last time; it's always and forever the last of everything that's here and now. This is the last time I'll be submerged in the ocean with this child (or children?) in my womb. This may be the last time I'll ever be pregnant again, because who can know the course of life? These are certainly the last hours of this particularly perfect afternoon. I feel another rush of fluid gush from my body. Suddenly I miss my mother, back in cold, gray Vancouver, waiting for spring so she can tend to the garden of the handsome stucco arts and crafts house where I grew up.

The sun begins its descent. Felix and I take turns paddling each other out toward the mouth of the cove, past the sole panga boat anchored a little way off. The water becomes choppier, and we're destabilized so we turn around, noticing the greater effort required to come back, pulling against the tide that wants us out to sea. In the shallow water we play, capsizing each other. Felix doesn't have to exert much effort—the weight of my ridiculous porpoise-like body as I heave myself onto the board is enough to pull us both over. Occasionally, my uterus contracts, and I have to stop for a moment, concentrating, welcoming the surge.

As the sun finally sinks below the sill of the earth, I abandon the board, swimming out, treading water, witnessing the world turn to gold.

Yolande Norris-Clark

INTERLUDE

I climb back into the truck, and settle myself on a towel, and the kids pile in behind me. Lee takes the wheel, steady, driving as slowly as he can over the pitted dirt road—every bump and impact sending more of the ocean inside me flowing out.

We pass horses loping lazily home, and the sometimes-baseball field, now empty, where the goats graze by day.

No one has considered dinner, so we decide to eat out. I'm feeling spacey, but hungry, so we head to The Beach House, one of the nicer restaurants in the bay, right on the water. The kids are squirrelly, and they play in the sand. The atmosphere is jovial and anticipatory. When my surf and turf arrives, I eat everything, surprised by my own ravenousness.

It's dark when we arrive back home. My yoni feels heavy, and I fall into bed, thinking about meeting my baby, so very soon. I drift to sleep, the thought of our child in my mind's eye.

In the morning I wake up again, still pregnant. *How curious. How interesting.*

I spend the day lazing in bed, riding the swell, the billow and heave. I call my mum and tell her the story of how her new grandchild is not yet here. The kids meander in and out of the room. I eventually make my way out to the garden, but I'm overwhelmed by the cacophony of the jungle, and I can't get comfortable. I certainly can't get dressed.

I nap fitfully. I read books to Iggy, our baby who is still so little, yet so eager to be a big brother. Our girls, Treva and Xanthe, come in and braid my hair. I fold baby clothes. Nothing is happening. Everything is happening.

I notice moments of annoyance appear on the horizon of my thoughts, and the occasional flash of fear. I allow these to pass.

PORTAL

Lee brings me water.

I watch light move across the room.

Now I've had enough of the stillness, and we decide that we'll go to the party after all—the weekly "expat" gathering at a luxurious resort up over the mountain that overlooks the bay of San Juan. I manage to put on a loose-fitting dress, but I forego underwear, and leave my hair undone.

The resort is decorated to the hilt for the holidays, with silver lights everywhere, and jazzed up Christmas songs playing. The kids run ahead, some to jump in the pool and others to join the foosball game. The scene is at once unbearably intense and hilarious.

I can't really talk to anyone—somehow this is far more surreal than all the inappropriate times I did drugs in my late teens then tried to show up at the family dinner pretending I was a normal human, yet like those earlier transgressions, it's also ridiculously fun to be here.

When my new friend Celia comes up to chat, I tell her that if I seem stunned it's because I'm sort of having a baby right now, open waters and all. She laughs and tells me I could just jump in the gorgeous pool and have a waterbirth right there, and I like her even more (but I also decline to swim, this time).

The sun goes down and the festivities ratchet up, and I tell Lee I've reached my limit. The edges are blending together, the scene pixelates, and my sensations have started up with more fervour. Lee sets off to gather up the kids, who are scattered this way and that, and we finally return to the truck.

On our way back down the mountain, the hills of Palermo and the lights of San Juan sparkle like a tropical snow globe.

Back home at Casa Rosa, I lounge around, restless, but I eventually fall asleep, because a while later I open my eyes in the still-dark morning, awakened again by the keening shrieks of the family of monkeys. (I found this sound uncanny when I first heard it—disturbing, even—but I'm comforted by it now.) I am somewhat nonplussed to still be pregnant. How many days has it been? I can't remember.

I feel like a giant sea creature. I am as elemental as a plant—the towel underneath me is soaked with amniotic fluid. I can see in the dusk that it's tinged with blood and meconium. I rest my hands on my enormous belly, and I waver back and forth.

Lee is still sleeping beside me. I admire his long tan body, hard from paddling out. *That's my husband.*

My baby is quiet. I tune into his ambiance for a moment. Suddenly, I know he is a boy, and I know there is only one of him. I feel his concentration. He is on the journey.

The howlers settle down and the sun comes up, bathing the undulating stucco walls in light, rippling like liquid.

The sensations come again in a gentle swell, soft and leisurely, occasional, fitful; fleeting. I realise that I love it. It's so easy, so delightful. Romantic, somehow.

Eventually the house starts to stir, the dogs bark, and the kids flock to our room—they too are surprised that their new sibling has yet to arrive. We snuggle, and read some books, then Lee ushers them all out for their breakfast.

I had made a playlist of minimal, ambient music weeks before and I put that on now. It's perfect. I am serene and grounded.

Another sensation builds. There's a sharpness to it that makes me stop and catch my breath, and I have to choose to inhale, and then exhale.

PORTAL

Our two nannies arrive for the kids' Spanish lessons, and Lee sends the children out to do their schoolwork. Once they are settled, Lee returns to our room and to me. We make love in silence, slowly and sweetly, one last time before our marriage and family change again.

Afterwards, I put my kimono on and make my way out to the courtyard, but it's too loud, too bright. I return to the bed, to the room. My head spins. Time starts to stray. The lines between my body and the outside world have elided. I put my hands in my watery yoni, perpetually seeping liquor or pee, or both.

I have discarded any impulse to distinguish, or to staunch my permeability. I feel stoned and heady. The sensations are still mild, and I ride them easily, but I see prismatic fractals, kaleidoscopic shapes. I'm drunk and tripping on the alchemical spirits of birth.

Now Lee enters. I can barely make out what he's saying, but I manage to discern that our lawyer needs us to sign some important documents. At first, I suggest getting dressed and driving into town with him, but when I look up, he smiles, and I see reflected in his eyes that I'm fraying at the edges. *No. Yes. Okay.* The world is a blur, and I cannot possibly organize myself to put on a shirt, let alone leave the sanctuary of our room. I'm not going anywhere.

But the papers can't wait, so I tell Lee to ask our lawyer, Sandra, to come here instead. This is when the shift occurs. Another sensation arises, sharper still than any other, and I suddenly feel scared. I feel the shadow of the story of pain and now, in a moment that descends like a revelation, I consider the possibility of calling out, crying out, screaming, but it's only that: one possible mode.

The other option—the other portal opening before me—is the prospect of entering into the sensation, embracing it, allowing it to flower, and yielding to it entirely. I notice myself deciding that I'd like to play here, in this realm of experiencing birth fully, accepting it completely, and loving it totally. I decide to see what this can be.

I rise to stand at the foot of my bed, leaning slightly against the edge of the mattress, and I begin to move, to sway and sinuate. The motion is necessary because now I am under water, treading water, feeling the undertow.

As the next sensation advances, questions form:

What if I were to decide that this birth is going to be sheer pleasure in its entirety?

What if I simply choose not to resist any part of it?

What if I choose to allow myself to feel every single fragment of what is happening in my body?

What if I were to choose to open fully?

What if I were to choose to open every single portal that I have access to, and what if the portals I have access to are infinite?

What if I choose to know that I am everything and what if this baby is me and I am he and we are meant to be here, doing this together, and what if it can all be utterly, boundlessly sweet?

What if I could simply choose to open my throat portal, my mouth portal, and the portals of my pelvis and yoni, heart, and mind?

And now…I do.

My arms are open, my legs are open, my heart is wide open, and the crown of my head is open. My sex is open, and I am shattering into a million pieces, and it is pure rapture.

I am.

PORTAL

Here, now, is the rest again: calm, quiet, internal.

Lee enters the room with a document, and Sandra, the lawyer, pops her head in. I register her wide-eyed astonishment at seeing me so wild and naked. I reach out and sign the paper, and the door closes. The last executive task is done.

The kids run in. I stand up, ferocious, and roar: *Out. Everybody out.* I have no space for distraction, no interest in accommodation or explanation. I am in communion with God now, and this is the spiritual work of my life.

INTEGRATION QUESTIONS

1. How do you feel when witnessing or receiving another woman's story of orgasmic birth? How does your body respond? What thoughts do you have?

2. Does her story seem possible for you? Are you inspired to make it possible? Does any aspect of your response include upset, disbelief, or trigger?

3. Can you identify any part of your own story or experience that might explain your responses? Take a moment to feel into what's available to you here. Anchor into it and claim it as your own.

CHAPTER TWO

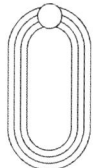

BIRTHING THE COSMOS

RENEGADE

At nineteen years old, and on the precipice of new motherhood, I had no understanding of the mechanics of transmuting pain, or what it meant to harness energy and to communicate with my highest self, with my baby, or with God. I lacked a true reference point for authentic self-responsibility and self-ownership, not to mention any comprehension of what it is to be a conduit for power.

Yet even as an innocent maiden, I did have a couple of things figured out. One was an understanding of my political power as a birthing woman—more specifically, that I had no political power at all within the obstetric system. The other piece of insight that I grasped fully from the beginning was that birth works, and that it tends to work best in the absence of interference and sabotage.

As a young mother, my initial inspiration for exiting the industrial medical system almost completely was both political and reactionary: I knew that many, if not all, of the diagnostics and testing methodologies that underpin what we know as "prenatal care" are totally unnecessary. They are made up, irrelevant, and unmoored from the intelligence of the natural world and experiential reality. I knew that most routine prenatal procedures have no real scientific or evidentiary basis, even according to the mercenary metrics of the establishment.

I also discovered, in part via research, but also simply through observation, empirical reasoning, and instinct, that many forms of prenatal assessment are actively *counterproductive*—directly damaging, even—and that engaging in what is offered (or in many cases, mandated and coerced) within the system is actually the *source* of a great number, if not most, of the problems, complications, and emergencies that for the majority of mothers would likely not materialize if not for medical interference.

I recognized, for example, that the use of surveillance diagnostics such as ultrasound, amniocentesis, the gestational diabetes test, and the GBS test (to name a few), are justified on the basis of only specious evidence, not to mention an autocratic standard of safety and risk. When I examined my own values and interests, I immediately saw that the potential downsides of these procedures far outweigh their purported benefits, especially given that they all involve various degrees of objective damage or toxicity to mother and baby—harms that are almost never revealed to women by their doctors or midwives, despite lip service made to "informed consent."

My reconnaissance was extensive and exhaustive, and I found endless discrepancies, contradictions, outright lies, fallacies, and loose ends to unravel in the industrial obstetric and medical midwifery paradigm. But alongside the shock and rage I felt at uncovering what I now see as a very real conspiracy hidden in plain sight, I also began to experience a parallel phenomenon, which I can only describe as a process of remembering.

I began to remember that I am whole, and alive. I remembered that birth is my mother tongue.

Given that I evidently had the capacity to breathe, register hunger, digest food, and eliminate waste without the need for any expert assistance, surely those same reflexive principles were operational within the domain of reproduction. After all, I hadn't needed any professional oversight or medical espionage to become pregnant, and I reasoned that both my body and the child in my womb likely had the capacity to organize our cells and systems automatically, according to the same logic of divine biological design.

I also came to the conclusion that breaking ties with the medical establishment might even be to my baby's and my distinct benefit. Very quickly, the entire cognitive framework of industrial prenatal care and institutional birth collapsed. At that point, I decided that I would no longer engage in any kind of testing, assessment, or measurement of my body during pregnancy at all.

I fired my licensed midwife once I recognized that she was merely replicating the same forms of medical pathologization within my home, and I very deliberately disavowed all the ways we have been taught to cultivate and channel fear into domestication and ritualized submission, including the internalization of medical ideology through the self-imposition of obstetric procedures, which I saw (and have subsequently seen) so many women perform.

It baffled me then, as it does now, that under the banner of "unassisted birth" or "freebirth" (or even in relation to the term *wild pregnancy* which I began to invoke in 2017 to describe the choice to allow pregnancy to proceed without any medical interaction or appraisal), so many mothers nonetheless impose medical technocratic rituals upon themselves. It is, apparently, quite popular among some women who nonetheless choose freebirth, to put themselves through many of the very same medical prenatal protocols and proprieties that an obstetrician or midwife might offer, such as routinely weighing oneself in pregnancy, performing DIY group B strep swabs, peeing on urine pH strips, frequently listening to a baby's heart tones with either a fetoscope or a home-doppler, and more.

This was not for me. Early on, I saw obstetric assessments as emblematic of submission, and inextricable from the fundamentally abusive system in which they were constructed. To my mind, it was not simply that most of these procedures bear no relationship whatsoever to real "care," (self-care or caretaking) or to actually supporting the health or safety of our babies, but that many of these forms of assessment, having been forged within an ideological program intended to subjugate and exploit, cannot be excised from the environment of that corrupt system with the expectation that the act will then somehow be rendered benign, or natural, simply because we have removed the figure of authority from the equation. We don't sanctify or legitimize symbolic cult rites by duplicating them, we only corrupt ourselves, inevitably taking on the essence of the institution in which the customs were manufactured.

Instead, I would be undergoing pregnancy and birth in a way that, as I saw it, epitomised freedom and autonomy. I hired, out of pocket, an underground traditional birth attendant—an authentic midwife, in my eyes—who was able, and more than willing, to respect my total authority. With that, I walked away from the Trojan horse that is Canada's "free" midwifery system. At first, the choice to fully trust my body's capacity to grow and birth my child was a form of resistance, and even rebellion. I was angry at what I saw as the deceptiveness of medical hegemony, and I wanted no part in the medico-pharmaceutical industrial machine. And I was determined to prove it, and them, wrong.

What began as a near-militant rejection of "the system," however, quickly morphed into an embrace of what I discovered to be the deeper reality. Pregnancy and birth are both processes that tend to work very well when they're not being messed around with. Childbearing is made up of normal, spontaneous, biological events that function as predictably and as impeccably as any other natural biological system. But pregnancy is also a liminal state that primes us for the mystical evolution of birth, and nature is the perfect mirror. This doesn't mean that the outcome is always to our liking, or according to our wants, but nature is always a reflection of the fundamental truth echoed by our bodies, our minds, our psyches, and our environment.

For the most part, when pregnancy and birth are not being interrupted, hindered, or sabotaged, they simply unfold. Babies simply grow, our bodies simply give birth, and our children simply emerge from our yonis, without any fixing, assisting, or modification necessary. I came to an understanding that the actions often taken under the auspices of helping or saving tend to constitute the very sabotage to which I am referring.

It is, of course, every individual woman's prerogative to either relinquish the medical paradigm altogether, or to engage with it as she sees fit, including mimicking the allopathic belief system within her own home, by weighing, measuring, and scrutinizing her body just as a doctor or midwife would (or by performing such practices on occasion, if and when she feels inspired to, for whatever reason).

As a young mother, I chose to believe that my body works, and to accept the truth as I see it, that birth is not only a physical experience, but also a deeply spiritual one. This revelation resonated with exquisite clarity as I claimed it, and its validity has been consistently reflected back to me in the years that followed, as I have lived out my ideas and theories to their fullest in expanding my own family, and through the relationships I have formed with other women.

Over the years, I held space for many birthing mothers in my community, and I began to offer birth consulting and obstetric trauma debriefs online, interspersed with the births of my own babies. I saw it all, and lived it, too. My own first seven homebirths ranged from that initiatory fifty-hour-long challenge, to our first daughter, Treva's speedy fifty-minute landing, to my fifth baby's birth surrounded by my raucous, joyous family celebrating with me as our sweet Felix tumbled into the world.

During each of my own experiences, and through every other woman's birth I witnessed, I learned something new, and at the same time I also saw, in each birth I was involved with, a confirmation of what was my central and most obdurate bias: that birth is a triumphant fusion of endurance, defiance, resilience, exertion, and, yes, *labour.*

Granted, there were a *few* women I supported whose births were tranquil and serene. But when I asked them to explain their technique, or their approach, some would tell me about books they had read (and I had read many of those same books), and some would talk about meditation (and I had done many of those meditations), yet it still seemed to me that those women must have been spiritually connected in ways I didn't have the skills for. I knew *(*or I *thought* I knew*)* that I could never give birth that way. I told myself the story that I just didn't have "it."

And, I didn't.

QUANTUM ENTANGLEMENT

What is "it"? What is it to be a body, to know ourselves as human, to experience this life in the flesh to its fullest extent, to taste beauty, love, embodiment, and to understand the world we occupy enough to delight in it?

For most of us, our beliefs and convictions about ourselves and our corporeal existence, including the processes of illness and healing, may feel serendipitous, or inevitable, or rational, or may even occur to us as a factual reflection of "reality." The nature of "reality" is, however, I suspect, quite different from what each individual is committed to perceiving.

It's difficult for me to imagine a less interesting topic than tiny invisible particles, but I am deeply interested in the psychology of those who spend their time investigating quantum physics, and how this field of study impacts the way we commoners understand our place here on earth.

According to the geniuses and savants who examine matter, energy, quirks, quarks, and quantum phenomena, the atom is the smallest unit that forms a chemical element of matter and consists of a central nucleus made up of neutrons and protons, around which electrons revolve. Electrons are negatively charged, protons are positively charged, and neutrons are neutral. This elemental formation constitutes *stuff*—all the stuff, so we are told.

In recent years, certain quantum physicists have proposed that neither electrons nor any other subatomic particles have a consistent substantive materiality. In fact, a trend has emerged among some scientists who submit that an electron can behave as either a particle—a point of materiality, a "thing"—*or* a wave, which is described as a kind of disturbance, or an oscillation, as opposed to a tangible entity.

In some cases, researchers are now suggesting that it is only when an electron is being observed under certain conditions, that it *gains* substantiality, and that prior to that observance, it's actually *always* behaving as a "wave"—as a vibration. This would mean that it is in the witnessing of a subatomic particle that it actually comes into material being.

This takes the observer effect (the theory that the act of observation changes that which is being observed) to another level. The observer effect has been tackled from various angles by the likes of Einstein, Heisenberg, Schrödinger (and his cat), and yet the notion that witnessing has an impact on the witnessed is also rather elementary. Most of us, at some stage following the often-sudden recognition of our own mortality (which, in my experience and by my observation as a mother, occurs at around age three or four[5]), realise that how we behold the world is unique to us as

---

[5] Our dear Ignatius, a few weeks before his fourth birthday, turned to me while we were in the truck heading down to the beach and said, out of the blue, *Mum, am I going to die?* I replied, *Yes, my sweetheart, one day, but probably not until you're very old, which is a a very very long time from now.* He said, *Ok,* and we moved on.

individuals; that all we really ever have is consciousness; and that while energy is clearly mutable it can never be extinguished.

All of this applies to birth in several profoundly important ways. Birth is, as much as death and the transmutation of energy, a philosophical matter.

Quantum theorists also wrestle with a concept which physicists call "non-locality," which in simple terms means that anything that moves also moves the entirety of all existence along with it. And, of course, each of us—from our subtlest feelings to our grandest gestures—are included in that constant interplay; the continuous motion of everything.

This is at the heart of the emerging understanding of the world as a holographic imprint: the essence of which is that every single notion or thing that exists in the world and which possesses any form of expression—whether seemingly static, or dynamic—is then replicated in all other things, objects, ideas, and realms, both large and small. The world as we know it is really just a hologram; a perpetual symphony of vibration and pattern, colliding and rippling outward, which includes every thought, emotion, and belief brought into existence and focus through our consciousness, and mirrored in the entirety.

In his work, David Bohm (physicist and student of Einstein's) explores what he calls the "implicate reality," defining this as the vastness of everything outside of our observation, which is also inevitably folded into the initial surface level of experience that we perceive—the layer that he refers to as the "explicate." In a sense, what Bohm is suggesting is that what we discern during our day-to-day experience—the table, the bowl of food, the sun streaming through the window—is but a holographic indentation producing a "secondary" reality (perhaps infinite numbers of them) registered in the shimmering, undulating ephemeral.

When I overlay the idea of the implicate and explicate planes onto world mythology, cosmology, the production of what we understand as "history" and collective belief—including the beliefs we hold about birth and the origins of life—things become very interesting indeed. It seems that across the earth and throughout time, folk traditions from even the most (seemingly) disparate cultures share the story of a great deluge that swept nearly all of humanity away, except for that one pioneering family. In the Judeo-Christian tradition, of course, this would be Noah and his brethren, but apparently there were similar flood myths in faraway places.

The Mesopotamian *Epic of Gilgamesh* recounts the tale of a Sumerian King who reigned for a respectable one hundred and twenty-six years, but who still sought after immortality. His want led him to a man who had been granted that very thing, after saving his relatives and every species of animal on earth by building a ship that sailed them to safety. (In the end, Gilgamesh comes to terms—more or less—with the anxieties of mortality.)

The Aztecs had a somewhat similar story. In it, a married couple named Note and Nena are warned of a flood and hide themselves in a hollowed-out cypress tree while the earth is inundated (they become fish after disobeying the god that initiated the total reset of the world).

There is yet another comparable story in Greek Mythology involving Zeus, who advises the son of Prometheus to build an ark, and after the destruction of the earth, the planet is repopulated, again, with the help of Zeus (who, despite his chronic narcissism and gaslighting, nonetheless seems to have a soft spot for humans).

Hindu and Buddhist mythologies also involve tales of deluge and repopulation, and beyond these there are Norse, Chinese, and Indigenous American accounts that feature similar themes. Some researchers believe that these flood myths describe literal events that took place in the past, and there are, ostensibly, several underwater cities that still exist today, located across the planet, including off the coasts of Japan, the Mediterranean, and Cuba, to say nothing of the lost city of Atlantis, which, phantasm or fairy tale, retains a mighty hold on the collective imagination.

PORTAL

When I began my (admittedly relatively superficial) excursion into the cultural parables of the past involving destruction by drowning, what struck me about these stories was the holographic reflection of the eruption of the waters of life—the contra-alluvion that occurs when the surging burst of our initial aqueous abode is punctured and the womb-sea pours forth, rousing us into the first act of agency in this life: the undertaking of our birth, as we follow the flow of the original estuary.

Birth is the autochthonic story. The blueprint of the myth and the quanta. Stories hold everything that matters most: the motherboard. The mainframe. The needle and thread. Stories mediate the implicate and the explicate.

Pain in birth is not a requirement, it is a vestige of a tormented version of the story of civilization, shadow-cast against the cave wall, cloned throughout the quantum field, and taken as the truth. It is both the journey of birth and the story of it that brings us into the world, and the effects of the chronicle run deeper than most of us know. It is not by accident that almost every woman who gives birth carries some degree of trauma or pain, upon surfacing for air following the event.

You, the mother, are not only bringing your child into the world. You are bringing the world into your child, and bearing into the world, *through* your child, the imprint of all the beliefs of your ancestors. That which you know to be true about pain and suffering is being encoded, too. And in the same way that your baby is being created, so too will you recreate yourself.

By way of birth, you are transmitting a new iteration of the story of civilization or wildness, drawing it forward into the future and in reverse, slicing through the seam of time, shifting the geometry of infinity and beyond. You are re-animating humanity, and the beliefs you hold about the power or fragility of your body and your psyche will be imprinted into your child's fascial memory as their body is being braided together, cell by cell, strand by strand, in the ocean of your womb.

Perception is kaleidoscopic, always. The quality and essence of how we perceive ourselves, others, the world around us, and the saga of our humanity, is penetrating and refractory, reverberating into and through matter, space, time, and consciousness. The question of whether, how, and by whom you are witnessed during your birth will inevitably alter the experience and the outcome.

Similarly, through the discipline of intentionally observing your future birth as present, now, the way you want it to be, and projecting your desire onto the celluloid of your mind, you disintegrate the old story; the story of the self, of any inhibitions from your lineage, of birth as suffering, of myth, and you build the world anew, paving the way in the process, for the literal collapsing of waveforms into bliss as your baby moves through your magnificent body.

THE MYTH OF PAIN-FREE BIRTH

I was aware very early on in my journey through motherhood and midwifery that some women *claimed* to have orgasmic, pleasurable birth experiences. And my initial, reflexive response to this assertion was, *Yeah right.*

I never felt that the intensity of any of my births was an issue—and it wasn't. In fact, I cherished the passion and the potency of what all my births had given me, and I still do. I always loved birth, and even the idea of describing my births as "painful" felt like a reduction of the immensity of it all. Instead, my impression of birth was that it was many orders of magnitude *more* excruciating than what the word "pain: can describe. Nonetheless, my attempts to avoid referring to pain in relation to birth didn't negate the fact that pain was undeniably a central element in all eight of my first birth experiences.

Prior to Helio's birth, I would have been a woman who would have argued for why pain-free, pleasurable birth just isn't possible for some or even most mothers—especially me. I didn't feel defensive about that, but simply settled on the matter. As the years went on, and I acquired more experience in birth than that of most other people I encountered—not only through my own (at the time) eight births, but my decades of birthwork as well—I felt very secure in my viewpoint which, looking back, I admit gives me a twinge of dismay.

Even when I witnessed a few of those orgasmic births with my own eyes as a homebirth attendant, I couldn't quite believe it. It just didn't seem logically possible for a baby to come out of a woman's yoni without some degree of discomfort, or without some measure of intensity, let alone for it to be absent of pain entirely.

It isn't that I doubted the truth of other women's experiences, but I couldn't fathom that pain-free birth could possibly be attainable and true for me—a mind-frame which I now recognize so clearly as being the very evidence of my commitment to *making* that unbelief a reality. Whether it was sublimation, or extreme control, or that these women were somehow super-human, I was sure that there was something about their way of being that I could never access.

I saw pain-free birth as a chimera—an experience which, I was sure, would remain within the realm of myth, for me, in any case. And I was at peace with that. I persisted in holding this view for many years, despite encountering several women during that time who described even their very first births as painless and pleasurable. Yet I was also keenly aware that there are many more women who have given birth to multiple children, as I have, and who have never experienced birth as anything other than an enormous challenge to vanquish. That was the reality within which I chose to dwell.

With the birth of Helio, everything changed. In the ceremony of it, which introduced me to the power that we always have available thanks to the art of choosing, I was gifted with the realisation of having been incredibly, shockingly, totally wrong about birth altogether.

Specifically, I was profoundly wrong in my assumption that birth just happens the way it happens, and that we handle it the way we handle it, and that we have no real agency in terms of how we experience it. I also discovered that I was wrong about agency itself, and about what choice and radical responsibility really mean.

IGNATIUS

Just as I love every one of my children wholly and completely, for exactly who they are, likewise each of their birth experiences are indescribably precious to me—each is a unique jewel in my memory, distinctly faceted, full of depth and character, while constantly providing me with a new refracted pattern when I hold it up to the light. Birth has taught me so much. And learning is almost never linear.

Despite my familiarity with birth, and all the insight I thought I had gleaned about how to "handle" the intensity of it, my eighth baby's birth in 2019 was perhaps the most challenging I have endured—more so, even, in some ways, than my inaugural first-birth as a naive girl full of expectations of easy victory.

As an expert (or so I thought, in my own comprehension of birth) I assumed during the leadup to my eighth birth that I knew what I was getting into, at the very least. Following the birth of my second baby, I had had no interactions whatsoever with any professionals at all during any of my subsequent pregnancies, and I approached the veil of my eighth birth fundamentally at peace with the fact that the process would occur according to instinct. But at the time, I still saw birth as a problem to conquer.

PORTAL

I armoured myself with the knowledge that at least I possessed the force and strength to withstand the struggle before eventually, inevitably, surmounting it. Subconsciously, I was preparing to do battle, and (given that disposition) I ended up carrying a significant burden of trepidation into the trenches. Unsurprisingly, in accordance with my unconscious plan, that birth was a full descent into the underworld: dark and terrible, a torment and a crusade.

I thought I was going to die. And in many ways, I did.

I died to my old self, to my previous notions of risk, to my long-established fortified beliefs about birth physiology, to my assumptions about how I "did" birth, to my understanding of embodiment, and to everything I thought I knew of "safety."

Instead of the swift landing I had been expecting based on the successively more rapid births of my previous babies, I felt like I was being re-initiated into the agony of new motherhood once again—I cried and bellowed and snarled and moaned for ten hours, and then...my baby still didn't come.

Finally, after several hours of grueling pushing while lying prone on my back—a position I chose freely, according to primal impulse—my child finally appeared, just as I blacked out. This momentary loss of consciousness was interrupted by my husband's voice, tinged with concern. *Yo. Get your baby,* he said softly. I came to, dazed, then sat up to see my child's body: a boy, limp, unmoving, and grayish white.

My first thought was, *Ah. He is dead. And I love him.* It was very curious to feel so much adoration intermingled with serenity, given my initial perception of his state of being as *not-alive*. I gathered him up into my arms, held him to my heart, and to my surprise, a few moments later, his soul seemed to enter (or re-enter) his frame, his face and form animated, he took his first breath, and came fully alive. Ignatius Shepherd was here.

This experience taught me everything I had no idea I was thirsting for, and it rocked me to my core. In retrospect, I was, and am, immensely grateful that none of the people in the room (including Lee, or the three friends I had invited to help with our older kids) touched my baby, or attempted to rescue him, or revive him, or to perform the allegedly critically necessary maneuvers that most certainly would have been employed in the context of any degree of professional supervision.

I was also relieved that I had declined to absorb or adopt the trend, which seems to have proliferated throughout the natural birth-world, of sucking, or clearing the airways of a not-yet embodied newborn by covering their mouth with my own. I suspect this may, in a very small number of cases, be a truly instinctive choice on the part of a mother, but I think it's mostly unnecessary, and may sometimes represent an unconscious form of mimesis driven by often performative social media depictions of what primal instinct entails.

In any event, there is no more effective method of clearing a baby's airways than the natural compression that occurs when a newborn moves through the birth canal, and any residual mucous or fluid is almost always either easily swept aside by a mother's hand, or cleared by the baby him or herself as they cry, cough, and then begin to nurse. I know that in the instance of Iggy's emergence, had I intervened to accelerate his revival, this would have deprived him of his ownership over his vital and truly enlivening experience of transitioning independently to full incarnation.

Supposedly lifesaving intrusions like resuscitation, the deployment of oxygen, intubation, and even overly-emphatic, verging-on-violent actions like vigorously rubbing a baby or suctioning their airways with a bulb syringe to "bring them around," have become so ubiquitous that the very notion of a newborn simply being offered the space and quietude to self-animate is an utterly foreign concept for many—one that is considered not only anathema but even highly irresponsible.

Yet it is precisely because we have been culturally entrained to fear the delicate and dependable orchestration of embodiment (and dispossessed of it ourselves as mothers) that so few babies are permitted the organic experience of being allowed to consolidate, materialize, and integrate their journey to earth in their own time.

While it is undeniable that, in a small number of cases, proactive support and encouragement might be necessary to facilitate a baby's adjustment to independent breathing, this is far less frequently necessary than most might expect. We have collectively lost nearly all appreciation for the holiness of the liminal space inhabited by a new child as they are suspended between worlds, and what it is to honour the importance of that child's ownership and agency over the instrument of their visceral selves.

In our eagerness to close the gap between emergence and breathing, we often sacrifice a timeless moment of profound spiritual reconciliation. We also, quite regularly, unwittingly endanger our babies' lives in the effort to rescue them from normal birth.

I no longer believe that much, if any, of the various forms of intervention undertaken at any point in pregnancy or birth (but especially at the time of a baby's emergence) are usually relevant to an infant's wellbeing, except to impede, complicate, or delay their survival, and of course to create a self-fulfilling justification for authoritarian medical saviourism.

There are exceptions, of course, but for the most part, we have been conditioned to perceive these managerial operations as *the* crucial factor for survival. We have been convinced that technological horrors like "vacuum extraction,"[6] along with various maneuvers, techniques, and imposed breaths, are what ensure that a baby makes it, or "succeeds" in

---

[6] "Vacuum extraction" is literally the process of attempting to "vacuum" a baby out of their mother's vagina using a suction device attached to the baby's head, powered by a motorized vacuum machine. This is often accompanied by internal fetal monitoring involving puncturing the skin of the baby's scalp with a tiny metal corkscrew which records the baby's heart-rate.

fully coming into their bodies, but I actually think most babies have to *overcome* these kinds of medicalized intrusion at the pivotal point that they are meant to learn to regulate their physical, energetic, and spiritual systems.

I now comprehend that most often babies breathe *in spite of* the meddling that we've been indoctrinated to see as essential, not thanks to it. This form of sabotage has been so normalized that it has moved beyond custom: the assumption that babies who are not-yet-breathing are on the verge of death and must be heroically rescued by suctioning or CPR has become fully intertwined with a number of distorted myths about our physiology.

As a result of our preoccupation with effectively eliminating what I see as the holy intermission a new human being occupies as they hover between two states of existence, we have impaired our capacity to even properly identify or interpret what it looks like for a healthy child to *be alive*, while resting in the pause prior to their initial inspiration.

What I came to realise through Ignatius's birth, is that The Breath is the most sacred thing we have. It is the essence of what we are. It is through the breath that we *become*. All action, expression, and creation derive from the breath. A child's calibration of breath and body, in that moment of initial intergalactic transition, is incredibly precious and important.

I also learned that Iggy's leisurely metamorphosis—and every aspect of his birth—was a reflection, in large part, of my own state of mind, my choices, and my fears leading up to and during his birth. I believe that birth is reflective of not only a mother's mental condition, but also her spiritual tone and, of course, her baby's soul-essence, and their own chosen path. Birth is very much a co-creation, always.

I find that my children's personalities invariably denote the energy of their births, but not necessarily in the ways that we might assume. Our beloved Ignatius—or Iggy as most people refer to him—is now almost three years old as I write this, and he is one of the brightest sparks. He is intelligent, perceptive, and the most loving big (and little) brother ever. While his birth had a certain shadow element to it, he himself isn't dark or dour at all, but he *is* extremely discerning, and careful, and contemplative in a way that, to me, is evocative of his languid emergence, and of the seeming consideration that he brought to the experience of his arrival.

Never, at any point, have I felt anything other than total gratitude for his incredible birth, including the aspects of tribulation that made it so rich and distinctive.

I was also fairly sure, in the wake of his birth, that I would *not* be having another child.

For one, I was in my late thirties at the time, and I had just the slightest niggling worry that maybe the naysayers were right, and that perhaps my "advanced maternal age" did indeed have something to do with the harrowing aspects of his birth (which I now know, without a doubt, has no basis in reality, or in my own belief system).

But more significantly, at the heart of it, despite how much I cherished Ignatius' birth (and always will), I could not imagine going through another voyage into that same backcountry of pain and obliteration again.

I was still operating from the perspective that Iggy's birth was something that had happened *to me* (as I viewed all of my births up to that point), as opposed to an experience that I had chosen, and created entirely. The truth is, I was afraid, and I was utterly unaware of having any power over my fear, or power over how birth occurred for me in general. Like we so often do, I had made myself an unwitting victim of the world I had single-handedly crafted—oblivious to having built it through my own being.

I did not yet know:

- how to *skillfully* bend time
- what surrender truly meant, and how to do it

- how to connect to God
- how to access my oversoul or Guide-Self
- how to choose bliss or beatitude as an ever-present option
- how to dissolve pain
- how sophisticated and reflexive my inadvertent commitment to victim-consciousness was, or how to clear it
- how to reinforce my energy field
- how to connect with the soul of my baby
- how to choose to function from a place of true self-leadership and mastery in the moment of dissolution
- how to rescript the past
- how to work with fear as an ally, and as an access to power
- how to collapse reality.

I wasn't really aware that these capabilities even existed, let alone that they could be learned or acquired.

But I am now, and it is this set of spiritual and energetic skills—and the potential they have to facilitate a totally painless, completely ecstatic experience in the context of birth—which constitutes the primary teachings of this book.

I now know that it is not necessary to go into birth as I did, believing that it would require the utmost of my courage, gumption, resolve, and grit, and that I could overcome the experience by mustering all my strength, emerging as the victor on the other side of it all.

Blissful birth—birth as I now believe it is ultimately intended to be— doesn't require *any* strength at all.

PORTAL

THE WRONG KIND OF BIRTH

Let me stop for a moment to clarify that if you are beginning to question yourself, or your past birth experiences, or to wonder if maybe you somehow did birth "incorrectly," whether on account of having felt pain, or for any other reason, I want to assure you that neither you, nor your births, can be "wrong."

No matter what kind of birth experience you had, whether it was intolerable, or relentless, or unbearably long, or hilarious and joyful, or if you transferred to the hospital, or chose to give birth there in the first place—whether you loved your birth or hated it—there is nothing wrong with you.

If you are among the many women who are experiencing residual trauma as a result of obstetric violence—whether enacted by hospital obstetricians or homebirth midwives, or a traditional birth attendant, for that matter— please know that whatever feelings you may have about what you and your baby went through (be they feelings of violation, betrayal, grief, or rage), *all* of those emotions are real and valid in every way.

There is no hierarchy of trauma, or grief, or triumph when it comes to birth, just as there is no hierarchy in terms of the "kind of" birth we experience. There is no "failure" in this realm. However your birth transpired is not a marker of your value, your fundamental strength, or your capacity to be a good mother or a good person. Birth is not a morality test, or a punishment.

Birth is, however, our responsibility. We create the birth we experience through the choices we make. What I know from my own experiences (not only in birth but also of obstetric trauma, medical abuse, and sexual assault) is that I was only able to fully recover myself, and my power by developing the willingness to acknowledge that I am entirely responsible for my choices.

Not only am I now in possession of the choice to move forward (or not) in my life once a calamity or a dilemma has occurred (and in what direction I take that strand of choices), but I own all of the choices that led me to each moment of crisis and fracture.

I recognize that this will be a difficult concept for many people to differentiate from "victim-blaming," but the way I am describing radical self-responsibility is, as I see it, the inverse of self-blame, and we'll be exploring this concept in great depth going forward.

What I want to focus on for now, though, is the idea that in the essential totality of existence—in the grand scheme of things—nothing is ever really "wrong," or rather, even wrongness has its flawless place. We *always* give birth as an exact expression of who we are during that chapter of our lives, and our way of giving birth—the time, the place, the quality of the energy field, and every aspect of birth's imprint—is always correct, and perfectly aligned with our being and our spiritual and energetic condition. Given that, there can't really be anything wrong with it, or us, or any part of birth, ever, simply because it is the result of our choosing.

Birth, like all of life, is the perfect mirror of our state of being. This is what I have observed in every birth I have witnessed, and it's absolutely true for me. Each of my births have been an expression of exactly who I was *being* and *becoming* at that juncture.

Every element within the construct of the world we are giving birth to, in every instance, is architected through consent. The choice is ours, in every moment, to recognize ourselves as the brilliant power plants that we are, and to conceive and actualize using that generative power—or, alternatively, to offer ourselves up to consume and be consumed.

Even when our birth experience is awful, or devastating, or traumatic, and in no way a product of *conscious* selection according to any preference we are aware of at the time, it is, even so, the outcome of our aggregated choices.

Now, when I reflect on Ignatius' birth (and especially when I review the documentary film I made about the experience[7]), I notice so many obvious examples of my total commitment to feeling like a victim, with all the drama that entailed. I also recall ways in which I created drama that are *not* necessarily evident in the video, but which I'm able to identify now in retrospect through memory, especially with the perspective I have as the new person I have since become—a different woman entirely.

Beyond what is evident in the footage of Iggy's birth, the subtlest, most granular, wiliest hooks into drama occurred within the recesses of my consciousness and had everything to do with my internal story about how the birth was proceeding (and birth in general), as well as how I was choosing to respond to fear, how I was positioning my body, and the antagonistic relational dynamics that I had unconsciously set up with the (wonderful, loving, and well-intentioned) people around me.

Since much of this drama, tension, antagonism, and resistance took place only within my own mind, I was especially susceptible to succumbing to the negative energy that I was so strenuously cultivating. By way of my unskilled choosing, I had managed to make myself both isolated and pregnable—which is a very vulnerable combination.

It's easy (and delightful) for me to notice, now, how I built the experience of agony during Iggy's birth from the ground up. I love seeing myself clearly. I love being humbled by my own honesty. But the sweetest aspect of this excavation is the reminder and the recognition that despite not having been overtly aware of what I was creating through my choices at the time, out there in the quantum field of looping eternity, my willingness to now lovingly hold my past self to account, and to receive my own observations of truth without defensiveness or dissembling,

---

[7] This documentary is available for purchase on my website, www.yolandenorris-clark.com.

creates a wrinkle and a fold in the fabric of time. I can see that what I know now I also, on some level, knew all along.

The world *is* an infinite hologram. Every imprint, every energetic charge, is reflected in every other iteration of being. Each lifeform and waveform and primal scream ripples or rumbles through the stratosphere and underlayers. All the sequences of growth and entropy, bloom and decay, are present and felt at all times, in all places, and in every corner of perception. Birth itself is a holographic reflection of how we live.

We *are* all one. And the intimacy of that oneness can only be apprehended when we know ourselves as the unique, quintessential beings that we are. Nothing about our particular dramas is special, really, but the effect we—you—have on the universe of existence is as signatory as a first kiss. Every decision changes everything, including the choices we make in every moment of which thoughts to allow, entertain, or embrace.

This is especially clear when we start to examine the nature of drama more closely, and to inspect how it is that we might be contracting into certain outcomes and states of being, taking into account our creative power. The macro-expressions of our occupation of and adherence to drama are as significant as the micro-expressions.

POWER AND PAIN

What I did not fully know during the pregnancies and births of my first eight children is that our conceptualization of pain, pleasure, and sensation itself, is also calibrated according to the thermostat setting of the people and culture around us: beliefs about birth are, paradoxically, more ingrained and deep-rooted than we might think, but also more temporal and changeable than we might expect.

Power, too, is socially engineered and shaped by expectation, along with how we perceive free will and the power it grants us. In many ways, it can be challenging to dislodge our calcified relationship to our own power, but we can change our minds, especially when we are able to expand the awareness we have of ourselves and our effect on the world, by broadening our understanding of choice.

Freedom in birth, and freedom in every aspect of our lives, is waking up to the power of owning every single choice we make. This includes the choices that lead us to give birth the way we do, and the choices we make in the midst of birth, of whether to embrace the force of it, or to resist.

Pain-free birth *is* possible for every woman, but not every woman will choose it—and when we are starting from a place of rationalizing our limitations, we diminish the likelihood of even perceiving the options before us. As confronting and triggering as this might be, it is a law of the universe that, ultimately, the proof of desire is in the having. If you didn't have a pain-free, orgasmic birth experience, you did not choose it.

This will be an uncomfortable declaration for many readers, but bear with me, as we will be plumbing the depths of this concept in the pages to follow.

WHY IS BIRTH PAINFUL?

At this point, you're probably asking yourself, *Why?* If pain in birth is optional, and especially if it is something that we can induce or decline by choice—through will, intention, and our own agency—then why is the pain of birth generally considered to be universal, and why don't more women simply decide to disavow it? Why, if pain-free birth simply involves choosing, don't more women just choose it, and carry on?

Let's explore, in brief, some of the reasons the majority of women experience birth as pain, or at least as a process that involves a significant degree of pain, struggle, and resistance.

Yolande Norris-Clark

Cultural Programming and Social Engineering

You may have noticed that almost every media reference to birth (whether in film, literature, the news, the internet, state messaging, or medical advertising) portrays it as dreadfully painful, gory, injurious, melodramatic, and even imminently deadly. This is purposeful. The idea of birth as dangerous, scary, and of course, excruciating, is heavily marketed to the public, and woven into the fabric of our families, our societies, and our psyches.

When we are born into a culture that fears birth, and that continuously reinforces from every direction the idea that birth is a tribulation to either be avoided through drugs and surgery, or a trial that some women just happen to be strong and savage enough to endure, that message will become installed in our consciousness as an archetype. This is how conditioning arises from our immediate culture and surroundings. The majority of the internal programs we run are ideologically constructed, including the program that tells us that birth is "labour," and that it is primarily a hardship to be overcome.

It is certainly possible for us to consciously de-program ourselves from the effects of intentionally negative and authoritarian social engineering, but this first requires a willingness to acknowledge that we have been deceived by it in the first place.

The story that modern obstetrics saved us from the perils of birth, and that prior to the dawn of medical management women were dying during childbirth in droves, is, in my opinion, an abject lie. Similar to the way that the injection fraud has been perpetrated on the public using propaganda and revisionist history, the idea that birth was the number-one killer before obstetrics saved humanity has been drilled into our heads and is repeated like a mantra, yet is nonetheless, I believe, a blatant fiction.

In fact, it is clear to many of us that the truth is most likely in direct inverse to the official narrative: obstetric management, in conjunction with toxic medications and prophylactic injections, was the foremost *cause* of any rise in maternal and infant mortality, and remains the primary reason for poor birth outcomes (including trauma, which is most definitely a negative, unnecessary, and far-reaching consequence).

No, there is no way to "prove" this using the same fabricated statistics and research methodologies of the monopolistic establishment which devised the deception in the first place. Thank goodness we all have available to us several far more salient forms of proof, including the abysmal and widely observable outcomes of industrial birth today: shocking percentages of babies born by knife[8] and subjected to a range of barbaric and torturous procedures; staggering numbers of women emotionally, psychically, spiritually, physically, and sexually scarred by birth; and a general population of human beings that are terrified of our most basic biological function.

Perhaps the principal substantiation that the accepted story of the inherent danger of birth is an absurd and monumental farce is embodied experience. My own first-hand witnessing of hundreds of babies' births, not to mention my own children who have all passed through my vagina and into the world, has offered me empirical corroboration of the self-evident truth that it was never the doctors with their drugs and tools, or even midwives, that brought about our salvation. Women have never needed to be saved from birth in the first place.

Medical Ideological Possession

Ideological possession (a phrase coined by Carl Jung, the father of analytic psychology) is the result of chronic cultural programming and social engineering, which transmits compelling sociopolitical ideas through propaganda. This programming then "possesses" an individual's worldview—not necessarily because that individual truly believes that

---

[8] One of Sister MorningStar's pithy sayings.

these notions are logical, correct, or beneficial, but because the ideas are so highly charged with symbolic relevance that the programming becomes enmeshed with their identity and sense of self.

We can see examples of this dynamic in politics, religion, and education, but the most comprehensive and invisibilized iteration occurs under the rubric of medical conditioning. The medical industrial complex is the most powerful institution on the planet, and its monopolistic influence reaches every corner of public and private life, from politics, to finance, to technology, to family planning, to our intimate relationships.

The central disciplinary branch of the medico-pharmaceutical establishment is obstetrics which has, for the past couple of centuries, successfully inculcated into each generation an increasing fear of life, death, and the body's biological processes. This is achieved in part through the constant public repetition of core conceptual mantras, such as "birth is dangerous," "birth is disgusting," "birth wrecks our bodies," "birth is pathological," and "birth is painful." This is also achieved through the most effective form of mind-control, which is, of course, the traumatic hazing that occurs during the medicalized birth process itself.[9]

The constant echoing of fear-based messaging primes us to expect abuse and mistreatment during birth, so that when the time comes, we anticipate the abuse that is then duly enacted upon us by medical professionals as simply *what birth is*. Regulated midwives are very much a part of this program as well. While midwifery is presented on the surface as a

---

[9] It is difficult to offer specific examples of this ritual hazing, because literally every single aspect of medically managed birth—including most homebirths with most midwives—exemplifies this dynamic, from the way birthing women are addressed, to the specific procedures to which mothers and babies are subjected. The fear, stress, and trauma resulting from every aspect of the birth process may not be remembered in specific by the babies who are born into this miasmic reality, but it is nevertheless etched into the psyche, the emotional and physical body, and shapes the world we live in. I have written and spoken extensively on this topic for many years, and this is also the focus of my upcoming book.

profession that is distinct from obstetrics, it is, in fact, very much incorporated into the obstetric model, and functions in many ways as a foil for the medical apparatus.

Regulated midwives are effectively state-appointed and state-approved controlled-opposition. Under the guise of "gentle birth," "family-led birth," "humanized birth," and coercive concepts like "informed consent," midwives inflict the very same forms of obstetric violence on mothers and babies as is perpetrated in the hospital, camouflaged by the pretense of "holistic care," all of which supports the continuation of the multi-layered deception, hiding in plain sight.

This arrangement is as convincing as it is because most midwives have no idea that they themselves are being used as operatives. If (or when) they do come to realise they are working for the biggest and most powerful drug cartel in history, they tend to rationalize their collusion with excuses about their livelihood, their sunk costs, or the potent fantasy that they're at least supporting some form of "harm reduction" with their heroic presence. The brainwashing which student midwives experience in midwifery school is so thorough, that they emerge truly believing that their treatment of women and their approach to birth is in contrast to the medical model, when in actuality it is just an embellished, euphemized replica.

Increasingly, women are becoming aware of this dynamic, but the majority are still taken in by the propaganda that on one hand glorifies all of obstetrics, while on the other hand makes a false distinction between hospital birth and regulated midwifery which is no more than a counterfeit "alternative."

A good rule of thumb if you are considering hiring a midwife is to find out who makes the rules to which she adheres, who she answers to, and who signs her paycheque. If the reply to any of these questions is any person, entity, or organization other than you (the mother) then you are electing to walk into a conflict of interest.

Though it may seem unlikely, the women who choose to exit the medical establishment entirely, and who opt for freebirth, or for the support of an unlicensed, unregulated, independent birth-witness, are still often (as I was, and as we all are to varying degrees) "possessed" by medical ideology, which exerts so much residual covert influence even on erstwhile defectors, that we remain to some extent captured by its framework. This shows up as an unconscious minimization of our own power, and of how our bodies, minds, and psyches respond to the birth process, including in the assumption that birth is inherently painful.

And yet, just as it's possible to extricate ourselves from the larger and more evident vortices of cultural programming, we can effectuate our own exorcism from medical ideological possession as well. Cultivating an awareness of our internal colonization is the required first step, followed by actually physically leaving the premises and then abdicating our co-dependent connection with all handmaidens and accomplices.

Subconscious Collective Agreements

Agreement, or consensus, is incredibly influential. This is because we humans are pack-oriented beings. We attune to each other's behaviours and we follow the group, partly because we want to fit in with the clan, but even more so because we are constantly calibrating to the vibratory resonance of the people around us.

Shifting this relationship to our fundamental subconscious beliefs necessitates that we deeply examine those beliefs in the first place. We must be willing to look at what our underlying assumptions really are, where our allegiances lie, who we look up to, who we knowingly and unknowingly seek to emulate, and, ultimately, whose opinion and approval we are pursuing, or driven by? Your own, or someone else's?

When the majority of those within our close social circle agree that not only is birth automatically painful, but that mothers have no agency over whether or not they experience pain, the cells in our bodies organize to make that belief true in the realm of the material. Whose vortex are you orbiting? Your own, or someone else's?

Layers of Individual, Societal, and Intergenerational Trauma

Every human alive today has been impacted by the trauma that results from birth rape and sabotage on account of our own arrival via the bodies of our mothers, which, whether we have specific memories of the event or not, creates a lifelong imprint on the nervous system. Many mothers also carry trauma from giving birth to their children, especially if those births occurred within the industrial obstetric system (and those children are subsequently affected by that trauma).

But in addition to our recent histories, the cellular consequences of intergenerational birth-related harm—the stories of our mothers, our grandmothers, and our great-great-grandmothers—is continuously reverberating throughout our bodies. Obstetric trauma specifically, is so ubiquitous that it has become almost entirely imperceptible to most people.

Pain in birth is always related to the set and setting of our birth experience, yet is also intertwined with existing obstetric trauma and other forms of trauma as well. Because birth is inherently sexual, obstetric trauma is a form of sexual trauma, and conversely, any kind of sexual wounding will always have a bearing on our births. Sadly, the vast majority of women not only carry existing birth-related trauma in the form of suppressed somatic memories from the past and from their own experience of birth as infants, but most women have also endured varying forms of sexual abuse or misuse.

Birth itself is not traumatic. Birth is literally enlivening, invigorating, and, as I now believe, designed to be as ecstatic and holy as the experience of loving, reverential, procreative sex. Yet the story that it is birth that destroys our bodies and our minds (leading to that mysterious illness we call "postpartum depression," which, of course, is simply a symptom of the monolithic, socially constructed psychological operation that is the desecration of birth) rather than the violation and harm that mothers and babies are subjected to during medicalized birth, is all-pervasive.

It is birth-rape and abuse that is the root cause of mothers' mental, emotional, spiritual, and physical fragmentation following the event, not birth itself. Yet so many women are unable to recognize that what they experienced during birth was rape and assault, because obstetric rape and assault is completely normalized, and perpetrated just as often by midwives as it is by doctors.

When these forms of trauma go unacknowledged, and, perhaps more significantly, when they are dismissed by the people around us, and by the entire culture in which we are immersed, the result is that we develop multiple layers of armouring, rigidity, and resistance to surrender, which can make it that much more challenging for many women to melt into the birth process, to trust it, to allow it to permeate our being, and to *become* the power of birth altogether as we are made to be.

The Manufacturing of Consent

"Consent" is blatantly weaponized. It is used as a tool for manipulating mothers and gaslighting us into compliance. The reason consent is such an important concept within the medical system is because it serves a dual purpose: consent is both a construct of coercion, and the basis upon which each and every one of us contracts into complying with not just false authority, but also pain.

Our "consent" is often extracted under duress, yet at the same time, by entering the industrial obstetric sphere, we are tacitly agreeing to submit ourselves to the worldview, program, and hierarchy of the medical establishment—a hierarchy in which we, as mothers, occupy the very lowest rung. This doesn't negate the discomfort and unpleasantness of (or the ethical violation implicit in) coercion, and it doesn't mean that choosing to withdraw or deny our consent (an option that is always available to us) will be easy. It only means that the choice is always there, and that the consequences are ours to decline, or embrace.

Intrinsic to full awareness is the recognition that consent is always operational in every part of life. No matter what kind of experience we are having, especially ones we claim *not* to want or enjoy, there is some point at which we have granted our consent, whether it's having walked through the doors of the institution that first time, or whether it's the choice we make to dwell on a particular thought-pattern or sensation. Every experience we have is architected through prior consent, at some stage.

Spiritual Fracture

Birth is ceremony. Birth is prayer. Birth is a hurricane, and a spring rain. Birth is a May morning. To give birth, and to be born, is to be summoned by God. Birth is more intoxicating and psychedelic than any exogenous drug, more potent than any plant medicine.

Birth is the foremost source of spiritual power and knowing. It is for this reason primarily that birth is sabotaged and broken, which invariably injures our sense of connection with the source and creator of all. This is the objective of industrial obstetrics, and this is also why mothers struggle to experience birth as the profoundly euphoric, easeful, and transcendent initiation that I believe it is designed to be.

Birth, in many ways, resembles what Carl Jung described as the *numinosum*. The numinous encounter, according to Jung, is an event that involves the breaking open of the psyche to a new dimension of consciousness.[10] Jung, however, specifically described numinosity as "an

---

[10] Carl Jung is said to have appropriated the term numinosum from Rudolf Otto who argues, in his 1917 book The Idea of the Holy: An Inquiry Into the Non-rational Factor

experience of the subject independent of his will," which I take issue with, especially given what I now know about birth as a spiritual shattering-open which is both uncontrollable and yet eminently malleable by the mind — a paradox we will be exploring soon.[11]

More than any other occurrence or phenomenon available to us in this lifetime, giving birth (and being born) offers the most significant, and prescient channel to the spiritual realm, through its totally unique nexus

---

in the Idea of the Divine and Its Relation to the Rational, that all religious experiences are numinous in that they invoke fear and trembling (the mysterium tremendum) along with a sense of attraction, fascination, and compulsion (the mysterium fascinas). Numen, however, is originally a Latin term for "divinity," "divine presence," or "divine will." Cicero (106 BCE, to 43 BCE), a writer, orator, lawyer, scholar, and statesman of the late Roman Republic, wrote of a "divine mind," a god "whose numen everything obeys," and a "divine power" "which pervades the lives of men." According to Romanian scholar Carmen Fenechiu, in their essay "The Term Numen in Cicero's Works," published in Les Études Classiques 76 (2008), "in the Late Republic numen was understood and used with two different but logically closely linked senses, namely "will" and "power" (imperium). These meanings have been recorded in several of Cicero's works, more precisely, in his speeches, but also in his political and philosophical essays. In most cases, the notion of the numinous is used with respect to a specified god or to the whole divine community without any specification regarding the exact identity of its members [p. 97]...[O]ne encounters in Cicero's works different meanings of the concept, which argue for its semantic evolution in the Republican Period (from the initial meaning "nod" to that of "will," "power," and even "divinity"), and imply that the term was already in use for some time… And yet numen did not originally presuppose a relationship to the divine world…But, gradually, as some of Cicero's passages show, the term comes to include the attribute diuinum and to express by itself (without any further specification) the sacred character. Thus numen as "divine power" is ascribed to the senate or to the laws." [p. 104] Cicero's use of the term — and, it seems, his characterization of the gods — is distinctly political and rhetorical, a far cry from the self-conscious psychoanalytic treatment of the term a couple of millennia later, all of which is delightfully reflective of the common threads of language, and both the similarities and distinctions in cultural preoccupations across the ages.

[11] Despite Jung's brilliance, and his immense contribution to the field of human consciousness, he nonetheless seemingly overlooked the topic of birth altogether, whereas I increasingly see birth as one of the most significant individual and cohesive experiences instrumental to the shaping of the collective imagination, not to mention a phenomenon that is at the very root of all archetypal personal dynamics. Given that Jung never had the exquisite privilege of giving birth — undisturbed or not — I am willing to forgive his necessarily somewhat limited perspective on the matter of consciousness in general.

of creativity, embodiment, and a cultivation of a relationship with the layers of our own internal awareness. We struggle with surrendering fully to the experience of birth and we tend towards resistance in so many ways, in part because we have become, over successive generations, ill-at-ease with the numinous experience overall.

This also explains why we are entrained to expect, and therefore conjure, pain during birth—in part to encourage and maintain dependency and victimhood, but also because pain, experienced as the endpoint instead of as a vehicle for further transformation, can inhibit the full efflorescence of our spiritual portals, and can dull our capacity to connect with the divine.

In short, alignment with the sacred is dangerous to the livestock managers who profit from our spiritual torpor and inertia, and who will discourage the realization of our divine potential through birth in any way possible, especially via the incitement of fear.

Fear

Fear—and the fear that individual women feel, cultivate, create, and absorb from the myths and stories of our culture—is one of the most effective disciplinary tools available. Fear, and its seeding, is one of the main reasons why birth is almost always depicted as a horrific emergency situation. Fear is what ensures that most women will willingly submit to the demonic rituals of obstetrics, and fear is at the heart of the expectation of pain and agony that is then imprinted in our subconscious minds from infancy onwards.

Fear also directly creates pain, through physiological and psychological tension and resistance. In Chapter Eleven, we will unpack where fear comes from, who it belongs to, how we consent to it, how we unconsciously nurture it, and how to powerfully disavow it.

Yolande Norris-Clark

Sexual Distortion

Birth is the ultimate culmination of sexual creativity. Orgasm is just as possible during birth (the zenith of sexual union) as it is during the act of procreation itself. The same hormones, body parts, organs, and physiological processes are at play during sexual intercourse as in birth. During birth, as with sex, the womb pulsates, the hidden yet highly-enervated network of the clitoris interwoven throughout every woman's pelvic lattice is suffused with blood as oxytocin and other intoxicating chemicals emanate from the pituitary gland, and we enter a state of heightened arousal.

Arguing that not all women can experience pleasure and orgasm during birth is no different from arguing that not all women can experience pleasure and orgasm during sex. This can be very confronting for many of us, especially given the seemingly endless inversions and distortions that exist in our culture surrounding sex and sexuality.

Increasingly, we are being groomed to think of sex and birth as totally separate entities—separate issues altogether—and this bifurcation is being fueled by the rapid development of biotechnology, from chemical birth control that formally established the decoupling of sex from procreation to the disintegration of the biological family and motherhood itself from birth, along with the rise of surrogacy and the approaching era of ectogenesis.[12]

---

[12] Sedgwick, Helen. 2017. "Artificial Wombs Could Soon Be a Reality. What Will This Mean for Women?" The Guardian, November 25, 2017. https://www.theguardian.com/lifeandstyle/2017/sep/04/artifical-womb-women-ectogenesis-baby-fertility. The term ectogenesis refers to the gestation of life outside of the womb. The word is derived from the Greek ἐκτός (ectos), meaning "outside," and γένεσις (genesis) meaning "origin" or "beginning." This technology has already been developed and is increasingly being promoted throughout the media and in popular culture.

Meanwhile, sexual norms have shifted to such an extent that the idea of the commodification of our bodies through degrading imagery and scenarios that feature forms of violation that have long been (rightly) viewed as taboo is now standardized and unremarkable to many. Sexual abuse has always occurred, but sexual crimes and the priming of potential victims now occurs within (and is facilitated by) the virtual realm, in ways that are far more insidious, complex, and darker than ever before.

The outcome is widespread confusion about how we navigate our relationships and sexuality, especially as mothers. Misplaced shame and guilt about the fundamentally sexual nature of what it is to be human abound, even to the extent that we deny our very origins and the inarguable fact that sex is a part of birth. Often the guilt and shame we feel stem from very real abuse which a shocking number of people experience in their individual lives, and through exposure to a culture of transgression, including the sexualized boundary violations that occur during birth.

This is rarely discussed publicly or in the media, and remains part of the collective shadow almost entirely, but the majority of the operations and procedures that make up the industrial obstetric experience (from early pregnancy onward) are pornographic and specifically sexually abusive. These protocols include vaginal exams, vaginal surveillance with the use of dildo-esque ultrasonic probes, strangers placing their hands on our labia, fondling our babies' heads while they emerge, slicing our vaginal portal open with blades (a practice called "episiotomy"), and using metal instruments to pull our babies out of our bodies, all of which constitute highly sexualized techniques.

Such methodologies are deliberately designed not to facilitate birth at all, or to support the health or safety of the mother and baby (although that would be the justification), but are rather intended to reinforce the dominance of both the practitioner and the institution under which they are practising, and to emphasise the submissiveness of the mother (and her baby).

Obstetric birth is primarily a sexual humiliation ritual. Therefore it is no wonder that humans in this day and age tend to be very disoriented when it comes to how we relate to both sex and birth. Just as some (or many) women have never experienced orgasmic birth, so too are there some women (and men, I assume) who never experience orgasm during sex. That doesn't mean they're wrong, or broken, and it doesn't mean there's anything to fix, or to strive for, or to try for.

As most adults who can and do orgasm know—including those who have learned to orgasm—it doesn't come from "trying." Yet for those who are interested in expanding the bandwidth of their experience and their capacity, orgasm is available. This is just as true when it comes to birth as with sex.

Our Commitment to Drama and Victimhood

The most effective form of population control is the perpetuation of victim-consciousness through the widespread endorsement of the notion that we have no power over the circumstances or outcome of our lives. Voluntary helplessness masked as impotence is commodified and stimulated throughout society.

In the context of industrial obstetrics, there are a myriad of benefits for the corporate institutions that seek to control human beings by preserving and propagating the notion that we require their drugs and interventions in order that we and our babies be "delivered" from the oppression of birth, which supports (and is supported by) the continuous stream of stories from women who were gaslit into believing that they were indeed saved by whatever interventions or procedures were justified by medical staff.

But the most insidious forms of victimhood are the subtlest, and the most controversial aspect of what I share about birth—and the key to whether or not (and how) we encounter either pain or pleasure—is that we invariably experience exactly what it is that we have chosen. Just as pleasurable birth can be summoned, crafted, elicited, and claimed, the necessary coefficient to this assertion is that pain in birth is likewise chosen.

We choose pain for a multitude of reasons, but many of these relate to the shadowy delight of having a powerful story of how hard we tried, how we almost died, that we prevailed in the end, or that we did, after all, need to be saved by the experts. We all have a different flavour in the way we opt into drama and suffering, and birth provides an incredible substrate for promulgating our preferred genre of theatre.

In my own case, I chose pain for my first eight births so that I could revel in the story of my immense capacity and my determination to prevail. Each of my birth stories was shocking and extreme in its own way—again, my first birth occurred at forty-three weeks' gestation, consisted of fifty hours of labour, a baby in a supposedly "posterior" position, terrible back pain, and on and on. And I loved it. But the most apparently subversive part of each of my birth stories has always been my long-standing assertion (which I still maintain), that everything I experienced is normal, and that most of what occurs spontaneously during an undisturbed birth is likewise fairly unremarkable.

Birth is, as I have been repeating for decades, the perfect mirror. We give birth as the fullest expression of who we are in that particular instance. Birth is *always* showing us who we are, whether we are looking for the answer or not.

True to my own lifelong chosen role as a whistle-blower and iconoclast, I have unconsciously made sure that each of my birth stories involved some element of crossing the boundary of what would be considered "tolerable" for most women, because I have, historically, reveled in drama—sought it out, wallowed in it, nurtured it.

The irony isn't lost on me that the more I have recognized my agency—and our personal and collective agency as human beings—and the more I have embraced what I see as our immense, expansive, God-gifted power of free will, the more shocking and unpalatable it seems my message has become, for some, while others are eager to envelop this newfound power into their worldview, and are galvanized by the prospect that we do not ever have to comply with the invitation to identify with victimhood.

THE STRUCTURE OF SURRENDER

Surrender is one of the core components of consciously choosing our birth experience, and yet many people misunderstand the nature of it. The experience of surrender is often misconstrued as acquiescence or resignation, but it's actually quite structured. Surrender lies between tension and pure relaxation. It is a liminal state, but one of presence, and awareness. Surrender is flexible, yielding, and connects us with all of creation, across the folds of time and space, through the embrace of pure reality, now.

Surrender is a discipline, a skill, and a choice, but it's also an instinct, or a facet of instinct—an aspect of our primordial makeup that, for most of us, has been profoundly wounded. Over aeons, trauma and imposed servitude have led to the erosion of numerous formerly reflexive impulses to the extent that surrender has become something we are called to relearn and to remember in order to step into power.

To heal and prosper (rather than succumb to the many forms of temptation laid before us) requires a form of intention devoid of endeavour, or aspiration, or of "trying"—one that is rooted instead in the implicit dexterity of surrender. This is the very same dynamic at play when it comes to choosing a birth experience that is either blissful, ecstatic, easy, and pain-free, or a birth experience that is scary, hard, and painful.

The holographic nature of life on earth also means that we can heal and change from a multitude of angles and directions, and we can apply the phenomenon of reverse-engineering to birth, through birthing into existence the reality that we have already chosen. This process is totally subconscious for most of us, but in the following chapters I'll share a very simple recipe for moving it into the field of your agency—not to necessarily make it explicitly conscious, but to bring yourself into an awareness of this dynamic as a *field* of consciousness.

And this is what wild, sovereign birth offers.

THE ULTIMATE EDICT

We are actively discouraged from learning the art of choosing. It is a cultural taboo to acknowledge that we wield the power of choice at every juncture, in every single instance, at every point in time, and with every thought. In fact, we are explicitly taught that our choices are inevitably curtailed by societal structures, who we think we are, our background, our economic circumstances, and our identities.

The impact of the collective agreements that swirl around us (even if we don't directly buy into them ourselves–or think we don't) have an effect, and carry a certain influence, although the weight of that influence ultimately comes down to consent, and the extent to which we allow ourselves to accord with, and enter the vortex of, the wider consensus. With regards to birth especially, our choices—the choices available to each and every woman—are far more expansive than we have been led to believe.

Most women are simply unaware that overwhelmingly, within the so-called "mainstream," the choices presented to us as constitutive of the array of options available, are actually incredibly limited, and generally represent only those choices that are sanctioned by the medical industrial complex. In fact, there are entire worlds of choice beyond the corral that our presumed handlers allow us to see from our blinkered frame. We have only to lift the veil.

The ultimate edict—one of the foremost laws of power and a key to personal and mutual ascendancy—is that we *always* get what we truly desire. And the proof of true desire is in the having.[13]

The skills that must then be acquired in order to augment our effectiveness in life (and birth) include learning how to know ourselves (and therefore how to differentiate between indiscriminate wants and true desire) and how to choose with proficiency. This requires that we first develop the capacity to recognize the shades, nuances, and layers of choice and how it arises as we create potential from the substance of our lives.

INTEGRATION QUESTIONS

1. Do you believe birth is painful? If so, which "reasons" did you identify with? What is your story about birth—what is birth to you, and what is it not?

2. What is your own origin story—the story of your cosmological mythology? Don't think; just allow the words to flow, whether internally or in a free-flowing journal exercise.

---

[13] Several people have pointed out to me that this phrase is similar to the expression "having is evidence of wanting," which frames Carolyn Elliot's hugely successful book "Existential Kink," in which, as I understand it, Elliot refers to and builds on the work of Carl Jung and his famous concept that until the unconscious is brought into consciousness "it will direct your life and you will call it fate." I was under the apparently incorrect assumption for several years that "having is evidence of wanting" was a widely used cultural maxim, but apparently the brilliant little saying was coined by Elliot herself. I have not read or engaged with any of Elliot's work—yet. But I look forward to doing so someday, especially seeing as years ago, I bought one of her courses. In keeping with one of my particularly shameful self-sabotaging habits, however, life got "busy," and I never ended up actually looking at any of the course material. But perhaps my interest in, and support for her work filtered through by osmosis.

PORTAL

3. Where did you come from? When you close your eyes and feel into the particle and the wave, what's there? What is your earliest memory? (Not a concrete memory necessarily, but the memory of feeling and being. Allow whatever is under the surface to emerge.)

CHAPTER THREE

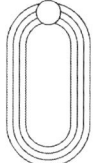

THE SOCIAL ENGINEERING OF BIRTH

BREAKING BIRTH

Motherhood is the most persistent, profound, and important form of love, connection, and energy on this planet, and birth itself is the portal to awakening within us our most significant and powerful form of insight. Birth is the basis for the activation of our deepest connection to our higher selves, and to God.

Birth is vast, fluid, and impossible to contain, to parse, or (despite my stubborn attempts) to articulate. It can be completely overwhelming—titanic—and utterly pacific. It is an astronomical coming and going, a merging into, a plunging inward, without and within the watery all and everything. Why then, is birth not typically experienced as the exultant free dive into the oceanic core of our being that it can be?

Why are the majority of humans alive on planet earth right now literally born into fear, tension, struggle, and significant trauma?

Birth is always an initiation into one world or another, yet very few mothers are aware that we can choose the world we initiate ourselves and our babies into. Beyond the question of pain versus pleasure during birth, most women are incognizant of the fact that the normalization of obstetric violence within the industrial birth system is a way of priming ourselves and our children for a world of nihilism and self-objectification. Most of us do not realise that we can create a reality in which our sense of belonging and connection with God and all of creation means that we are never lost or alone.

Unfortunately, reality creation is not (or is no longer) the norm, and to understand why, we need only look at the general state of birth today. Birth inevitably leaves a potent spiritual imprint upon both mother and baby, and we have each been programmed with the cellular memories of our own arrival into the world, which are in turn overlaid by ancestral baggage and media messaging, all of which tells us to be afraid of birth.

Industrial obstetric birth is the most dominant, commandeering form of mind-control that exists in society, and (due largely to its influence) most of us see birth as something we have to battle or survive. Our societal beliefs about birth have been aggressively engineered to ensure that most of us are terrified enough of the process to willingly submit ourselves and our babies to the horrors and brutality of the industrial obstetric system.

There are many layers to the conditioning that drives mothers to acquiesce and consent to the hijacking of their bodies, beyond simply financial profit and the overwhelming success of the medical hegemony. The deeper purpose of this programming is to separate us from our connection with God, and to uphold the prevailing mindset that our lives are both at odds with, and at the mercy of nature; that we are feeble, impotent victims of the meaningless, random phenomenon of being.

This is achieved through highly specialized, ritualized forms of ceremonial obstetric abuse that are contrived to break both the mind and the body of the mother, initiating her into a reality in which her perception of power and security as sourced from within is obliterated. Our internal authority as mothers is subsequently externalized to surrogate figures, state administrators, and institutions. Instead of referring to our own essential, instinctive, God-connected (and God-given) clairsentience and dominion for guidance, we are trained to farm out our jurisdiction to pediatricians, governments, social workers, schools, and parenting experts.

This may sound conspiratorial. You may be wondering why fear and submission would be the goals of our obstetric institutions? And if this is true, what nefarious actors or influences are behind this intention?

While I do believe that many of our institutional structures have been founded upon the principles of fracture, separation, deracination, and alienation, I *also* know that the impulse to use others, to take what is not ours, and to enact evil in whatever way, is present in all of us. There is no one extraordinarily demonic family, or corporation, or entity to blame. There are, certainly, figureheads, and functionaries, some of whom remain enthroned over several generations, but eventually those who rise will fall, and are replaced once they have served their purpose in the schema of dark and light by the next appointee waiting in the wings, eager to sell their soul in turn.

The answers lie within the domain of power, the spirit, and our relationship with nature and the divine. We all have the option of following the inverted path. We all have the capacity to fall from grace, and we often do. No one is exempt.

When the cord that connects us to our creative, generative power is frayed or severed—as occurs most significantly via the traumas of industrialized, medicalized birth—we become easily manipulated, controlled, and susceptible to the allure of entering into agreements with those same forces that champion the cannibalistic organizations and individuals who have become indentured in their servitude to the frequency of the diabolical.

Those who actively participate in the abuse of mothers and babies are representing and acting out sheer evil, yes. And they are just as much victims of this desolate system as anyone. Their collusion only proves the truth of this terrible dynamic.

Yet it is only by consent that we bind ourselves to these luciferian urges and energies and grant them ingress. These entities feed on coercion, manipulation, and the extraction of the soul-essence of human beings that becomes available when we choose to ally with evil.

When we consent to hate ourselves, to poison ourselves, to seek solace in substances and habits and thoughts that offer only surface consolation, we are making a choice to betray ourselves and our children by choosing the path of destruction, instead of creation, thereby replicating the trauma of our original psychic rupture during birth.

Breaking birth, not only through direct abuse and trauma, but also through the myth that birth is inevitably and even purposefully painful, leads to the fracturing of our greatest power: the Knowing that we possess infinite resources, innately and through birth, for connecting with Spirit and to each other, and the ability to create from a place of limitless expansion.

The barbaric traumas and spiritual vampirism of industrial birth constitute the primary fissure in our divinely ordained aegis of protection. Sovereign, autonomous birth, on the other hand, is the nexus of creation and offers us the most significant path to self-healing, self-knowledge, and our greatest potency as human beings.

VESTIGES OF VIOLENCE

During the months before I gave birth to my first baby, someone lent me a video tape (yes, those were ancient days—streaming didn't exist, the internet was very new, and if you wanted to watch a video it was on VHS tape) called *Birth into Being*, a documentary about the waterbirth movement in Russia in the 1990s.[14]

The documentary depicts several instances of what I now see as totally unnecessary forms of disturbance and even the violation of birthing mothers and babies, but I vividly remember watching it for the first time and marvelling at the ability of the woman suspended in a glass-sided pool, to release her baby peacefully into the water with only the softest vocalizations.

I also remember immediately having the thought that that could never be me—I'm just not *that*. Not only did I see myself as too angry, anxious, obsessive, and analytical to give birth that way, but I also believed that I was not, fundamentally, a *good enough* woman to have that kind of birth. I wasn't sweet enough, or soft enough. I didn't have that kind of grace. I wasn't enough of *something*, to give birth in a state of serenity.

I *did* know that I could, and would, give birth "successfully," because the story that my mother unwaveringly transmitted to me since I was tiny was that everything that had been done to me and her in the hospital on my birth-day had been barbaric and unnecessary. My mother had prevailed in giving birth to me vaginally not thanks to, but *in spite of* it all: in spite of the goons coming in and out of the room, in spite of the epidural she was violently forced to accept, in spite of the obstetrician who cut her yoni open with a blade, severed my umbilical cord prematurely, pulled me out of her vagina, and then took me away—and in spite of all this happening while my father was engaged in a verbal altercation with the anaesthesiologist that only marginally fell short of a full-on fistfight.

But the considerable, longstanding trauma which I still carry from my own hospital birth was tempered to a great extent by my mother's continual gift

---

[14] "Birth Into Being." 1999. https://www.cultureunplugged.com/documentary/watch-online/play/53925/Birth-Into-Being. The video is, as of this writing, available to watch for free.

to me of radical honesty, and along with it came a total belief in my body's fundamental capacity. What I learned and absorbed from my own birth experience was not fear and dependency at all, but rather defiance, and rage.

I was never handicapped, in the way so many women are, by my mother's story that medical professionals saved us, because at no point did she ever believe that to be the case. The form of trauma-bondedness that leads us to believe that we were rescued (when in actuality we were abused) is, however, the most common response to obstetric rape—the extreme, highly sexualized, and intimate kind of abuse which has become so prevalent in birth that it's seen by the vast majority of human beings alive today as utterly normal, and even to be expected.

Instead, throughout my childhood, my mother maintained that the medicalization of our birth was completely uncalled-for, and that birth itself is no big deal (if you can avoid doctors)—it's just a lot of hard work, and thus I was eager for it, and delighted to finally become a mother. I had spent my teenage years depressed and disembodied, but when I became pregnant, I felt for the first time in years—maybe for the first time in my life—a sense of complete ease, comfort, and safety in my flesh and in myself.

Thanks to my miraculous fertility, I felt whole, and I had no doubt that I could give birth. While I am immensely grateful to my mother for her grit, confidence, and strength, I realise now that the story I had created for myself out of the constituents of my lineage, was, nonetheless, still a highly distorted, damaged, trauma-informed, misconceptualization of what birth is. Yet I took that narrative, and from it I built my overarching identity: I was a warrior.

Just as life was a struggle for my foremothers, so would I fight in whatever way necessary, from my first breath to my last. It couldn't be any other way, I believed, and it was from that assumption and that state of being that I gave birth to my first eight children: birth was the antagonist, and I would never let it win. No one was more ferocious, savage, or determined than I. I had warred my way through my own birth, and I would armour myself again to bring my own babies forth.

Little did I know that in following the urge to protect myself—to steel myself against birth—I was reinforcing not only my preexisting traumas (and those of my ancestors), but unwittingly choosing pain. At that stage, the term "surrender," to me, signified resignation and defeat.

THE OBSTETRIC DILEMMA

When I was seventeen years old, I was informed by a doctor (during one of the last visits I would ever make to a gynaecologist's office prior to exiting the medical system almost entirely) that my pelvis was likely far too "narrow" and "masculine" to ever give birth naturally (let alone painlessly). While I recognized immediately how ludicrous this pronouncement was, the exchange stayed with me and over the years the significance of that physician's prediction in the context of how I have come to understand the larger story of birth throughout the ages has— perhaps in an expression of rebellion—become a source of inspiration (and contrarian delight).

As I discussed in the previous chapter, the impact of birth on the body, the psyche, and the nervous system is invisibly shaped by our beliefs—both conscious and subconscious—and those beliefs are embedded through personal experience, cellular memory, storytelling, and transmitted through the collective consciousness via cultural lore. This is certainly true when it comes to the majority of birth practices and prejudices which are grounded in the assumption that birth is an inherently dangerous medical event. But even what may seem like automatic or autonomic physiological responses to the sensations of birth have far more to do with the archaic remnants of inverted doctrine, held in epochal layers of politicization, than most of us are aware.

My own process of breaking the spells by which I have been variously enthralled over the years has been at times dark, occasionally enlightening, and often disturbing. The more I have opened myself to questioning my previously held beliefs, the more I have found that every concept, structure, institution, and system in the world relates to birth, from the shape of the earth to the mysteries of the cosmos, to God, and to the various lenses through which we interpret and perceive the idea of history. My lived experiences in birth have been the catalyst for some of the most fundamental shifts in my apprehension of the nature of reality, my relationship to what I know to be true, and of what truth is.

For example, when I was first establishing myself as a birthkeeper and a mother, I saw the field of midwifery in relatively idealistic (and in retrospect somewhat simplistic) terms—as a profession that had, until recently, been firmly anchored in biological reality, deep compassion, and ancestral wisdom. But when I began to study (and question) midwifery and birth customs and formalities more deeply, to examine first accounts of midwifery, and to compare current medical dogma with contemporary midwifery practice alongside the midwifery perspectives and conventions from the 19th century, the Renaissance, and even the medieval era, what I realized is that the history of midwifery is largely the history of the various ways that birth has been sabotaged.

I had assumed that midwifery was a casualty of corporatism and industrialization—a time-honoured profession deserving of reverence, which had been predated upon by the medical industrial complex, appropriated by it, and subsumed by it. But I now recognize that midwives, midwifery, and the long-established ideological frameworks and cultural beliefs entrenched in every society as tradition and authoritative knowledge, were highly distorted well before the medical takeover.

There is very little evidence, in any written accounts, of any birth-tradition from any culture that didn't involve multiple forms of unnecessary or detrimental physical and psychological interference. Yet every kind of intercession upon birth, and every distinctive ethnic version of the violation of our bodies during birth—not least of which is the kind of vandalism enacted on birth and birthing women today—has almost nothing to do with the preservation of life but has always served a deeper purpose.

That deeper purpose is the management of power in order to establish and fortify a given society's hierarchical structures, and to ensure that women—and humans in general—know their place. Birth is the foremost source of power and, because of this, birth is also the most important experience to modify and manage, for those who seek control or who act as functionaries for the would-be controllers.

Midwives have always served as the unwitting administrators of social and cultural discipline. It was traditional and indigenous beliefs and assumptions about birth that informed, to a large extent, what has now become standard obstetric practice. I am in no way suggesting that human beings have *never* known birth as the spontaneous, glorious, self-directed, God-connected experience of ecstasy that I now believe it was always designed to be, only that there are very few, if any existing historical records of such a time (almost none, to my knowledge), and I believe that too is deliberate.

I want to acknowledge that we cannot separate our often-warped misconceptions about birth, from the doctrinal ideas that form the basis of our communally held worldviews. One such fundamental concept, which has profoundly affected how we understand birth today, is the gospel of evolution which underpins not only agreements about the origins of our species but has moulded our consensus on the [dys]function of the birth process, including how we *feel* birth as mothers, and how we feel *about* it.

The idea that humans have "evolved" to be incapable of giving birth without the assistance of technology, professional management, or outside expertise is one of the most significant and persistent deceptions that has shaped the human story. Ironically, the theory of evolution postulates that we are essentially no more than somewhat socially advanced animals. According to pet intellectual of the ruling class Yuval Harari, we are simply "hackable animals." Yet the only thing that we purportedly do *not* have in common with almost all other mammals is a facility for birth.

While every other mammalian species manages to procreate in the absence of outside supervision, surveillance, and interference, the story yet persists that human beings happen to be the exception: we are both bestial, and yet somehow unique among beasts to the extent that our inexplicably metamorphic evolution from sea-dwelling creatures to apes, to homo sapiens, has granted us immense intelligence while also magically rendering us physically deformed to the point that autonomous birth is believed to be a near-impossibility.

None of this makes any sense at all, of course. But women, like me, who have been granted the illumination of knowing through embodied experience that the hardship we endure during birth is largely fabricated through culture and consensus, often find ourselves exiled to the margins of not only established fields of study built on certain unquestionable premises, but of the birth-world as well. Heretics.

The mythical illusion that human birth is dysfunctional on account of our large heads and our stunted, defective pelvises—known throughout the discipline of anthropology as "the obstetric dilemma"—must be maintained to perpetuate the fantasy that macroevolution is real, and the destruction of birth is central to reinforcing this conceit.

We are indoctrinated into the belief that our bodies are so structurally ill-equipped to allow for easy passage for our babies, that most women must be drugged, subdued, cut, sliced, and our babies hauled out of our bodies with barbecue tongs, not only as an ingress for the siphoning of dark energy, but as one of the central justifications for, among other things, maintaining the supremacy of the absurd and laughable theory of macroevolution.

I also suspect that, in reverse, the long-term belief that birth is inherently dangerous and damaging—augmented by the exceptionally awful treatment of birthing women around the time that "the obstetric dilemma" hypothesis was coming into popularity—informed and buttressed some of the core theories about where human beings come from.

What I know, however, thanks to my two decades of work in birth and the births of my nine babies, is that our morphology is not flawed at all, nor is it the consequence of becoming less fish-like, or of shedding our simian guise over time, or of having ancestors that once cowered on all fours while they walked. This is utter nonsense, and I think it would be self-evident as nonsense to anyone who has had the opportunity to become intimately acquainted with normal, undisturbed birth.

Alas, very few people alive today have any context for what birth can be. This is certainly the case for all obstetricians, nurses and the majority of midwives, whose job it is to derange and destroy the birth process, in order to rationalise the procedures that constitute their employment and justify their positioning as hero and saviour. Even the work of some of the most beloved, and seemingly "holistic" midwives and pelvic health specialists is informed by the fundamental belief that the shape of our bodies is the result of the maladaptive reconfiguration of the human skeletal structure, and that consequently our anatomy is somehow a challenge to be overcome, especially during pregnancy and birth, as opposed to an exquisite example of divine design.

This is what props up and sustains some of the core narratives of obstetric and midwifery ideology, not least of which is the mythological utility of "pelvimetry"—the absurd, objectifying practice of playing at measuring the diameters and dimensions of a woman's pelvis, to ostensibly attempt to predict the degree of difficulty with which a baby might be born—which, of course, so often ends up being a self-fulfilling prophecy. The true purpose of pelvimetry however, like most forms of assessment and enumeration during pregnancy, is to cast upon the birthing woman the spell of doubt in her body's ability to enact what is, and always has been, our biological inheritance—our most precious endowment—which is our capacity to bear and bring forth life.

The fallacy of widespread physical disproportionality extends to our babies as well. Foreboding estimates about our infants' size in utero, based on divination derived by ineffectual methods ranging from high-tech to low-tech, such as ultrasound, palpation (the laying-on of hands), and the manual penetration of our vaginas, are all used to support the story that our baby's position or size is in some way pathological. This, like so much about obstetrics, is almost exclusively nonsense.

Contrary to the persistent belief that the position of our babies is indicative of the alleged ease or challenge of our births, or the length of time our babies may take to be born, or even the degree or type of pain we may experience, I have witnessed babies in almost every position prior to the birth process emerge without any problems, and I have likewise observed babies in what we are told is the "ideal" position (vertex, anterior) emerge after long and even formidable birth experiences—and this has been true for many of my own births as well.

In short, our view of birth is predicated upon numerous underlying obstetric "dilemmas," which, stacked together, create a vortex of belief that we are incentivized to conform to blindly, precisely because our attitude towards birth structures the way we relate to our fundamental humanity, and to our own agency. This is the quintessence of what I see as the false matrix—the upside-down world, clown world—that is presented to us as "authentic," but which is a direct inversion of all that is truly life-giving, affirmative, and holy.

Yolande Norris-Clark

EMBRACING THE MATRIX

You may have noticed the term "matrix" being frequently bandied about in recent years—sometimes almost glibly, and in other instances with a ponderous pseudo-spiritual sense of doom—to signify the contorted morass of post-industrial reality, or unreality.

I continuously hear people referring to "breaking the matrix," or "exiting the matrix," or being a "glitch in the matrix," as a way of describing the experience of being or becoming awakened to the dynamics of spiritual and cultural domination and control.

I am all for that awakening.

But, in fact, *matrix*, from the Old French *matrice*, means "womb." The Latin derivation suggests the word *matrix* also signifies "source," "origin," and "mother." Other interpretations include "the place of beginning," and "the enclosure."[15]

It is significant, I think, that the introduction of the term "matrix" into popular culture and consciousness came via the Wachowski siblings, Lilly and Lana, who wrote and directed the four-part movie series, *The Matrix*, and who have described the central theme of those films as a metaphor for the so-called gender transition that both siblings underwent in the years following the release of the first installment of their now-iconic franchise. This, in itself, given the current social dynamics and climate, world events, and the rapidly approaching convergence between reproduction,

---

[15] Just before this book went to print, I was informed by @safia_doula, who follows me on instagram, that in Arabic رحم (pronounced "rahim") means "womb, matrix, blood-tie and safe place," and its derived noun, رحمة (pronounced "rahma") means "mercifulness and compassion." The beauty, complexity, subtlety, and commonalities of language across cultures gives me hope for humanity, and is one of the endless reasons that I know God is real.

technology, artificial (supposed) intelligence, and transhumanism, is quite stunningly emblematic, not to mention conflicting.

And yet as I see it, "The Matrix," — the veritable matrix — is not the venal, technocratic unreality that lures us into the mire of artificiality, dependency, despondency, and resistance to life and its unfolding as the term has come to be used today. "The Matrix" is, instead, the primal place of origin, the source of all.

Matrix is the mother, the father, the child, and all the holy trinities, lattices, and holographic networks that keep us forever connected to God, through the instrument of our bodies, minds, and souls in concert.

The matrix is the womb, the dawn of life. Birth is the original matrix. The earth is our matrix. Woman is the beginning — the first terrain, steward of the earth, mother to us all, created, as I know it, by the word of God. We, mothers, are the matrix embodied.

That so many truth-seekers invoke the term "matrix" to denote the illusion, the fragmentation, and the falsification of nature, is significant. Words are a form of spellcasting, of bringing the notional and the possible into the realm of the material.

To misappropriate the word "matrix" to signify the murk and muck of technocracy is, I think, to carelessly participate in the very contra-positioning of dignity and righteousness that is at the heart of the desecration of birth, and life itself.

We don't need to smash the matrix, or free ourselves from it. We need to re-enter it, reacquaint ourselves with it, embrace it, dwell in it, and learn to harmonize with our place in it once again.

Yolande Norris-Clark

ANCESTRAL MEDICAL DEPENDENCY

I come from a family of very stoic women—endlessly forbearing, self-controlled, and incredibly strong women who never bothered to complain or explain. Dauntless, my foremothers survived wars, famines, and deep trauma. You too come from a line of dauntless women, surely. No matter the specifics of your personal story, somewhere in the boughs of your family tree, your great grandmothers or great-great grandmothers simply *gave birth*.

Learned dependency, however, is also a very present reality. Mental slavery, and the farming of the human spirit is a part of the individual and collective story, and the repercussions of the social engineering of thought and consent is an aspect of our ancestral psychophysiology.

There may be certain individuals in your recent ancestral background or current immediate family who have been especially captivated by the teachings, instructions, and programming of the allopathic model. Through their internalization of this program, they may believe that their bodies won't work without being modified or medicated. Perhaps you too believe this doctrine. This is nothing to be ashamed of, but you're most likely reading this book because you're interested in shifting that dynamic, and birth is a lush, productive ground for making that shift.

If changing your relationship to allopathic programming is your desired path, it is immensely important to allow yourself to recognize that the attitudes, beliefs, assumptions, and sensibilities which you hold in relation to birth may not actually be yours to carry forward, and to remind yourself that the fact that you are alive today means that you come from a line of survivors.

No matter the specifics of your history, there are women in your past who were resilient and robust enough to give birth to live babies, somehow, perhaps against immense odds—odds which, in all likelihood, are thankfully not even remotely relevant for you. Your willingness to participate in the dance of life by having your own babies, and honouring the wisdom of your body to do so spontaneously, is a form of invocation — of calling into presence the spirit of your grandmothers who so courageously created you.

NAVIGATING TRAUMA

We live in a relational grid, wherein the forces of cause and effect have infinite repercussions. We are all wounded, surrounded by our fellow wounded, and the tears in the tattered fabric of our communities, societies, and relationships prime us for drama, while offering very few spaces or opportunities to integrate and to fully heal after experiencing trauma.

One of the first and most essential steps in taking responsibility for your birth experience, and intentionally moving into the process of creating the reality of your blissful birth, is to examine any imprints you have absorbed from past birth experiences, from your own birth, or from any other inscriptions that birth has made on your consciousness that might be impacting your energy field. Undertaking a process of internal disclosure is at the heart of expanding your capacity to fully own the results and outcomes of your choices.

On a very basic level, the more responsibility you're willing to assume, the more you will be able to see yourself as the *cause* of everything in your world. This is a fundamental shift for most of us, and a central key: knowing yourself — claiming yourself — as both the cause and the effect.

Drama and self-victimization (which we will be focusing on in Chapter Four), are, I would argue, significant elements — and symptoms — of residual trauma. When I look back on the experiences of my life that have involved major trauma, those experiences were not primarily traumatic because of the experience itself, but because of the shame, fear, and feelings of persistent victimization (either in the form of helplessness, or through my own villainization and dehumanization of myself or the other party).

In my case, the process of acquiring the ability and willingness to claim my ultimate agency has been multi-faceted, and has involved exploring my story of origin, travelling into my early past, and investigating my own perinatal experiences and development. Delving into the beliefs, impressions, and artefacts patterned onto us from our family lineage can seem like dense work, but the more joy, curiosity, and delight you can conjure as you set about this voyage of discovery, the easier it will be. Even the minutest shift in attitude or perspective will change everything.

I also want to emphasise that, in my view, it is not necessary to excavate every single area of our past in order to begin to heal. We can "work on" (or even better, play on) even just a small part of what has led us to where we are currently. When we initiate a cycle of healing in one discrete area, this will inevitably—and profoundly—affect the whole of our lives. The act alone of considering the past, and reconsidering our state of power and awareness in the context of past experiences, will modify our relationship to those events.

Revision, a concept that I was introduced to through the work of Neville Goddard[16], is a central aspect of integrating our prior experiences—including traumatic ones—so that we can move forward in power. Goddard, who died in the 1960s, was a leader in what was known as the "new thought movement." A controversial figure, Goddard wrote and published several books in the 1940s, and the perspective he put forth in

---

[16] I have enjoyed all of Goddard's books, and I recommend reading his anthologies. Newcomers to his work are often advised to begin with *Feeling is the Secret* and *The Power of Awareness*, though perhaps my favourite of his works include the underrated *The Search* and *Seedtime and Harvest*. His lectures are also excellent.

his work is that our existence is pure consciousness, and that we are wholly integrated with God.

One of his foremost notions is the idea of the continuous circular motion of time. In service to the intentional creation of our reality, Goddard strongly recommended practising a process that he called "revision," especially in the event that we have an experience or an outcome that we feel conflicted or dissatisfied by, or that doesn't serve what we intend as our larger vision.

In Goddard's book *The Law and the Promise*, he describes revision as follows:

> *The perfectly stable or static state is always unattainable. The end attained objectively always realizes more than the end the individual originally had in view. This, in turn, creates a new situation of inner conflict, needing novel solutions to force man along the path of creative evolution…today's events are bound to disturb yesterday's established order. The creatively active imagination invariably unsettles a pre-existing peace of mind.*
>
> *Imagining Creates Reality. What it makes, it can unmake. It is not only conservative, building a life from images supplied by memory— it is also creatively transformative, altering a theme already in being.*
>
> *Because imagining creates reality, we can carry revision to the extreme and revise a scene that would otherwise be unforgivable. We learn to distinguish between man—who is all imagination—and those states into which he may enter.*
>
> *…Imaginal change goes forward until at length the altered pattern is realized on the heights of attainment. Our future is our imaginal activity in its creative march. Imagine better than the best you know.*

To revise the past is to reconstruct it with new content. Man should daily relive the day as he wished he had lived it, revising the scenes to make them conform to his ideals. For instance, suppose today's mail brought disappointing news. Revise the letter. Mentally rewrite it and make it conform to the news you wish you had received. Then, in imagination, read the revised letter over and over again and this will arouse the feeling of naturalness; and imaginal acts become facts as soon as we feel natural in the act.

By mentally falsifying the facts of life, man moves from passive reaction to active creation; this breaks the wheel of recurrence and builds a cumulatively enlarging future. If man does not always create in the full sense of the word, it is because he is not faithful to his vision, or else he thinks of what he wants rather than from his wish fulfilled.

Much of the language here may sound obscure or arcane, and there is a lot of room for analysis.[17] My interpretation of this passage suggests that rather than encouraging a literal misrepresentation of the past, or denial, Goddard is referring instead to a deliberate traverse into past events in a way that resembles entering the Akash—the idea of a continuous accordion-like unfolding of all experiences through all times and all spaces and all layers of the cosmos at once. By accessing this "database," so to speak (which is alive in everyone's subconscious), we can shift the state of being that we are still functioning *from* as evidenced by our ongoing relationship with the past, as we create the future we're stepping into.

As I understand the mind, we form beliefs through both memory and collective programs, and through the largely unconscious process of living

---

[17] I also find Goddard's characterization of revision as a "falsifying" of the past somewhat troublesome, but I think this is perhaps more of an anachronism than anything else.

a version of our past into the present and beyond. Our entrenched unconscious beliefs are always running scripts in the background. When an event occurs that we don't like or we don't think we want, this indicates that our feelings in the present are not actually in alignment with what happened, and we are therefore being offered an opportunity to "revise" who we were in the past so that we can step into a new form of being as we move forward.

What I find especially fascinating about Goddard's process of revision is that in my personal and professional experience, it presents a powerful, sophisticated, and practical approach to working with trauma, despite having been written well before "trauma-informed care" was shaping the public conversation.

"Trauma," as most of us are aware, is a term that attempts to describe the struggle so many people have with integrating the Self, identity, self-ownership, and feelings of not quite belonging in the world following a shocking, unexpected, abusive, or difficult event. We each have varying thresholds and triggers, and what may be experienced as traumatic by one person will differ for another.

In most instances, trauma takes hold when disturbing events are fixed in our memory and intertwined with feelings of fear, anger, and shame in such a destabilizing manner that our perception of responsibility—again, of what belongs to us—is disorganized. For many people, trauma is ingrained so early on in our lives and becomes so comfortable, that we end up unconsciously re-playing or replicating our traumatic experiences, either in the realm of our imagination, or by making decisions that re-create the feeling of activation, fear, dependency, and victimization, precisely because *who we are* remains set at the frequency of self-devaluation as familiarity.

Broadly, there are two principal parts to releasing trauma in a way that frees us to move into the future with lightness and clarity: firstly, diverging the energy of trauma from our cells and tissues through and out of the body and, secondly, shifting and clarifying our perception of ownership over feelings of confusion, shame, and guilt in the realm of consciousness.

There is no right order to this, nor is there only one way to go about it. Thoughts are a form of action and have a material impact. The thoughts we choose to think change our physiology, as does the discipline of quieting our thoughts in meditation or prayer.

Similarly, in reverse, somatic exercises and experiences also inevitably change our thoughts. Embodiment is always the mind and body working in conjunction. For many of us who have been raised in a westernized culture however, it may feel more comfortable to begin the process of transmuting trauma with a mental framework, prior to attending to our primal animal self though it's often ideal to combine both approaches.

We are not only animals, nor did we evolve from apes or whales, I don't believe (as I mentioned earlier in this chapter). We do, however, share many characteristics with other mammals, including our fundamental reproductive physiology, our ability to heal spontaneously, the intuitive urge to move energy through our bodies, not to mention our capacity to give birth with ease. Movement, dance, and various forms of somatic expression have always been important parts of the daily rhythm of my life and healing, yet it has always been birth itself that has constituted, for me, the most potent avenue for trauma-release.

I now recognize the discharging of trauma as one of the primary purposes of the birth-dance, though this is directly prohibited by the use of chemical and physical restraints during birth, including drugs that numb the body, wires and tubes that hamper movement, surveillance devices that keep mothers strapped in one place, and of course, the coercive disciplinary social pressure to allow our bodies and minds to be occupied and controlled by outside authorities in the first place, all of which begins the moment we enter a hospital environment, or allow medical personnel into our homes.

Some of the most effective forms of intentional trauma-release therapies are based on the observation of other mammals, and their instinctive genius for clearing trauma through tremoring—the process of facilitating the spasm-like motions that allow every creature to complete the fight-or-flight cycle that is interrupted during an event that threatens our survival. Tremoring is inherent to human beings as well, and it's also an intrinsic part of what occurs according to instinct, when women give birth unhindered.

It is almost universal among women who give birth in power that we will shake and tremor during, but also between sensations, especially as the energy builds immediately before and after our babies are born. Equally important to the diffusion of tension during birth is the rhythmic cycle of sensation and rest that occurs as the uterus knits together to build its fundus— the all-powerful muscular structure of the womb that gently yet insistently pushes the newborn out into the world as the baby supports and responds to that propulsive force—all of which incorporates an incredibly adaptive, optimal form of stress *and* release.

Healing is innate, and healing is built into our psychology and physiology, especially as we move through the normal biological processes of life. As any sexually expressive and active adult knows, orgasm too inevitably involves trembling and tremoring.

But humans also create, innovate, and heal through the intellectual and imaginal realms, in ways that animals do not, and for us, unlike animals, a core component of discharging and integrating trauma can involve recognizing intellectually and even academically, that either:

    a) we were indeed clear victims in the situation, and we can therefore let go of that experience with the clarity of knowing that it is not *ours* to hold onto, or

b) we can allow ourselves to own that the indignity, shame, and guilt we may feel about the experience (if it's something we enacted toward someone else, or an event that on some level we recognize we overtly or subconsciously contracted into) stems from an iteration of who we *were* that is no longer who we are now.

When we are facing and working with our own birth-trauma, it can be very challenging to allow ourselves to consider that we *did* unwittingly create the situation. We manifest the experience of birth, simply by occupying the iteration of ourselves that formulated the outcome by selecting, one after another, each option from among the infinite array of possible choices. Thus, we built the experience that occurred.

This does not negate the potential (or the likelihood) that we were lied to, manipulated, treated poorly, or abused. But it does mean that we ourselves established the framework and conditions for the event to take place through the continuous stream of decisions which led us to that point.

Goddard refers to this kind of access to our internal archive of choices as the "bridge of incidents." I like to describe the stepping-stones we freely and voluntarily lay along the path to any outcome as "choice-points"—the series of macro and micro choices that forge our progress through life, but which often go unnoticed as being discrete intersections of selection except after the fact, when most of us are better able to perceive the archival register of instances in which we made a voluntary move one way or another. Even the most perceptive and self-aware among us tend only to recognize the "bridge" we have built from one state of being or reality to the next in retrospect, after hardship, often burdened by guilt and shame.

For most people, acquiring the skill and discipline of orienting our attention to the logical conclusion of our choices prior to reflexive action requires practice, especially in a culture in which trauma is commodified, and delayed gratification is disincentivized. Furthermore, visiting the past can be either stagnating or fruitful, depending on our approach. Goddard's brilliant invitation to us is to enter into this kind of time-travel soberly and calmly, with the confidence of knowing that we can deliberately set the past events of any given situation aside, and consciously re-build the experience with vivid intention so that the mind is reset to create from a new state of consciousness moving forward.

When we revisit the past, and reorient our perception to a position that sees previous event(s) as having unfolded optimally, we are, in a sense, collapsing the "reality" of the past (as we have revised it) into the present and emergent now from a completely new state of awareness. This is in some ways in contradiction to the disposition that originally engineered the event we didn't (and do not) want, and facilitates a shift in the energy that we hold about ourselves in the now, while transposing the relationship we have to any other players involved in the theatre of our story to a new octave.[18]

How do we do this? Through the technology of the daydream, often described as meditative hypnosis,[19] but which I think of as *realming*.

REALMING

Our son Cosmo came to me one morning when he was seven years old, and he described a dream-state that he entered into, in which he could retrieve himself and move between different locations in the universe with

---

[18] I use the term *octave* several times throughout this book to describe a plane of awareness, a term I first encountered through the work of psychic Paul Selig, who has written/channelled several acclaimed (and fascinating) books including *Beyond the Known: Realization, Alchemy*, and *The Kingdom*.

[19] I have several audio meditations available on my website. www.yolandenorris-clark.com.

his mind. He noted that he could also choose to do this while awake, and he referred to this practice as *realming*.

This was a revelation to me. The term *realming* is evocative, poetic, and exceptionally precise, describing the common thread between lucid dreaming and induced hypnosis, both of which are core components of how I overcame the fear and trauma that had been installed in my sense of self through the shockingly difficult journey of giving birth to Ignatius, my eighth baby.

We all possess the ability to realm, and through the process of deliberate realming we can revise and release any tethering that might be holding us to the version of ourselves that chose and created any adverse experience. Realming is a kind of self-induced hypnosis, a state toward which many people carry a sense of suspicion, associating it with New Age ideology and mind-control.

I certainly agree that the New Age movement has been specifically constructed in a way that allows it to be instrumentalized by certain dark forces which may be in conflict with the purity of heart that alignment with God offers. I have my own personal beliefs about God, Spirit, and the workings of the divine, just as I have feelings about the way that the New Age movement has indeed been co-opted.

While I don't doubt that forms of hypnosis can be (and have historically been) used for the nefarious programming of the mind, this does not necessarily mean that there is anything inherently sinister, partisan, or occult about hypnosis itself. In fact, we move in and out of hypnotic states constantly throughout our experience of waking and sleeping life.

Whenever we find ourselves drifting off into the territory of imagination, we are entering a state of hypnosis. When we allow others to induce in us a hypnotic thrall, we are simply opening up, through consent, a particular channel of awareness, and we can learn to access power in that state on our own as well, in alignment with God (I believe).

For me, hypnosis or realming in conjunction with prayer and frequency medicine (for example, the use of tuning forks, immersing ourselves in curated soundscapes using binaural beats, and meditative music recorded at specific healing frequencies) has been amazingly beneficial in rerouting my subconscious mind, especially as panic attacks began in anticipation of giving birth again, when I became pregnant following Ignatius' arrival.

It was through realming and revision that I was able to perceive that during Ignatius' birth, I was operating as the whiny, self-indulgent, little-girl version of myself. This is so very obvious in the video footage I have of Iggy's birth: I was a disaster, and I can recognize that with so much love for who I was at the time. I must emphasise that I adore that iteration of myself, despite having been so committed to the struggle, and so tender and lost. I was lovely in that perfect state, and I feel deep compassion for the woman I was then.

I know now that not only was I embedded in a larger cycle of victimization during that period of my life, but I was also reinforcing that cycle through every sensation I was offered within the enclosed structure—the world—of birth.

During the pregnancy that followed Iggy, which resulted in the blissful, orgasmic, pain-free birth of Helio, I travelled back to that previous birth experience many times, back specifically, to the state of mind that I was then occupying. I observed in those imaginal voyages, the cycle of victimization that I was playing out in the smaller internal cycles of my awareness. In every moment of Iggy's birth, I saw that I was recreating the larger spirals of resistance, fear, and pain, which were patterned as a kind of recursive loop—a vortex that mirrored every level of my reality at the time.

In oscillating with the frequency of this vortex, I was reconfirming my familiar story, and deepening the neurological grooves which made that particular mode of thought and perception habitual and reflexive. This is the essence of what makes up behaviour and identity. Identity is really just the repetitive act of thinking certain thoughts about ourselves, which we then translate to more overt motions in a particular direction or pattern. This means that by simply shifting our thoughts we are, effectively, adopting a new behaviour.

With thought alone, we can utterly transpose ourselves to a different domain of existence, thereby becoming the woman for whom that original pattern is not only rendered unfamiliar, but nonviable. Any alteration of fundamental perception modifies our internal ecosystem to the extent that our interior landscape becomes inhospitable to our former expression of self.

When we allow ourselves to apprehend our lives in reverse, we can then learn to reconfigure our stories and our existence as a formation of our outwardly pulsating energy, which in turn can bring about transformation into both the past and the future. I will always love the woman who fought so hard to save herself from the churning hellish depths of pain and agony in birth, but I barely know her now. She is no longer me. I have sorted through the parts of her that propelled the story forward, and left the pieces of the mask that I don't need anymore.

It is crucial for me to note, however, that I had no way of knowing that this process had really "worked," until I found myself in the midst of birth once again, this time, aware that every atomic element of thought, perception, and sensation was a choice. The transformation occurred both as a result of reaching a saturation point in my capacity to tolerate the self that I had become, but it was also only *during* the crucible of my next birth that I was able to bear witness to the fact that I had had enough of who I had been committed to being for so long until then.

PORTAL

CURATING THE VIBRATION

The body, too, is forged by our frequency and worldview. It is possible to reform and modify the way our bodies feel and even look, through curating the vibration of our energy field. By re-shaping our expression, we call in the experience that we have committed to choosing through assuming whatever posture we inhabit.

The language of being that we adopt in the present moment (expressed in word, thought, bearing, and execution) elicits our future reality as a reclamation from the past. In so doing, we harness our intrinsic capacity to bend time, evince, and bring into the present the reality that we are invoking through the articulation of our essence.

This is not an abstract concept. "Manifestation" of this kind is an empirical fact, and a co-creation with God. Our thoughts and beliefs literally manifest our reality from the inside out—from the expression of our cells, to our reflexive response to stimuli, to the force of our muscles, to the movement of objects through space, in response to the exercising of our free will.

The actions we take arise unerringly from the wellspring of beliefs intermingled within our consciousness, which creates the substance of our lives.[20]

---

[20] Supplementary resources for this book are available on my website at www.yolandenorris-clark.com, including a guided hypnosis journey that will invite you to re-enter the world of your previous birth (or your own birth), and support you in revising that experience in order to gently let go of the outdated, no-longer-relevant characterization of yourself from that time. These recordings are designed to take you on a journey into different timelines related to excavating your relationship to birth, and bringing into your field a greater degree of responsibility and responsiveness in a way that is very gentle, very loving, and sweet. The recordings are my own, but they're inspired by what I have learned through my study of Marisa Peer's Rapid Transformational Therapy (RTT) method.

INTEGRATION QUESTIONS

1. What is revealed to you when reflecting on your past birth experiences? If you haven't had children of your own yet, reflect on your own birth into the world. If you work in the world of birth, what have you experienced while witnessing other women's births?

2. Who are the women that came before you? What is their story of birth, of the body, of healing?

3. As you recollect your stories and the narratives of your ancestors, what do you notice in your body as you reflect on them? What is the truth? What actually happened? Are you ready to let go, to rewrite these stories?

CHAPTER FOUR

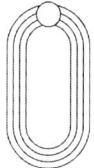

CHOICE AND VICTIM CONSCIOUSNESS

CHOOSE YOUR OWN ADVENTURE

Each of us creates the conditions of our lives and experiences from our fundamental state of being. The concept we have of who we are, from which the substance of our lives evolves, is consolidated through the stories we construct within our consciousness and brought into the material realm by the actions we take that arise from the refrain of the self. Habits and behaviours always—*always*—align with and reveal our state of being and our internal condition.

Our commitments and our values too, are revealed in the reality that we express by the way we live. There is no hiding from the mirror of truth (although many of us delude ourselves into believing any number of fantasies about who we are, usually in the form of hopes, dreams, and good intentions).

Yet how we actually spend our time during our day-to-day (what we physically do, the thoughts that we give energy and space to, the people to whom we offer our attention, our degree of reverence or contempt, the extent of our devotion or indifference to any aspect of our existence) is written on the body, inscribed in our attitudes, expressed through the spiritual and physical order (or disorder) of our homes, reflected by our children, our relationships, and exuded through the vibrational field of our energy.

All of this, we choose. We are always choosing. To be alive is to choose our own adventure. Whether we are aware of the choices we are making or not (or of the very existence of choice or not), to decline to choose in any instance is not an option. The progression of human life is encoded in a binary system. Both stillness and action constitute the movement of energy. Entropy is incompatible with—and antithetical to—animation.

Choosing is continuous and layered. Some choices present themselves undeniably as a major crossroads—a clear divergence on the trail. But most choices are less distinct: we are offered a constant stream of atomic choice-points that arise within every exchange, in every nanosecond. Both micro and macro choices and choice-points continuously feed into each other, inform each other, and ultimately shape our life-stream. Where we go, what we do, and how we set ourselves up in the material world, has as much an impact on our experience as does the choice of where we allow our minds to roam and to dwell.

Most of us move through life assuming that we are at the behest of chance, that life occurs *to us*, and that we have very little influence, if any, on how our experience unfolds. This is especially so in regards to the body, the parasympathetic nervous system, and our state of health or dis-ease, not to mention apparently irrepressible, unruly, extreme experiences like birth. But none of this is true. This sense of helplessness is a deception. Our thoughts, beliefs, and the most minute choices about where and how we direct our energy bears monumental influence even over what has come to be seemingly dismissed as the vagaries of our physiological systems.

The more we can develop an attunement to the subtlest ways in which choice often presents itself as reflex, routine, obedience, or even as a mere inflection in the mind, the more we can then choose to step into full responsibility for our lives. Once we recognize that we have contracted into, at some stage, at some phase of the journey, every event, situation, and outcome, we can then begin to choose with much greater discernment, responsiveness, and receptivity to the monumental power that we wield as human beings in possession of what might be God's greatest gift of all: free will.

But be prepared: this can be a deeply humbling, and even frightening process. Radical responsibility and self-ownership can feel terrifying, especially initially. Ours is a culture in which dependency, obedience, docility, and victimhood are increasingly rewarded and incentivized. Most people cannot tolerate the discomfort of freedom, which is, by definition, the recognition of ourselves as the sole authors of our lives.

The dark tunnels of our past are always ushering us forward. The hardship you have lived through, and survived, is not the barrier to your growth that you may think it is, but the rich loam of your flowering. Till it. Work it. This is the foundational element that will create the path to your blissful birth. Choosing to be mindful and assuming responsibility for our individual choice-points—or not—shapes not only our experience of birth, but also co-creates the material reality that we are all perpetually living into.

As time continues to accelerate and we move into a new era of awareness, convergences, and intersecting revelations (as political, spiritual, and relational disclosures are increasingly made known), we are being presented with what might seem like an array of choices that are more complex than the ones humans faced even a decade ago. As always, in every age, all is in perpetual motion, and so are you. While this may feel overwhelming, especially as the elision of technology and biological life-forms continues apace, one of the gifts of being alive now is having the opportunity to hone our skill in choosing in accordance with the living world, our conscience, and God-consciousness.

When we do make the leap into self-ownership through embracing the art of attuning to the subtlest frequency of choice and the ways that choices often appear as infinitesimal, fragmentary articulations of thought, we open ourselves to a vast new range of opportunities and possibilities, and we transform ourselves from the inside out, becoming the mavens and creatrixes of not only our birth experience but of our entire lives.

The most surprising aspect of this process might just be how much *fun* it is. Choosing from a space of creative inspiration and infinite possibility is powerful, but it's also exuberant, light, and joyous, and it is this energy of ebullient felicity and play that we always have the option of conveying during birth.

It's not that I believe that all of existence is a game. Instead, my sense is that there are multiple layers of reality that are largely imperceptible by the intellect or even our primary senses, and that the life of the soul exists outside of the material realm (as well as within it). But our navigation of the concentric rings of enclosure here on earth—the enclosure of our bodies, our homes, the geographic landscape, and all the contrivances of society—reveals certain laws, properties, and illusions that we may discover, test, and modify with our own influence.

This interchange can be wonderfully playful if we allow it to be so. In fact, throughout life we get to decide if we are the player or the played. Whether lovers or haters, killers or life givers and preservers, our bodies are dowsing rods and our minds create the atmosphere. Every choice we make modifies the pattern in the monumental tapestry of all existence.

Most of us struggle from time to time with the feeling that we're out in the cold, and maybe we read books like this one as reminders that we are not alone. Yet the world is both as it is and what we make of it, and while that might at first seem like another nanoscopic or irrelevant distinction, the power we have to move our minds across time and space, to test the tension, and then to pull the drawstring of awareness to bring the vision of who we are into the space of now, is what it is to remedy, recover, ascend, and become the leaders we can be for ourselves, our children, our families, and the wider world at large.

THE DRAMA TRIANGLE

"Neuroplasticity" refers to the human brain's capacity to build neural networks, maps, and pathways in response to new information and stimuli. Yet my impression is that the term "neuroplasticity" slyly denotes the same Cartesian mechanistic partitioning that has informed our cultural understanding of the self as a dualistic, bifurcated entity since Plato, and that this characterization of humans as conflicted by the purported schism between mind and matter is now being used to support various justifications for the merging of biological systems with digital technology.

The increasingly seductive notion that via transhumanism we can extract consciousness from the body and upload it to "the cloud" creating digital "twins" of ourselves—avatars—and that this will somehow lead to liberation, is in part an effect of the hyper-rational, dualistic thinking that has dominated philosophical thought for ages. No matter how technologically sophisticated, however, the electronic severance of mind from body can never lead to liberation, or be anything other than a gruesome simulacrum of life, not to mention a form of escapism from true responsibility, and a commitment to exponential forms of (increasingly deviant and macabre) drama, as opposed to authenticity.

I do believe the soul is eternal, but that does not, in my view, negate the fact that we are offered the experience of embodiment as composite, unified entities, in our rendition of life as human beings. Our body/brain/heart/soul plexus is indeed highly malleable, but I don't think it will ever be possible to distinguish the brain from the mind, from the body, from the spirit-self.

Creative learning and change are God-given superpowers. The paradoxical flipside of our pliancy—our programmability, if you will—is that through the repetition of certain actions, thoughts, and circumstances, we can also tend to become rather fixed in our ways.

Human beings are, in a sense, addicted to drama, or at the very least, highly attached to drama, accustomed to it, and often fixated on it. And all drama is rooted in the posturing and nurturing of victimhood which is, in essence, the abrogation of responsibility. As we discussed in the previous chapter, this propensity to shift accountability is very much related to early traumatic experiences. Playing the victim doesn't mean we're weak, or bad, or flawed. It's simply a learned behaviour, a survival mechanism, and a habitual response we can consciously deprogram.

One approach that primed me for the immersive transformation of choosing blissful birth was learning about the dynamics of what is widely known as the *drama triangle*, a term coined by clinical psychiatrist Stephen Karpman in the 1960s. I was introduced to a deeper understanding of this model by one of the most brilliant coaches I have had the privilege of encountering, my colleague, collaborator, and closest friend Emilee Saldaya, the founder of the Free Birth Society[21] (who first learned this framework from the Conscious Leadership Group[22]).

The drama triangle describes the dynamic by which victimhood is primarily assumed in one of three ways: by playing either the role of the classic victim, the hero/rescuer, or the perpetrator/villain. The Victim, Saviour, and Villain roles are all expressions of an overarching theme of victimization; they're just different ways of revealing victim-consciousness, which, in simple terms, is what it is to lie to ourselves.

---

[21] Emilee Saldaya's incredible programs and offerings, along with our collaborations together, including The Complete Guide to Freebirth and MatriBirth are available at www.freebirthsociety.com.

[22] The Conscious Leadership Group can be found at www.conscious.is.

Most of us spend our lives haphazardly drifting between the three primary victim postures. The classic Victim is who we become when we are continuously *at the effect* of the world around us. The Victim feels trapped, helpless, powerless, or incompetent. Sometimes this is obvious—when we whine, complain, or plead (*Why me?*), we are firmly entrenched in the role of the classic Victim.

But the Victim act can also be quite insidious and covert. Victims often attempt to fool themselves by positioning their victimization as a form of confusion, or even depression. (This is not to say that depression is not real, but that it is often very much intertwined with the Victim posture.) Classic Victims take *less* than their share of responsibility in their lives, or in a given exchange or situation—*I can't help it, it's not my fault, I didn't know, I just don't know what to do*—and this behaviour is often characterized by various forms of paralysis or dejection.

The conspicuous helplessness of the blatant Victim is often what mothers are unconsciously conjuring during pregnancy and birth, and this is rooted in ultimately declining to take full responsibility for our choices—*I can't have a homebirth because my partner really isn't on board*, or *my midwife sabotaged my birth and that's why I ended up with a transfer.*

Any time we are feeling at the mercy of a circumstance or an event in our lives, there is some element of the Victim stance that we are playing out. In such cases, there is always a point at which we can track back to an instance in time during which we bypassed our intuition, our better judgement, or our knowing, and sacrificed ourselves, handing over our power to an external or perceived authority in some way.

Another form of victimization that we often tend to let slip into in our lives is that of the Rescuer, or Hero. Heroes and Rescuers *need* other victims around (whether those happen to be individuals who are themselves actively playing the role of Victim, or whether the Rescuer has fashioned others as victims in their own minds) in order to get the charge they're unconsciously looking for. In either case, the Rescuer is ultimately instantiating victimhood in taking far *more* of their share of responsibility, so eager are they to relieve the discomfort of the present moment, be that their own discomfort or the discomfort of others. Activists, healers, therapists, and teachers can often fall into this category, and there is frequently an element of superiority involved in this brand of victim-identity.

Heroic Rescuer-type victims find themselves burnt out, frustrated, and feeling stymied by their own efforts, even while they delude themselves into thinking that their behaviour constitutes generosity or magnanimity, when it's actually a kind of stealthy arrogance or condescension that allows us to feel better than the one we have "othered" as requiring our salvation. The actions we take while assuming the stance of the Rescuer are ultimately selfish and constitute an effort to relieve our own unease, and to artificially elevate ourselves by swooping in to save someone else through self-sacrifice.

We also often "hero" or rescue *ourselves* with food, overwork, distractions (the Netflix binge, social media scrolling), or through consuming alcohol or other suppressants, stimulants, or substances in a deliberate (or thoughtless) effort to shift our state of consciousness. Anytime we seek to escape our current reality, our sensations, ourselves, or our families, or when we check out of full awareness to relieve the pressure of a feeling or a state of being that we would prefer to simply mask or negate, rather than acknowledge, accept, untangle, integrate, or allow, we are adopting the act of the Rescuer.

Then we have the Villain or Perpetrator. This is the part we play when we blame others when things go wrong. The Perpetrator is the hyper-critic who is always lashing out, and projecting onto the other person, or institution, their disappointment and outrage. This can be big, bombastic, and offensive, or more subtle, and expressed through statements and responses like, *If you hadn't done that, none of this would have happened,* but it can also be a more elusive, muted, passive-aggressive articulation of this dynamic. For example, *Well, she can't really help it, but she forgot again, and therefore..."* etc. The Villain's assignment is to control the narrative, to evade accountability, and to deny that responsibility is theirs to bear. In the context of birth, we may blame our partners, our obstetrician, or the institution for choices that ultimately, we stepped into.

As women especially, we often persecute ourselves, making ourselves the villains in our own lives. This is such a frequent covert pattern for many of us that it may become the refrain of our internal dialogue. *Why did I do that, I'm so stupid, I hate myself, I'm disgusting, I'm broken, I'll never be able to...*xyz. We also often villainize our bodies, and this too is very subtle—*I would really love to have a homebirth, but I have to have a c-section because my pelvis is too small.* In this way, we play both the Rescuer and the Persecutor, by relieving ourselves of what may seem like a desire to give birth at home by villainizing ourselves, using the excuse that we are simply too broken and dysfunctional (and I see this dynamic constantly in women who are navigating birth).

The ubiquity of the drama cycle is evident not only in the way that we engage interpersonally, but is also reflected in how governments, institutions, and corporations are puppeteered to push agendas and to deflect responsibility, while also exerting inappropriate degrees of domination and control (which we as individuals must consent to, in order for that pattern to continue). I certainly recognize my own propensity to evade my own power and responsibility, and how beguiling it can be to succumb to the temptation to see myself as trapped and impotent. But once we allow ourselves to be aware of how these tendencies are permitted, nurtured, and even encouraged (and how easily we can slip into these various frames) we can begin to change the patterning, and remove ourselves from what is essentially a delusion bubble of bypassing that for many of us can become a reflexive guiding force.

Let's look more closely, for example, at the fictional woman who says that she wants to have a homebirth, but also believes that she can't because her pelvis is too small. This woman may be unaware that:

- there is no scientific or rational basis for assuming that an adult human female who is able to become pregnant through sexual intercourse would ever be physically incapable of giving birth to the child that grows in her womb
- pelvimetry is pseudo-scientific nonsense
- pregnancy changes the chemical and physiological structure and composition of our bodies in a multitude of ways including augmenting the production of a chemical known as *elastin* that ensures that our ligaments can stretch to allow our bones to accommodate the passage of our babies through our bodies, and
- babies are brilliantly and exquisitely created with malleable skull plates that will mould themselves to their mother's frame as they emerge.

Setting aside these points, however, the most salient and indisputable fact is that no woman "needs" to do anything merely because a random medical professional has told her to do so. To accept such a narrative is to position herself as the child-like victim of both her own anatomy and of the tyrannical yet heroic authority-figure primed to save her from biology, as well as from her (supposedly) poor decision-making.

Apart from false information and medical conditioning, however, what if, instead of stating that *I'd love to have a homebirth, but I can't, and I have to have a c-section because my pelvis is too small,* this imaginary woman simply acknowledged the following: *I love the idea of homebirth, but I'm afraid of it. I was told by my doctor that my pelvis is too small and that I'll need a c-section, and I trust the medical establishment and its representatives more than I trust my body to give birth spontaneously.*

The differences between the two sentiments may seem vague or impalpable, or even inconsequential, but the distinctions are actually quite monumental. In the first version, the woman has accepted the pronouncements of an outside authority about her body (and the purported consequences of these assumptions) as true, and has already revoked her own agency (*I can't, I have to, I'm too xyz*).

In the second statement, even what may seem like a minute shift in ownership changes everything: the frankness, transparency, and emotional honesty which are now present, allow for an exponentially expanded set of possibilities. The mother is no longer a victim, no longer reacting to an edict, but is now responsive, responsible, and is in a position to untangle her beliefs from those that may have been imposed on her, if she so chooses. When we are willing to speak the truth to ourselves, above all, we create pathways for inquiry that can open up new worlds.

Each individual possesses an indelible right—a divine right, in my opinion—to take responsibility for any and all decisions about our bodies and our babies. When we operate from this position of inherent self-sovereignty, and we speak what we know to be true with integrity, we alter the fundamental basis of every conversation, decision, and outcome.

THEATRICS AND SELF-OWNERSHIP

How do we know we're on the drama triangle? How do we know we are choosing to step into the theatre of the Victim? It's quite simple, really. Any feeling of dissatisfaction, irritation, annoyance, exhaustion, self-pity, rage, distaste, disgust, contempt—any situation at all in which we feel triggered and experience an emotion that puts us in a reactive, contracted state, indicates that we are occupying one (or more) of the three victim positions: the classic Victim, the Rescuer, or the Persecutor.

As most of us do, I live approximately 98.9 percent of my life camped out on the drama triangle. The most familiar and comfortable version of the victim role I play is the Villain, or the Villainizer. I'm always ready for a fight. I'm prepared to argue at any moment, I'm perpetually outraged at this or that, I can see every other person's glaring flaws like high-beams (and often my own as well, thank goodness) and I can deconstruct all the ways that the institutions of this world have failed us.

I'm also a dedicated martyr, and the urge to hero everyone around me and to save the broken world has been one of my foremost distorted directives. When that gets exhausting, I wallow in feeling utterly dejected and sad because life is so very hard, and no one appreciates my epic efforts. Believe it or not, I have undergone some massive upgrades in recent years in my ability to, at the very least, recognize when I am mired in this dynamic, and what might be a 1 percent differential from the 99.9 percent of the time that I was in this pattern in the past, has been transformative.

Occasionally, these days, I honour myself enough to say no. Once in a while I mind my own business. From time to time, I listen to my body. There are brief instances when I choose to shut up, to not insist on proving how smart and right I am, and I let go of my craving to control other people or an outcome. Lo and behold, this is when I get a taste of what real power and freedom feel like.

Any kind of growth in this area is remarkable and positive. I also know that minute, incremental nudges forward in self-awareness are what allowed me to have the blissful ninth birth that I did, which in turn has continued to prompt further (very positive) modulations in every corner of my life.

The drama triangle is relevant to birth in a multitude of ways. We choose the drama of victimhood either through abdicating responsibility or by assuming an inappropriate degree of it, and the allocation of responsibility is always established through choice.

Faced with the evident large-scale choice-points leading up to our births, most significantly the question of where, how, and with whom we give birth, many women avoid responsibility by capitulating to the wishes and interests of family members, doctors, or partners, placing other's desires over their own internal sense of knowing, and allowing themselves to believe that doing so will reduce friction, tension, or conflict. Women also override their own inner knowing due to a sense of obligation to tradition, or to the mores of the wider society.

When we submit to what is expected of us in an effort to seek approval, validation, or as a way of attempting to control the responses of others, we are, in effect, betraying ourselves and our babies. We are also expressing a fundamental lack of respect for the other people in our lives by proving, through our self-betrayal, that we don't trust that they have the capacity to handle our truth, or to fully know us.

At every stage of pregnancy, we will be presented with opportunities to either practice maintaining robust boundaries—prioritizing instinct, spiritual centredness, and fierce mothering by honouring ourselves and by extension, our babies—or we will, step by step, build the outcome of our births out of decisions rooted in self-deception, self-denial, and infidelity to our intuition.

We also tend to create inadvertent drama through choosing to don the mantle of victim-consciousness even in the way that we elect to think about birth, not only through the choices we make in advance of birth which establish the set, setting, and tone of the ceremony itself, but during the inevitable moments of cataclysm once birth has begun.

The first step in disavowing drama, claiming self-responsibility, and choosing alignment and pleasure over pain, is to practice self-ownership over all the parts of your life. Begin with acknowledging that whatever it is that you possess right now (and conversely, whatever it is that you lack) you have, in some capacity, chosen, appointed, designated, or in some way accepted for yourself, as evidenced by the fact of it. This is true for any experience from your past that you continue to carry forward into the present (and therefore the future) including your prior birth experiences that may have ended in disaster, or trauma, or pain.

You are not the victim of your birth or your life, although if you believe the contrary that will always be true. To assert that you are an ongoing victim, and that you have no agency, is to choose the very behaviour that makes such a declaration accurate.

In effect, to claim the identity of the victim instantly establishes a perfect causal loop, and immediately shunts us into a very constrained reality enclosure. This is rarely undertaken consciously, and this phenomenon is usually far more readily observed in others than in ourselves. Yet it is not only unremarkable that you may have the capacity to see victim consciousness in other people, it's overtly counterproductive to focus on others' victim orientation, and we do so at the expense of our own expansion.

If (and when) you find yourself fixating on someone else's victimology (which we all do, at times), simply bring your attention back to your own business. (Repudiating victim-identification, however, is not synonymous with blaming yourself or anyone else for anything, nor does it imply the necessity to ignore or excuse anyone else from their responsibility for wrongdoing.)

Many people will claim that they are embracing self-responsibility and then, in the same breath, make excuses, conjure caveats, blame their current standing on parents, other people, the government, or their history, to rationalize their particular situation or circumstance on the basis of supposed exceptionalities, and in effect, argue strenuously for their own confinement and incapacity. We all, to some extent, express the reflexive tendency to make up stories to justify our shortcomings, but our power and agency are commensurate with the degree to which we can unlearn this behaviour.

This kind of power—the power of asserting agency through choice—is a requirement for manifesting a pain-free blissful birth.

A precondition of even *beginning* to open ourselves to the possibility that we can choose the positive things or experiences that we truly desire in life (such as easeful, ecstatic birth), is to allow ourselves to at least experiment with the idea that we chose everything in our lives that came before, even (and especially) that which we have allowed ourselves to believe that we didn't want.

Stepping into creative potency demands a reckoning with the fact that over the arc of time, through the succession of choices made at every micro and macro fork in the road, we selected the problems, the struggles, the suffering, and the negative outcomes that came into existence as a result of our progression through the world. And this is where many women falter.

THE THRILL OF VICTIMHOOD

For so many of us, the notion of the presence of choice or desire in the co-creation of adverse events might sound profoundly contradictory—no one *wants* to be in a state of suffering, illness, dis-ease, grief, or misfortune, do they? Surely no one really desires such a thing. In fact, the suggestion might strike you as downright offensive. *How dare she? No one chooses misery or privation.* Well, not on the surface of things.

But in the shadowlands of our consciousness, in those lower octaves of the deeper reality, I think we all get a charge from seeing ourselves as victims of negative experiences and outcomes, and from wallowing—luxuriating, even—in the muck of suffering. I think most of us, if we're honest with ourselves, can acknowledge that there are rewards to hooking into our victim story.

There is always something to receive in exchange for acquiescing to the belief that we have been forsaken. There is a kind of delight—a dark, grotesque, and even shameful pleasure—in the prostrations of victimhood. This is the essential allure of victim-consciousness, and the drama cycle. Most of us revel in the drama of playing the victim in the theatre production of our assumed version of reality. It can be very confronting to explore the idea that we contract into our suffering, or that we often love, and even cultivate the breakdowns that inevitably befall us, and which we so often turn into agonies.

The spectrum of opinion regarding whether or not human beings really have free will, or if we are simply informed by programming and animal impulse, is vast and varying. Most people, when faced with the idea of infinite agency, will reach for the most extreme and uncomfortable examples that challenge and complicate this assertion. *What about child-victims of abuse? What about cancer?* These are the usual go-to defensive responses, whenever the theory that suffering might involve a subliminal choice is brought up.

Let me be clear, that in no way am I suggesting that a child, or anyone, consciously chooses to experience assault, violence, heartache, wrongdoing, or death. This is not a simple calculus.

My experience and perception of choice and free will is inevitably tied to my understanding of God, a topic we'll wade into more fully in Chapter Seven, but I am well acquainted with the fact that those who tend to disdain the idea of free will are often self-proclaimed atheists. It's also very interesting to me that many of the individuals who are most highly lauded for their reputed intelligence often strike me as the most simplistic in their thinking about faith, although this shouldn't be surprising, seeing as doubt is consistently promoted as a symbol of intellect and sophistication.

I recently encountered this phenomenon in American theoretical physicist and Nobel laureate Steven Weinberg's book *Dreams of a Final*

Theory: The Scientist's Search for the Ultimate Laws of Nature. In it, Weinberg describes himself as "unsympathetic to attempts to justify the ways of God to man," arguing that "[i]f there is a God that has special plans for humans, then He has taken very great pains to hide His concern for us." Weinberg suggests that the fact that "the God of birds and trees would have to be also the God of birth defects and cancer," indicates that human suffering represents a contradiction to God's power, compassion, and presence, and that this reveals the implausibility of God's existence altogether.

For Weinberg, and others who share his secular position, the "problem" of evil is generally taken as the justification for unbelief in the divine and in our autonomous volition, which is perhaps the ultimate expression of both victim-consciousness, and denial. For those who do believe in God (such as myself), the presence and possibility of evil is a primary reason for faith and the [very much living] proof of our God-granted agency.

I won't pretend I have any of the answers, but the changeability of our beliefs is yet another form of evidence, to my mind, of infinite choice. I also see choice as existing outside of our known or material reality, and independent of the realms of time or memory. I believe that we each have a kind of soul-contract with the basic sketch of our lifelines, and that in an obscure and impenetrable way, we assent to the initial setting of the lives we are born into, based on our soul's pre-existing burdens, and the lessons we are required to encounter (which we may or may not choose to learn in this life).

Again, this certainly does not mean that I think any child ever deliberately decides to be abused. Children *are* innocent, and that innocence is concurrent, and consistent with the overarching celestial or cosmic choices offered to us pre-birth, which I regard as part of each individual's path. Once we arrive here, we are all co-creating the scripting of the story of the world with every decision. When an adult makes the choice to harm a child, they are not only engaging in a horrific act of violence, wrongdoing, and evil, but they are affecting the course of that child's life in imposing upon them the force of their will, and in the process, marring their own life by etching onto their soul the indelible story of their abhorrent moral choices.

As a woman who has, myself, experienced childhood abuse, trauma, rape as a young woman, multiple forms of sexual assault, abusive relationships, a devastating divorce and the subsequent separation from my two oldest children (along with many other experiences of hardship, including severe illness), the element of choice as it relates to loss and affliction has been a difficult thing for me to wrap my mind around as well. But what I know from my own experience is that at a certain point, the trauma I suffered became my responsibility to face, to look at, to honour, to nurture, to heal, and to make choices in contrast to.

Nonetheless, I carried my pain and shame with me well into my late-adolescence and adulthood. Long after the abuse of my innocence had ended, I allowed it to occupy my mind, my heart, and my body, and I lived my life in a state of ongoing resentment and hostility, imitating and re-emphasizing through each of my own subsequent choices, the abusive scenarios that I claimed to find intolerable.

At the ripe age of forty-two, I think of myself as a late bloomer in this area especially. I have spent a considerable amount of time in therapy, absorbing ideas and material that were designed, I realise now, to maintain and nurture my identity as a victim. Talk therapy is generally not focused on the efficient resolution of past hurt or trauma, and often has the effect of reinforcing the very programs and self-perceptions that keep us leashed to the victim animus, and therefore habitually cultivating results in keeping with that persona.

This makes sense in light of how embedded the psychology and psychiatry industries are in the same systems of power and control that are intended to keep us hooked and dependent on external validation, and in the thrall of the cult of victimization (most therapeutic modalities are branches of allopathy, like obstetrics, after all).

The glaring shortcomings of therapy aside, at this point in my life, it's not only easy for me to see how I co-created all (and I mean all) the situations of hardship and strife I survived, it's honestly truly *exciting* for me to continuously plumb the ways in which I now recognize that I did, in fact, choose those experiences for myself, and to realise how rich those events ultimately were for my overall development, as strange as that might sound.

This does not mean that I blame myself at all, nor does this indicate that I absolve others of *their* responsibility; it simply means that I recognize where I have willingly (if unconsciously) entered into an energetic covenant with those who may indeed have done me wrong, therefore binding myself to that oppositional or even predatory force which can function as a kind of chrysalid, enclosing us within a drama that rightfully belongs in the past.

I want to be very clear that taking full responsibility for our lives and learning how to (a) identify when we are playing the role of victim, as well as (b) hone our capacity to step *outside* of the spectacle of performative drama, does not mean that there aren't very real victims or perpetrators, or that we have any obligation at all to dodge or ignore experiences or feelings that are real—it's actually quite the opposite.

Discovering how to discern when we are caught up in victim consciousness and how to exit that state of being requires a reconciliation between acknowledging situations in which we *were* victimized, while also declining to continue claiming victim*hood* by calmly observing how we bought into those situations, contracted into them, co-created them, and, on some level, *chose* them. This is the apex of power, authority, and liberation.

PORTAL

Being willing to move forward in our lives without dragging past experiences with us, and (crucially) without perpetually re-creating the same or energetically similar experiences because we're stuck in the same consciousness that produced them, is the reward of awareness.

Again, this does not mean that anyone is to blame for having been victimized, but it does mean that there is an element of choosing in every moment of our lives, and that the concept that we are co-creating a universe that is perpetually responsive (the fundamental idea of "karma"), is always at play.

Releasing ourselves from our fragile dependency on oppression as a source of identity (including taking responsibility for healing our traumas) is one of the most significant distinctions between childhood and maturity. Sadly, many, if not most adults in our day and age never psychologically or emotionally move beyond an adolescent stage in which we feel at the mercy of our past experiences, our parents, or the dominant authority symbol.

For those suffering from what has now become a socially-sanctioned, normalized state of arrested development, the focus of the desire for validation often shifts at some point from the parent figure to the institutional delegate, namely doctors or other medical professionals, enabling greater numbers of people to live out their entire lives in a state of emotional stuntedness, ever-reliant on external directives and approval.

INTEGRATION QUESTIONS

1. Examine the beliefs you have about birth and your body. Are there any areas where you can identify that you may be responding from either the position of Victim, Villain, or Hero?

2. Reflecting on the idea of responsibility and that we are always choosing, what do you believe this reveals about who you *are being*, now, or who you were at that time?

3. Be honest with yourself while reflecting, without judgement. What "position" on the drama triangle do you most often find yourself taking (Victim, Villain, or Hero)? How does this show up in your daily life?

CHAPTER FIVE

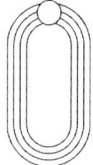

THE PROOF OF TRUE DESIRE

FOUND WANTING

Every single woman on earth has the power to choose a blissful, pain-free birth. I know this, precisely because I used to be a woman who would have loudly disputed such a declaration, although I now recognize this truth as archetypal and decreed by God. We always get the birth we choose, though we may not get the birth we think we want.

Just as pain in birth can be transmuted and dissolved entirely by any woman who chooses to do so, likewise, pain, struggle, tension, and hardship can only be experienced during birth, through choosing. This is a biological and spiritual law—it is absolute, and axiomatic. The methodology is fool-proof, and the fundamental concepts and principles are universal and immutable–and we are all free to prove this for ourselves through direct experience.

Yet not every woman who reads this book will choose to implement its teachings, and many more may claim that they did, but then declare that it "didn't work," and thereafter ardently deny that what this demonstrates is that they did, in fact, choose pain, struggle, suffering, and unnecessary drama. Everything I share in this book can "work" for all mothers. For some women though, this is an extremely triggering position.

The assertion that pain during birth is ultimately a choice, and that we establish every aspect of our births through choosing (and that we always have the power to choose differently) strikes many people as profoundly offensive, and may even bring up feelings of rage, incredulity, or inspire rationalizations and extreme defensiveness (all of which I can personally understand and relate to). If one is unfamiliar with what choice really is, how it works, or how we choose (or have chosen in the past) unconsciously, then the idea that we have selected something frightening, or terrible, or even painful, can seem irreconcilable with our understanding of the world and our place in it.

What I hear from many mothers, is that despite having "done the work," or "prepared extensively," or "cultivated the right mindset," or "reframed the idea of pain," they still experienced suffering, intensity, and struggle, and this is therefore the proof that choosing was outside of their capacity.

But the art of choosing bliss and the transmutation of pain in birth is not about "doing the work," because there is no work to do. It's not about "reframing," it's not about pretense, and it's not even really about mindset. It's about learning to choose, and choosing to surrender, which first requires becoming a woman who knows that everything is possible for her, and that the scope of her power *always* includes the potential to select with precision, extending to every single aspect of how her experience of the world—and of embodiment—transpires from her innermost condition.

This can be an incredibly threatening proposition for many of us, because this power cannot be claimed unless we are also willing to own the choices we made that created everything in our lives that came before, and to differentiate between true desire, and what we think we want. As I have previously stated, the proof of true desire, is in the having. True power lies in our capacity to fully possess the incontrovertible fact that everything we have chosen is evidenced now, by the reality of its existence. This is accurate not only in birth, but in every other potential scenario in life.

Often, we may think we want something, but wanting is not the same as true desire. True desire can only ever be verified in retrospect, by the materialization of the thing, the situation, or the achievement itself. You might think you want it (whatever "it" might be), and as a result, you may experience longing, or craving. But wanting or even yearning is not the same as actual desire, and as I keep saying, *the proof of true desire is in the having.* Correspondingly, if we are making choices that take us away from what we think we want, our true desires are being revealed to us.

The expression "to be found wanting," is a very revealing one. The phrase comes from the Old Testament of the Bible, in the *Book of Daniel*. The New King James translation reads, "You have been weighed in the balances, and found wanting."[23] This is widely interpreted as a reference to the judgement of a person's character by God as inferior, or inadequate, and so it may be. Yet my understanding of this passage is that it also refers directly to the ubiquity of victim-consciousness, and the widespread repudiation of God's immense generosity in granting us free will, and the potential to materialize love and goodness in action, through our embrace of reality, by which, paradoxically, the seemingly impossible can be brought into being.

God has also bequeathed to us the capacity to judge, and to discern. Most of us use this endowment to judge others, and to justify or excuse our own behaviour. But when we can humble ourselves enough to see our own willing acquiescence to the enslavement of victim identification, we free our minds. We are all, from time to time, "found wanting." We find ourselves wanting this, that, or the other frequently. But we also have the

---

[23] Daniel 5:27

power, always, to choose to earnestly behold that which we truly desire, which is always and only ever demonstrated by what we end up having.

This works in all directions, and it is always true, in part because until we have the thing, the relationship, or the experience, we cannot know what it is to have it, let alone whether or not we truly desired it in the first place. If we refer back to the idea of the ever-presence of choice and its binary nature, the absence of something, someone, or some situation is a possession of a different kind—the possession of scarcity, or dearth, even. This proves in turn, that our true desire was in fact lack, or whatever other, different thing we actualized (including nothing) instead of the thing we thought we wanted, which, as always, we choose through every discrete thought and action leading to it.

Most of us, when we come up against any kind of barrier, or perceived limitation, tell ourselves that it is unattainable to us simply because we have not yet attained it, and we use our existing frame of reference as an excuse for why it remains inaccessible, and then we apply this circumscription to others as well, all in subconscious service to denying that whatever experience we have is a result of our choosing, including birth.

I had no idea—not even an inkling—that I truly desired the experience of euphoric, orgasmic birth, until I had it. The having wasn't simply the moment of my baby's emergence—it occurred through the transformational process of expanding my perception of both what it is to choose and how to choose, which began with shifting my capacity for responsibility and self-ownership, then subsequently, propelling an evolution of what I knew to be possible for myself, transforming who I was (and am).

This was rooted in the all-powerful recognition that until that turning point, I had, despite my lack of awareness theretofore, nonetheless chosen everything that came before, and that my true desire—as evidenced by the reality I had lived—had been to experience birth as the most flamboyantly dramatic, ostentatiously intense, exuberantly painful experience imaginable.

If you have already given birth, how does it feel in your body, in your heart, and in your nervous system, to reflect back on everything that occurred during that birth (or those births) and to declare dominion over every part of it, knowing, and accepting, that at some point along the way, it was your choice—your agency—that established the conditions for whatever specific experiences you had at the point of culmination?

This can be a very difficult thing to contemplate. Again, if you are among the many women who were mistreated, violated, or abused by a midwife, an obstetrician, or any medical professional or bystander as your precious child was moving through your body, there is no excuse for the behaviour of those individuals. You have no obligation to forgive them, or to relieve them of their responsibility. But you do have an opportunity to neutralize the force they exerted (and may still be exerting, energetically) over you, and to reclaim your power, by acknowledging that you architected that final outcome, even if indirectly, even if unconsciously, through the various choices you made—hours, days, weeks, months, and even years—in advance of the moment of birth.

Most women, who open themselves up to this kind of radical responsibility, will begin to see that there were red flags all along the path that led to their birth-rape—red flags that they ignored, justified, pushed under the rug, or allowed themselves to remain in denial of, in order to placate other people, or to fit into society's expectations. The very same is true if you experienced a previous birth that you loved, except for its intensity or pain, or with the exception of any aspect. The only difference is that the choice-points—the intersections during which you selected one path or another, one form of support or another, one context or another, one response or another, one way of holding your body, or of breathing, or another—will likely be finer, subtler, less evident or distinguishable, at least immediately.

If you can lovingly guide yourself to a state of openness to the idea that you chose the way your birth played out—however it occurred—your subconscious mind will respond to that newfound receptivity by offering you clues, signals, and fragments of memory, bringing those particulate moments into the conscious realm, to show you even the most attenuated instances in the timeline of your story in which you may have opted into choosing pain or tension, via the drama of victimhood.

The distinction between birth in power, which so many women experience during their freebirths and homebirths (and much more rarely, but occasionally, in medicalized situations) and orgasmic, euphoric birth, with no pain whatsoever, lies in first knowing that it is possible, and then knowing how to choose it.

EGO AND SACRIFICE

The process of bringing some thing, state of being, or experience into presence, always requires sacrifice. There is always a price to pay. We can only ever "manifest" something different (that is, to invite into the material that which we truly desire with conscious intention), if we are willing to sacrifice our former state of being, and to give up the version of ourselves that maintains a commitment to the other, prior reality as we step into the new, immaculate Now.

The most uncomfortable, yet fundamental and essential sacrifice we are called to make for transformation to take place is of the Self whose state of consciousness remains beholden to the belief that the reality from which we have created our current bondage is immutable. The fantasy that we are helpless victims of the ongoing stagnancy we remain committed to is often immensely comforting.

To actualize your desire for a blissful birth, you must be willing to abandon your identity as a victim. You must be prepared to sacrifice your excuses and your justifications. You will be required to release the pretense that you can't have anything other than pain, or that you have no agency to choose the conditions of your birth, or that your body or mind are somehow unique in their impotence, inadequacy, or ineffectiveness. You must be willing to relinquish your attachment to drama, which is a kind of worship of the derivative, lower self: a form of idolatry.

And yet it is the purpose of the ego to maintain the identity framework we have developed that has allowed us to survive and to navigate the world (however dysfunctional and limiting the ego-driven habits, behaviours, beliefs, and perspectives might be), and the ego has some very covert, and even devious ways of attempting to convince us that we *are* the maladaptive, victim-oriented limiting beliefs, thoughts, and assumptions that we entertain about ourselves.

ARGUING FOR OUR LIMITATIONS

I was so inspired and enlivened by the revelations imparted to me following Helio's euphoric birth that I felt a compulsion to shout from the rooftops, to as many women as might possibly hear, that not only can birth can be rapturous, pleasurable, and easy for every mother, but also that we can have anything we choose, limited only by the structures imposed by our own commitments.

A small subset of women knew exactly what I meant, because they too had stepped through the portal to bliss in birth. But for the most part, the responses I have received to my joyous proclamation that pleasurable, orgasmic birth is available to us all, without caveat or restriction, or exception, has ranged from a reserved curiosity to skepticism, to defensiveness, and even aggression and rage. And in every response, the subject's internal state of being, the nature, quality, range, and texture of their particular flavour of devotion, and their degree of victim-orientation is on full display.

I read all the books, I did all the exercises, I was completely prepared to have a painless birth but no matter how much I told myself it didn't hurt, it hurt. I'm not sure why I couldn't get there, explained one woman in a public forum, revealing the underlying assumption that not only did she believe she had done everything she could, but that she had also allowed herself to think that she had done everything that was *possible* for her to do. In the end, having exhausted all of her apparent options, she maintained that she was simply not capable of experiencing anything other than the reality that she did, which is that birth *hurts*.

It bugs me to no end that you can do all the prep and mental work, but still be in the worst pain of your life, expressed another woman. And yet, if we truly believe that it is possible for us to do, be, or have something, and we fall short of achieving that state, or position, or thing, then by definition, the absence of that experience is the confirmation that, ipso facto, we could not have exhausted all the options or "done all we could"…unless what we are tacitly admitting to, is that we never actually thought the goal or the yearning was viable in the first place. Furthermore, the notion that transmuting pain in birth is simply a matter of "telling ourselves that it doesn't hurt" is diametrically opposed to the principles we will be unravelling in the coming pages.

Many women have come forward to ask me if choosing blissful birth is a matter of simply duping ourselves through a form of mental trickery, into masking the pain. One mother wrote, *You're supposed to try to change the pain into something you enjoy, and that just didn't work for me, period.* But as I've said, bliss in birth has nothing to do with effort, or striving, or telling ourselves a story that isn't true, or denying what *is* true. It comes from learning how to choose to yield, to trust, to surrender, to allow, to connect with God and the energy of the eternal, and to dissolve all resistance into shimmering, exquisite love through radical embodiment—a process we are about to deeply examine.

Enacting the sequence of dissolution and transmogrification, however, is almost out of the question for someone who has staked a claim to impossibility: *It didn't work. Period.* This is a woman utterly committed to "it"—whatever "it" might be—not working (period), offering another very interesting example of clandestine victim identification. Furthermore, no woman is "supposed" to do anything, and if what you are committed to is the experience of the sensations of birth being painful, effortful, wild, primal, or gloriously, spectacularly expressive (none of which is wrong), then by definition, you will likely succeed in knowing birth as some variation of that.

Personally, I don't mind pain in labour, one mother asserted. *I don't really think of it as pain, just my body working perfectly. I have given birth drug-free several times. I wouldn't seek to have a "pain-free" birth. I enjoy the labour journey as it is.* This is wonderful, and perfectly valid. No woman has any obligation to modify her perspective on birth, or to explore new ways of experiencing birth, embodiment, or consciousness. The ideas in this book will only resonate with those who are ready, willing, and able to receive them. That said, I do think that the "ping" of being activated enough to comment on, or to explain why one isn't interested in even exploring a topic like this might be an indication of subconscious curiosity, at the very least. Often, resistance is the first indication that we might actually have a repressed urge to shift our attitude towards something.

Very few people truly "enjoy" pain. I would argue that no one really does. Some individuals certainly seek out pain for various reasons (almost always related to trauma), and pain and pleasure do indeed exist on something of a spectrum, but they are also, paradoxically, in conflict, and even mutually exclusive. Despite this, most of us, perversely, delight in pain to some degree (even when it's not being masochistically conflated with pleasure), and the majority of us positively relish the drama of it. I hear the echoes of this kind of gratification in the tone with which so many women maintain their incapacity.

On several occasions I have been asked why I was suddenly able to choose a pain-free, pleasurable birth my ninth time around, and why I did not therefore make that choice during my earlier pregnancies. The answer to this excellent question is simply that it was only prior to my ninth birth that I got sick and tired of my old story, bored of perpetuating my identity as a victim, and open to the realisation that pain, struggle, suffering, and drama were inauthentic states that I had chosen only because fighting — resistance, toil, and, in a sense, being in combat with myself and all of existence — was familiar and habitual, but not, I realized, actually *true*. And in every part of my life, I am increasingly interested in and devoted to authenticity, and coming into relationship with the deepest (even ugliest) truth about who and what I am.

This distinction between authenticity and inauthenticity can be a tricky one. Let me be clear that even though I am avowing that we choose our state of being (including suffering and pain), most of us are unaware of having chosen, and genuinely ignorant of the breadth of choices available to us. To be sure, there are always reasons for choosing a certain path, and often these include simply being oblivious to the fact that there also exist other, different paths, options, or ideas of which we might avail ourselves.

It is also certainly true that we have been entrained not to seek out alternate information or possibilities. This is, in part, the point of this book, which brings us back full circle. Yes, we live in a society in which we are actively discouraged from being accountable for ourselves, and we are spurred to outsource responsibility for everything from birth to death. But we don't have to. You do not have to be as careless and as ignorant of your power as the profane world wants you to be. God, I believe, has given us so much more.

Another aspect of the enigma is that it is never the case that any experience that we choose is really wrong. Everything does, indeed (I can now finally accept to a great extent) happen for a reason (as trite and as irritating as that adage often sounds to me). Ultimately, every choice we make is always in divine alignment with the larger purpose of life as a sacred training ground—including bondage and subjugation. We are all here on earth to fulfill our purpose *if* we choose to; to fulfil our mission(s) *if* we choose to; and to reach our potential *if* we choose to. And if we choose not to, well, that's also part of the tapestry, and there is a kind of perfection in that as well.

Learning and growth are never linear (and are often circular, and recursive) and each of us has the potential for monumental—exponential—shifts in awareness. At the very heart of every variety of learning and growth, is responsibility. The most consequential forms of burgeoning, however, cannot take place unless we're approaching our lives as the source of our own power, our own outcomes, our own capacity, our own solutions, and ultimately, the source of our own frame of consciousness, while simultaneously, I believe, in full surrender to God's boundless, constitutive grace.

EXCEPTIONAL CIRCUMSTANCES

Another tactic that many of us employ as a way of unconsciously arguing for our own limitations, is framing ourselves as atypical; as somehow different from other women, and special, on account of our (or our baby's) anatomy, physiology, or the composition of our births. This is a cunning strategy on the part of the subconscious mind, to justify our victimhood, and it's one that most of us tend to cling to with remarkable tenacity.

In particular, stories about so-called "back labour," or other narratives around our babies' positioning ("asynclitic," "posterior," etc.), and the purported "cervical lip," (a term used by medical professionals to pathologize a situation in which a mother simply needs more time for her cervix to open fully, but which conveniently establishes a pretext for various intrusions and interventions) are all frequently used to defend the notion that the suffering we experienced was inevitable.

I did the work. I reframed my experience. I had a supportive midwife and doula in my corner. My husband did everything right. I was confident, and ready for birth. But I couldn't avoid the pain that came with back labour. My birth was beautiful and empowering, but unless there was some way I could have prevented back labour, there is no way I could have avoided the pain.

This comment, as relatable as I'm sure it is for so many of us, nonetheless exposes a very strong commitment to the story that what this mother endured was "unavoidable," and that ultimately, she had no agency over what she sees as the most definitive, unequivocal aspect of her birth. As I have said, experiencing birth as bliss has nothing to do with "doing the work" or "reframing" anything. There is no "work" to do at all—it's quite the opposite.

More significantly, this mother's commitment to believing that it was "back labour" that prohibited her birth from being anything other than it was is in full evidence, and she is utterly convinced that her capacity to expand beyond the known or expected was thwarted by the fatefulness and certainty of her recalcitrant, stubborn body. Short of somehow circumventing "back labour," she views the experience of pain as predestined.

This perspective also exposes that sneaky dualism coming into light. Ultimately, according to this account, the mind is constrained by the body, rather than the whole self being an indissoluble, intrinsically elemental totality, capable of the diffusion of energy and the quantum spanning between realms. What is also apparent, is that while this woman confirms that her birth was "beautiful and empowering," and that she enjoyed the experience (which is truly a positive thing, and not something to be diminished or dismissed at all), the undertone of defensiveness and her emphasis on what she believes was the inevitable and crucial deficit resulting from the special kind of birth she feels she had, is, again, a way of deflecting responsibility, revealing her ongoing pledge to see herself as simply at the mercy of the overpowering vicissitudes of birth.

The term "back labour," especially, has become a signifier for a birth that is considered almost deviant, and suggests a kind of exclusivity in its awfulness and difficulty. Women frequently share war stories about whose "back labour" was worse, with a sense of near-competitiveness (and, at times, with what can seem like exhilaration or glee). Yet as someone with a fair degree of experience from all directions—as a birthing mother, and as a birth-witness—I know that the construct of "back labour," like the assumed, automatic pain of birth itself—is thoughtlessly fostered, promoted, and passed around like a virus, which women internalize, and then unconsciously replicate in their own births, via belief.

But while "back labour," has almost taken on the codification of a pathology, it isn't anything other than a phrase that indicates a self-reported (self-selected) and entirely personal phenomenon. It simply means that the mother, according to her own subjective experience, felt the sensations of birth primarily located in her back (as I have, during three of my nine births), as opposed to lower in her pelvis, or closer to the top of her fundus. And? So what? There is no objective form of assessment to determine what actually constitutes "back labour," or "front-labour," or "up" labour, or "down" labour, or the severity with which any of these may present. In truth, birth can only ever occur in the present, in our own bodies, minds, and souls. The moment our babies emerge, what we think of as our "experience" of birth, becomes a story. And "back labour" isn't really any different than any other kind of birth at all. It's all just birth.

One of the most significant reasons the myth of the exceptionality of "back-labour" persists lies in the distortedness of the lens of midwifery, a profession that legitimizes itself through the perpetuation of the "soft" pathologization of the female body, and the manufacturing of problems justified by our always unique, nonconforming morphology (every woman's body really is one-of-a-kind).

"Back labour," is often framed as the result of our babies' supposedly suboptimal positioning, and this, of course, often ends up being a self-fulfilling prophecy, not to mention a rationale for the pre-emptive sabotage of birth via the imposition of all kinds of ridiculous, nonsensical, and highly stressful rituals including adopting special poses, exercises, chiropractic maneuvers, and proscriptions against sitting and even sleeping in specific ways, in an effort to inspire a baby to change their position in the womb, none of which are "evidence-based," or falsifiable.

In my twenty years of birthwork, I have witnessed countless babies in the so-called "correct" position take days to be born (along with intense back-pain for the mother) and I've seen babies in the "incorrect" position born with ease (with no overly intense back sensations at all). In fact, with very few exceptions, there is no right or wrong posture for our babies to take as they gestate—the way our babies choose to lie in our wombs in the weeks, days, and hours leading up to birth rarely has any bearing at all on the ease or difficulty with which a birth will occur. And yet positioning is used not only as a pretext for a variety of forms of interference, intervention, and sabotage, but positioning fixation is also a primary method of scapegoating the body before, during, and after birth, whether as way of foretelling the ostensible certainty of pain or of rationalizing it.

With respect to pain specifically, it is emphatically not your baby's position or "back labour" or any aspect of your physiology that is the "cause" of pain during birth. It is, instead, your preexisting beliefs and commitments, your misunderstanding of how to properly prepare your mind *and* your environment for birth (not to mention misjudgement of how mind and context are connected), and it's your misconception of your own power and of how to use that power to choose to dissolve and transmute pain—any kind of pain—which is, in fact, possible for every woman to do (no matter how her body or baby presents) but which not every woman will choose to do.

DESERVINGNESS AND ORGASM

When women feel personally affronted by the implication that they had (and have) just as much a capacity for orgasmic, pain-free, blissful birth as I do, it almost comes across as though my proposition—that all women might be more powerful than they are allowing themselves to know—is taken as an accusation. How could I, a random stranger, have the gall to believe in their potential for more? *How dare you suggest to me that I create my experience of the world?*

The regularity and reflexiveness with which my proposition that every woman is mighty and masterful is taken as an insult and a provocation is both fascinating and disturbing—but also, sadly, predictable. I wonder if perhaps there is an element to the issue of intense defensiveness of the prevailing response that relates to the ongoing, pervasive themes of both sexual repression and the accompanying lack of sexual boundaries in contemporary culture. Not only do many women unconsciously see themselves as undeserving of pleasure, but as undeserving of power as well (not to mention confused as to what power truly comprises).

Birth is the completion of the sexual cycle—the apotheosis of sexual fulfilment. It is as normal, natural, and biologically and spiritually ordained for birth to be as exquisitely blissful and orgasmic as sex can be (and hopefully is) for all of us. As I discussed in the latter part of Chapter Two, birth and sex are on an unwavering, inarguable, self-evident continuum.

Birth *is* sex. The unease that many people feel about this very idea, is another relic which I hope will increasingly be seen as belonging to a bygone era. Arguing that not all women can experience pleasure and orgasm during birth, is no different from arguing that not all women can experience pleasure and orgasm during sex.

I will never participate in promoting the claim that certain women, for whatever reason, are prohibited from the full spectrum of pleasure we are granted access to in this life, and that includes birth. What I am capable of, every woman is capable of. Orgasmic birth is no different than orgasmic sex.

It was only a few decades ago that sexual bliss—especially for women—was seen as something that many, if not most of us, just simply did not have access to. This was explained away in part as a result of biological peculiarities, none of which were logical in any way (somewhat like the "back labour" excuse), but the most prevalent view was simply that enjoying sex (especially on the part of women) was considered unnecessary, and even indecent, obscene, or prurient. That undertone is very much present today when the topic of orgasmic birth is broached, and I can't help but wonder if there are threads of residual shame or embarrassment for some of the women who have expressed feeling offended and even angered by the universality of my position.

Why do you so arrogantly presume to think that your narrow, restricted personal experience, values, lens, and insights, are applicable or relevant to all women? asked one mother, outraged by the audacity of my generalization that every woman has the potential to have a blissful, pleasurable birth. *Some women can have orgasmic births and others just don't have that capability. You can't insist on claiming that what's true for you is true for everyone.*

Well…I can, actually (I can even write a whole book about it), and of course, anyone is free to disagree. But what is especially fascinating to me about this particular stance, is the apparently blind double-standard: while my viewpoint that every woman possesses the capacity for, and the potential to choose a pain-free and orgasmic birth is seen as "narrow" and "restrictive," this woman (and others who share her perspective) see their own emphatic insistence that certain women are simply prohibited from calm, euphoric, pain-free births (whether by nature, or physiology or some other special reason) and that they are therefore simply doomed to birth in pain and agony, as somehow *more* open-minded and *less* proscriptive and censorious than my contention that if choosing ecstasy is possible for one mother, it's possible for all.

I do, indeed maintain, that every single woman on the planet possesses the capacity to choose her experience of birth, down to whether or not the sensations are exquisitely pleasurable, or bitingly painful. It is entirely up to you, however, whether or not you decide to engage with these ideas wholeheartedly, to choose to implement them, and then, when the time comes, to allow yourself to expand beyond the boundaries of your beliefs and perceptions, to crack open, and allow for beatification through birth.

If, however, you don't believe that this is possible, the likelihood that you will then experience it as true for you, will be exponentially diminished. Nonetheless, I will always stand for your, and every woman's worthiness and deservingness of everything that I know is available, and more. I also acknowledge that you are free to choose differently—no matter how infuriating that might be.

One of the most noteworthy paradoxes we are called to wrestle with when it comes to the art of choosing, is that whatever you believe about the power you have to select your experience, is correct. If you are absolutely committed to the idea that I am special, and that what I discuss in this book doesn't apply to you, you cannot be wrong.

In fact, if you are determined to discount my assertion that a completely different kind of birth is available to all women, you will *always* be right about that. If you don't want it, and can't have it, you are correct. Whatever it is that you believe about your own capacity and the extent to which you have the power to choose anything in your life, is always going to be perfectly, utterly true.

MANAGING OUR EXPECTATIONS

The way women describe their birth experiences (and the remarkably consistent features of those descriptions) makes evident their degree (or lack) of self-responsibility. What I have observed over the years is that the women who do *not* have births that they think they wanted or enjoyed tend to attribute those birth experiences to chance, bad luck, or physical dysfunction—or even to the possibility that their bodies failed them—because this is so often the story that we are encouraged to believe, even when birth is subverted or stymied by a well-meaning obstetrician or midwife. The narrative becomes a version of *I tried so hard, but my birth just didn't work out* or, *the stars just weren't aligned* or, *God chose for me and it was out of my hands.*

On the other end of the spectrum, women who believe birth is going to be a disaster often succeed in creating exactly that, and frequently end up with highly medicated births. Similarly, women who, for whatever reason, desire to escape birth on a conscious or subconscious level (and there are plenty of legitimate reasons for that desire) will almost always find a way to fulfil this commitment—usually through heavy medication or surgery.

Women who believe birth is going to be easy, but who decline to fully consider and take responsibility for the implications and logical conclusions of how they establish the set and setting of their births (where they decide to be, who they invite, the way this will affect the profoundly psychedelic, psycho-spiritual elements of the experience, along with how their overarching and atomic choices will form the essential scaffolding of the process), often struggle, and may end up with far more interventions than they initially thought they wanted.

Conversely, women who believe birth will be hard, yet also know that they will ultimately prevail, generally tend to choose to cultivate the mental fortitude and an environment conducive to moving through the process with a sense of self-ownership. These women often experience birth as both a massive challenge, and as a source of immense power. This is the mental framework from which I was operating during my first eight births.

In further contrast, women who have exactly the births they dreamed of usually describe their stories from a very different angle, situating themselves in the retelling as the protagonists, the deciders, and the power generators—not as the *sole* source of power, mind you, but as the willing, grateful, and responsible recipients of the power that God has bestowed. These women see themselves as the instigators and creators of the birth they desired, and they view birth as a project to be undertaken with exquisite precision, deliberation, and intention. At every step of the way they have guarded their vision, cultivated that vision, and consciously brought that vision into reality at every choice-point.

I acknowledge that these are general observations, and I am very aware that there may be some readers who fall somewhere in between all of these broad categories; there can be lots of overlap. I also want to emphasise that this is not a condemnation of those who succumb to a victim mindset. I *do* understand the dynamics of the experience of feeling "at the effect of" the circumstances of our lives. I have been there many times myself.

But when we are willing and able to exist in the perfection and mystery of birth; to *be* the energy of birth completely; to surrender fully to the divine will of God (or Source, or however you prefer to understand the Creator of all) through birth, and to connect with our babies on the level of soul and embodiment simultaneously, while knowing that ease and ecstasy is ours to claim and is available at all times, we have already chosen an experience of pure bliss.

PORTAL

INTEGRATION QUESTIONS

1. Which of these "exception" stories have you subscribed to in the past? Which stories feel, or have felt, true in your system (e.g., cervical lip, back labour, etc.)?

2. What would it feel like to let go of these stories? How might you think and behave differently if you were to release these stories, to remind yourself how powerful you are, and to play with the idea of what's truly available to you (i.e., pain-free, blissful, orgasmic birth)?

3. What do you actually want? Does it align with what you believe you can have?

CHAPTER SIX

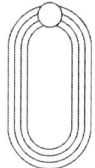

CONSENT AND THE ARCHITECTED UNIVERSE

THE VORTEX OF INDUSTRIAL BIRTH

The idea of "choice," in any context, is often highly misunderstood. This is certainly the case with regards to birth, and especially industrial birth, whether at home (because industrial birth is often enacted in women's homes) or in the hospital.

Many women believe that "choosing" the birth we want, or creating the reality of our births, is simply the practice of thinking happy thoughts. There is a popular and pervasive myth in the birth-world that regardless of the setting, as long as we can affirm the idea in our minds of having a wonderful birth (along with hiring a great doula), we can easily materialise "the best of both worlds"—a lovely peaceful birth, with all the safety features of modern obstetrics. This is a fantasy.

Yes, we always get to choose. But so does everyone else around us. Every choice we make expands and contracts the possibilities available to us—expansion in one direction, contraction in another. Every choice creates an enclosure, lifting certain veils, opening certain portals, bringing certain influences closer, and distancing others.

We never have the option of controlling or dictating the choices of another, or of deciding how someone else might respond to the world that they create and occupy. We confront this law when our choices bring us into a direct intersection with another person's (or institution's) energetic field or authority. Every universe possesses its own indelible laws.

In making the choice to enter a particular universe, we have already dictated to ourselves the palette of the outcome. To presume to enter another's world, believing that we can re-shape its codes, constitutions, and ordinances in conformity to our preferences, is to attempt to defy reality—and this will always end in frustration.

As an example, let's look at birth within the context of the hospital or the sphere of institutional influence. By showing up to the hospital when your birth sensations begin, or by hiring a government midwife to come into your home, you have made the choice to limit the choices available to you to only those that exist within the boundaries of the world you have chosen to enter. When we willingly enter the world of birth-as-pathology, under surveillance, framed by external regulation, sovereign birth is therefore precluded.

The universe of industrial birth—whether enacted in the hospital or imported into your home by one of its agents—is its own vortex, cast by the resonant framework of the beliefs and assumptions that created it. The possibilities offered by this universe are limited by its internal structure.

When you elect to oscillate within the frequency of industrial birth, you are choosing to be subject to its laws. By becoming one who participates in that world through choosing it, and who now exists within the resonant field of that world, you have inevitably contracted into the internal ordinances of that universe.

You can, indeed, choose anything you desire for your birth. In accordance with the world you have chosen (which coheres with your Being), in alignment with the reality that you have constructed for yourself and your baby, you can have anything you desire for your birth *as long as* your true desire is consonant with the laws of the vortex of the universe you have chosen to occupy.

Giving birth in freedom is a possibility that always exists now, and forever in the infinite Now, within the paradigm of the universe of sovereign birth. Everywhere in the world, no matter the laws, political expectations, or social customs that hold sway, there will always be some women living in the world of liberated birth and freebirth (a term I use specifically to denote giving birth without the presence of any formal outside support-person).

Conversely, industrial birth is also a universe architected through choice. There are women all across the planet living in the world of assessment, monitoring, surveillance, and the extraction of a child-as-product from her body. These women, of course, are now among the majority.

Especially if you are interested in giving birth in coherence with the laws of nature versus the dictatorship of technocracy, you must know that these two worlds—the world of servitude to the cyborg, and the world of birth liberation—are distinct, and incompatible.

By choosing to live in the world of freebirth or birth-in-freedom, everything is available to you *except* that which is *only* available within the vortex of medicalization. By choosing liberated birth, you can have anything you desire, as long as you are at peace with the fact that you have automatically forfeited the following:

- being watched by strangers
- having someone suggest or insinuate that your baby is malpositioned
- having a doctor or midwife tell you your baby is "late"
- being hooked up to an external fetal monitor

- having someone put their hands inside your vagina
- being offered surgery
- being offered drugs
- being saved by a professional
- deferring responsibility to an external authority.

If the former options are what you want, you must go to the hospital, or invite a regulated, licensed midwife into your birth-room. And if you choose to enter the universe of institutional, medicalized birth, with the expectation of anything other than what has always been the guarantee and promise of that context, you are residing in a state of delusion.

Outcomes are fairly predictable when the larger (macro) choice of the world we have selected to occupy aligns with each discrete (micro) choice we then make. For example, given that I have chosen freebirth overall, I no longer even have the option of feeling upset by the overbearing, gaslighting behaviour of medical professionals, because the issue doesn't arise for me. I don't interact with medical professionals at all—they simply do not exist within the realm of the universe of freebirth.

However, I work with women all the time who are frustrated by the experience of having medical professionals frequently talk down to them. This is interesting, given that infantilization, manipulation, psychological games, and coercion are utterly definitive of the world of industrial obstetrics. No medical professional can possibly proceed through graduation or residency unless they have proven their mastery in exercising power through covert bullying and intimidation—it's simply intrinsic to the cognitive ecosystem and belief structure of the medical institution.

A significant part of every medical professional's educational programming involves conditioning that, by the end of their training, becomes so naturalised, the inductee has almost no capacity whatsoever to perceive their own exaggerated sense of authority and self-importance. Considering the embeddedness of this dynamic, the idea of expecting—or even hoping—that a medically-trained professional could possibly behave in any way other than exactly like a medically-trained professional is simply incoherent. Water is wet. Fire is hot.

Delusion and denial are both the cause and the result of a discrepancy between our larger macro-choices (context, environment, support-system, etc.) and the fluency of our micro-choices (how we allow ourselves to be spoken to, the atmosphere of our birth, the ease with which we enter an altered state, etc.).

Arguing with the reality of the universe within which you have chosen to live or operate is illogical and self-defeating. We all do this, of course, to some extent in certain areas of our lives. In order to survive the outcome of a core misalignment in our choices (which, in birth and in every other context, involves being confronted with the fact that what we truly desired wasn't actually what we thought we wanted), we have a few different options:

- We can whine and cry about how unfair life is, and how we didn't know how unpleasant and awful the experience of birth in captivity was going to be, and make lots of indignant noise about how the system needs to change (classic victim).
- We can blame the bad mean awful hospital system and its deranged sadistic operatives, or, conversely, we can blame our doula or partner or someone else for not having protected us well enough (victimhood through villainizing another).
- We can blame ourselves for not having fought hard enough, or for failing at our own self-advocacy (victimhood through villainizing ourselves).

- We can dissociate and convince ourselves that everything that was done to us and our baby was unavoidable, necessary, and lifesaving, and that our birth was great (bypassing).
- Or, we can acknowledge that we contracted into a particular set of possible outcomes by choosing, initially, the universe of the experience, and then crafting the walkway to that outcome with every subsequent choice, brick by brick.

The latter option is, without a doubt, humbling, painful, and often quite heartbreaking, especially at the point of departure. But it's also profoundly, stunningly redemptive, and incredibly expansive and powerful.

SPIRIT AND BIRTH-PLACE

As we have established, the environment and context of your birth — the universe that you decide to enter into (and therefore enter into agreement with) — is possibly the most salient factor that will affect the tone and resonance of your child's homecoming, and your rebirth as a mother.

Most of us are aware of having at least a few different options available to us when it comes to the kind of support system and environment we select for the birth of our babies. Whether or not you give birth at home, in the hospital, with a midwife, with an independent attendant, or alone, the conditions of the external environment (and thus the internal conditions that are created as a result of the external) will impact you inexorably, and may determine the extent to which you experience bliss, pleasure, embodied transcendence, and effortlessness during your birth.

But we have also been conditioned to view certain birth choices through the highly ideological and politicized lens of the institution, and many options offer a far different kind of experience in reality, than the illusion that is presented. For example, contrary to what is promoted, hospital and birth centre births are largely indistinguishable.

The birth centre "experience" is idealistically sold to women as a "natural" alternative to hospital birth (along with the "best of both worlds" trope), but it is illusory to believe that there will be any measure of greater "naturalness" or spontaneity at a birth centre versus a hospital. The most discernible difference is that birth centres usually have better interior decor.

Not only that, but because birth centres are construed to be "alternative" and "holistic," birth centre staff are often, as a result, far *more* concerned about liability, optics, and their reputation, and this often means they carry a greater burden of fear of variations of normal and complications (and may therefore be more likely to create them) than the staff at a hospital. When women give birth at a birth centre, it is often the case that at the very earliest sign that her process might not be following the narrow preordained notion of what is "normal" or "acceptable," transfer to the hospital will likely be deemed necessary (although this trend is rarely divulged during an initial interview or walk-through).

When birth occurs within the walls of the hospital, in contrast, the health professionals there enjoy the very highest level of legal impunity, and authority. The hospital is seen, socially and culturally, as "the safest place," and so (paradoxically) hospital practitioners—especially full-blown obstetricians—may be much more relaxed and more "willing" to "let you" "get away with" having your birth process take more time, or declining various procedures that have been standardized. This doesn't amount to much of a concession, but many women discover this surprisingly dissonant distinction to be true when they hire a midwife for their homebirth, believing that this will therefore mean they will automatically avoid being mistreated, which sadly isn't the case.

If you are considering a homebirth, it's very important to know that birth at home can range drastically, from a wild and primal spontaneous emergence to an event that is even more highly medicalized and interfered with than what many women experience within a hospital or birth centre. This will largely depend on the beliefs, convictions, education, experience, and affiliation of the support person you end up inviting into your home — or whether you end up inviting a support person into your home at all.

The beliefs and perspectives that midwives hold vary widely and will be indelibly coloured by the philosophical underpinnings of the kind of training she (or, ludicrously, he) has received. A medically educated regulated and licensed midwife who answers to a governing organization will not only be legally obligated to perform certain rituals and procedures, but her entire cognitive frame for understanding what birth is and how it works will have been shaped by the attitudes of the establishment in which she was instructed.

Midwifery has, overall, become increasingly institutionalized, and the vast majority of midwives undergo some degree of medical hazing. If you, as a mother, sign up to be supported by a medical practitioner (whether they call themselves a doctor or a midwife) who has been taught and conditioned to see birth as a medical problem, to collect evidence to support that assumption, and who answers to a central medical authority, they will, in all likelihood, find *something* about your body or your baby that can be interpreted as a medical problem, and your birth will be medicalized.

An unlicensed, non-medical, independent traditional birth attendant, or birth-witness, on the other hand, only answers to the mother, and for many women this represents the baseline requirement for a relationship founded upon mutual respect and trust, although (of course) there are also many other considerations, including energetic compatibility, and whether or not the two share a philosophical congruence. Additionally, given how pervasive the cultural pathologization of birth is, there are many non-medical, unlicensed birth attendants who are nonetheless operating from a medicalized perspective.

The hospital system, whether we choose to have it replicated in our homes or not, is rooted in a deliberately manufactured misunderstanding of birth, creating a self-fulfilling cycle in which the sabotage imposed by the system itself then has to be remedied through further interventions. In the majority of situations, it is the *system itself* (or the way the system is imparted and imposed by well-meaning birthworkers) that creates most complications in the first place.

In greater and greater numbers, women are beginning to recognize the inherently dysfunctional dynamics of medical birth—especially as the institutional structures of the corporate kleptocracy continue to crumble before our eyes—and this realization leads many women to freebirth. Freebirth too, however, can look very different depending on numerous fine distinctions. For example, a freebirth surrounded by family and friends will have a drastically different tenor than a quiet solo freebirth, or a freebirth with only the father of your baby present.

THE ENERGETICS OF BIRTH

As I've mentioned several times already, I have encountered a very limited number of women who have had "pain-free" hospital or birth centre births, so of course it is *possible* to have a blissful birth in those settings or in the presence of medical professionals, because anything is possible when we harness the power of our minds. These women are, however, few and far between. I have to emphasise that in my experience, according to what I have observed and lived myself, the more distracted a birthing woman is by external influences and interferences of any kind—from individuals to machines to technology—the more challenging it is for her to enter an altered state of transcendent bliss.

I suspect that employing the methods that I'm sharing in this book while giving birth in the hospital would be far more challenging than in other contexts, and that it would take a far greater degree of focus and mental filtering than most people are capable of. It's very challenging to call oneself into full presence and to inhabit an experience completely when our bodies are being violated. Violation usually leads to necessary forms of dissociation.

I identified dissociation as a very likely response in myself early on, and this is one of the reasons I have always chosen homebirth. Yet what I have also learned over time is that, for me, *any* form of distraction—any ripple in the energetic fabric of my birth space—occurs as a disturbance and a form of interference. We all have slightly different set-points and triggers for a trauma response, but birth is a biological and spiritual experience that, at its core, is common to us all. And what is common to all medically managed births is violation, the modus operandi of obstetrics.

I have seen, first-hand as a birth-witness, the acute sensitivity that most women have to the energetic frequency in the room as this plays out in homebirth situations. Over the years, I have observed that when I enter a mother's birth-room, no matter how quiet or respectful I am, the mother feels my presence, and in turn, I can feel her perception of my energy. I have developed a very highly cultivated sensitivity to the nuances and undertones of what a birthing mother is experiencing when I am in her field, and I know I am *very* good at navigating that energy with deep reverence.

But no matter how attuned and devoted a birth witness might be, it is a mistake for any of us to believe that we can *actually* "invisibilize" ourselves while in a woman's birth-space. Self-awareness is one of the most important virtues to develop as a birthkeeper, and this begins with acknowledging that our existence within the mother's vicinity will always shift the energy in the room.

Many women assume that if they hire the right doula, or create the most epically detailed birth-plan, they will manage to avoid abuse, but it's a mistake for any mother to believe that if she enrols in a medical birth, she can somehow mastermind being the exception to the established norm of sabotage. Some women do, but this is exceedingly rare, and it happens by chance, not by will or design. Most of the women who book birth-trauma debrief sessions with me are those who believed that they could "game" the system by orchestrating a team of helpers to "advocate" for them, or by priming themselves for either a fight or preemptive self-abandonment.

The very reality of believing that we need "advocacy" during birth is itself a glaring red flag, signifying an underlying awareness that we are not safe. Entering into birth from a defensive position is already a loss, and is often a form of reflexive re-traumatization, usually indicative of existing layers of trauma-bondedness. Even inviting individuals into our birth vortex whom we care for or even love (and who love and care for us) can be distracting, and must be very carefully considered.

I certainly recognize the way I sabotaged my previous births, specifically by welcoming people into my home and my aura who didn't belong there, or whose attendance was not specifically to my benefit. It's also possible to allow other people's energy into our field during birth even if they are not actually physically present. This can occur by way of intrusive fearful thoughts that don't belong to us, and this can also arise from an over-dependence on the desire to be saved or "delivered" from the experience of birth. We can momentarily (or even in more extended ways) allow others' frequency to infiltrate our consciousness which can constitute a profoundly impactful form of self-sabotage.

What I have ultimately learned is that the full flowering of a mother's utmost power and connection with herself, her baby, and the divine source of creation in a state of bliss, can only be realized in its totality through complete individuation. It is through the individuation of Self that we open ourselves to being utterly supported by the universe, and God.

That said, any expression—even that which might be considered self-sabotage—is a powerful form of choosing; it's a form of limiting ourselves so that the experience we are having remains in alignment with what we feel we can handle given where we are in our development. I also know this means that, in a way, there is no "self-sabotage." In the end, there is only choice. It was not until I fully chose to know that I can experience birth in complete resonance with my inner world and with God that I then automatically set up the conditions for that to occur.

This process of choosing occurred well before my birth began—it happened over the course of my pregnancy. I became a different person. My resonance shifted, and this established the terrain for the practical choices that I ended up making. Those practical choices involved, among many things, declining the option to invite other people into my birth-room, my home, or my head, and setting boundaries when it came to my kids' and my husband's involvement as the birth unfolded.

The fortification of myself—a harmonization of my own self-knowledge—had to occur in a context of complete peace, in a similar way that most of us learn to meditate: first in an environment that is set up to be conducive to that experience, which then becomes available to us more broadly. The capacity to meditate, to connect with the Source of all, to be in a state of serenity, is always within us. We have it, we own it, it's a part of who we are. But uncovering the instinctive capacity for enacting and accessing it requires stripping away distractions, and paring down the interferences that might pull us out of that state of being, until it's embossed into our consciousness through practice.

SELF-SABOTAGE

Some of the primary ways women create unnecessary drama, in what might otherwise be straightforward experiences of pregnancy leading to easy (not to mention ecstatic) homebirths, include rushing off to the hospital or to a doctor on the basis of fears, questions, or variations of normal that are unlikely to be solved or answered by the allopathic system, or that are simply made up, and unmoored from empirical evidence or reality altogether.

Given that medical professionals are trained and incentivized to find problems that usually pose little to no danger, or to create problems as *a result of* their interferences, most of us are aware, at least subliminally, that entering the system to be "checked," "monitored," or "scanned" is a guarantee that we will become enmeshed in a medical drama of some sort. This can be as a result of an official diagnosis, or simply on account of intensive fearmongering and coercion which often leads us to submit to further testing and procedures, which (as most of us know) almost invariably puts us on the conveyor belt to the assembly line, to be reconfigured as the product we become in the factory of industrial obstetrics.

This is not to say that entering the medical system is wrong at all, or that any woman should ever ignore what might be a truly intuitive sense that she requires medical assistance. Furthermore, no mother ever visits the midwife's office, clinic, or hospital without a reason (and no reasons are "good" or "bad"—they simply are).

But often, the real reason for taking ourselves to the hospital or engaging with the system is not medical necessity at all, but conformity—or, in the case of women who believe they want a homebirth, it's the mother's latent desire to either find or create a justification for relinquishing herself to the professionals, so she can be absolved of bearing responsibility for the leap into the unknown that birth outside the system represents.

For this woman, the covert attempt on the part of her subconscious mind to ensure that her birth will become medicalized means that she will be delivered—even before her baby is born—from the psychic discomfort of relinquishing her loyalty to the obstetric system, a cleavage that is *inevitable* when we prove to ourselves empirically (through birth itself) that we do not need the professionals or their technology.

Most self-sabotage—in any area of life—is enacted because "success" is edifying and unfamiliar, and most of us live out the majority of our existence (as strange as this may sound), actively—if unconsciously—avoiding enlightenment. We think we want it, but for many, the threat of achieving a distinction that moves us into a new realm of being, especially if we're not prepared for the larger implications of this expansion, can be deeply disagreeable, and so we find a way to abandon our mission while deluding ourselves into believing that it was chance, or luck, or fate, or our capricious biology that decided for us, and we replace choosing powerfully with compromise, or contingency.

Bypassing our own integrity in this way engenders defensiveness, which is a potent signal of victim-consciousness. The strongest indication that we don't actually believe our own story is that we create an identity around it, we defend it, and we are triggered when that story is challenged in any way, sometimes to the extent that we will argue (passionately and even angrily) for our lack of agency, or for our body's dysfunction—as women so often do when it comes to birth. (Are you feeling triggered right now? Check in with yourself. This isn't about you at all, unless, of course, it is.)

For many women, the victim-hero story that she "tried" to have a homebirth or a freebirth but that it just didn't work out on account of whatever condition or complication was used to rationalize medical intervention—or because her body was uniquely flawed, and therefore she had to be rescued by medical experts—becomes a deeply embedded part of her persona. As a result, it is then necessary to defend and legitimize the impermeability of this identity at all costs. To allow herself to acknowledge that, in actuality, she chose to remain tethered to the medical industrial complex, and found a way to ensure that outcome because she was scared of birth, and even more afraid of releasing the version of herself who conforms to the expectations of the clan (and is therefore validated by the clan), is deeply threatening, and often unbearable.

In the end, it is almost never *truly* the circumstances, or context, or other people, or our bodies and the stories we make up about them (our pelvis, or our baby's position, our baby's size, the cord, etc.) that thwarts our blissful birth. Set and setting are incredibly important, of course, but we choose the material and structural aspects of our birth, according to who we are, and in accordance with our state of internal alignment and resonance.

Instead, the outcome that you thought you wanted for your birth was likely thwarted because you chose to be dishonest with yourself about your true desire. When we continuously obscure what we truly desire, the internal conflict that we have manufactured will establish so much dissonance, that even if we do ultimately end up being at home when our birth begins with homebirth as the goal, it may be challenging to achieve the mental fortitude and resolve required to ensure that the experience is easeful and pain-free, and integration after the fact may also be more complex.

We often enact this kind of self-sabotage as a way of subconsciously reinforcing our preferred identity as a victim, and to mask or avoid what for many of us is the deepest, darkest, truest fear: the fear of what would happen to us—of what we would become—if we were to ultimately discredit all the excuses and reasons for having configured and constructed the previous avatar that we call the Self. For most of us, the prospect of revealing to ourselves that none of our stories were actually true is terrifying, and this is what we risk when we play with the tinder of actually powerfully claiming total custody of ourselves.

Another common scenario which will distort the activation of the principles shared in this book, is projecting onto your partner the assumption that he bears any form of responsibility for making your birth one way, or another—that he needs to behave in a certain way, think a certain way, connect with you in a certain way, be a certain person, or support you with certain specific words or actions. This is a key form of self-sabotage and drama-creation. Look at your partner, acknowledge who he is, recognize his strengths and weaknesses, and plan your birth — and your expectations — accordingly.

I do know that there are some women who have orgasmic births while gazing romantically into their partner's eyes, but not many. And more importantly, this kind of connection almost always arises organically, as opposed to being premeditated, or contrived. I have encountered and worked with far more women who have pre-scripted an expectation of (or an attachment to) their partners being the person who will facilitate their orgasmic birth for them, and this tends to be a dead-end — a way of setting ourselves up to blame our partners when reality reveals to us the result of shirking our responsibility and displacing it onto someone else.

Over the past twenty years, I've walked with women in every kind of domestic scenario and relationship imaginable (including physically abusive, violent situations) and what I have observed is that, while most women hope their partners will be supportive (and that's entirely understandable), having an unsupportive partner is actually almost never a true barrier to choosing the birth you desire.

Women who are determined to give birth in a particular place, in a particular way, and with a particular form of support, will make that happen. They will take responsibility for lovingly informing their partners of their unequivocal choice. They will offer their partners resources should they decide to open their minds to the possibility of shifting their perspective, and then they will release any attachment or need for external validation from them or anyone else, and carry on, single-mindedly, becoming themselves.

Birth will *always* alter our relationship. Choosing to recognize and honour our responsibility for the setting, circumstances, and outcome of our births will create a certain pattern as it ripples outward, just as sacrificing ourselves for the sake of maintaining the illusion of peace in a dysfunctional and domineering marriage or partnership will have a very different reverberation. What kind of change for your partnership are you choosing?

Pick your transformation. It's all you.

The You that is willing to step up and handle these situations with loving nonattachment and easy, incisive discernment regarding what belongs to you and what does not, is *also* the You that is going to have the power to choose—at every emotional intersection of your birth—pleasure, joy, gratitude, and surrender.

EYES WIDE OPEN

The horrors and abuses of the obstetric industrial complex persist, and continue to be viewed as normal, precisely because they are offered up in plain sight. The essence of this particular brand of sleight-of-hand is always that the revelation—the declaration of truth—is so outrageous and so deviant, that we (the good, innocent people of the world) read the articles, or watch the videos, or listen to and witness our doctors enacting the violations, and in our nobility—in our innocence—we experience a cognitive break.

When we observe a midwife fetishistically fondling a woman's vulva as her baby emerges, or cutting a woman's perineum then roughly pulling at and manipulating her baby's body through the birth portal—as though the mother herself isn't perfectly capable of birthing her own child, or of receiving her baby into her hands, and as though babies are incapable of birthing themselves without being molested—we impulsively justify the situation.

The reality being presented to us by the controllers as ordinary is actually so outlandish and preposterous that we experience an extreme form of dissonance in beholding it. Recognizing the harm being done would (we subconsciously believe) require that we either condone or resist it.

Because both of those options are so seemingly unattainable, most of us either disqualify the facts laid before us—which comprise the confessions and admissions of biological imperialists—as exaggeration or exception in order to survive mentally, *or* we rationalize the motivations of the collaborators. We may even consent to, or defend them. Most of us will grasp at whatever it takes to soothe our sense of inner conflict.

Consent is a political construct and a grooming tool designed to facilitate submission. Consent is used in a multitude of ways, including interpersonally, but also for the management of the thoughts, mentality, and beliefs of groups of people. One useful way of understanding the engineering of consent is through the convention of predictive programming. This is the idea that various forms of media (including TV shows, and even literature) present to us a future that has already been delineated by governments and corporations.

The idea of predictive programming, however, is widely misunderstood as constituting a future that is being entirely planned for us without our involvement. This is not the case at all. Predictive programming is not actually a "prediction," nor is it a forecast of machinations already put in place. It is, instead, a form of dark prophecy—an invitation to audition a potential future scenario first in our individual imaginations (the workshop of worldly creation), which we then co-construct through collective imagining, laying the substrate for the materialization of any future into reality. The focus of our attention is the foundation of innovation and destruction.

Well before the act or the object exists in the world, consent is usually extracted preemptively using psychological manipulation, through propaganda, movies, fabricated conflict, and social media. Everything we know and perceive, from our political structures to how we understand and therefore experience all of existence, from the rays of the sun (which we absorb—or not), the food and information we consume, the beliefs we assume, and the choices we make during pregnancy and birth, is crafted by agreement.

The more we are shocked by the newest strategically-presented schemes and ideas, the more acceptable and seemingly innocuous (by contrast) the previous iteration of supposed advancement will appear, in hindsight. Each new divulgence is introduced as a sort of social concussion, or mini-reset. In this recursive way, we are continuously nudged, in incremental steps, to sanction the changes to our conceptualization of what is normal, natural, and acceptable. The overall effect is that all of what is biologically integral and holy—like our primal need for sunlight, connection, birth, attachment, motherhood, and family—is eroded from all sides, simultaneously. And we agree to it all.

It does take an exponential degree of power and courage to see this for what it is because, for most of us, the initial point of discernment is an excruciatingly painful departure from the comfortable lull of numb, dumb reliance on the fictitious altruism of external authority. Most people do not want to see these dynamics at all. But this conundrum—the apparent choice between submission and rebellion—is a false dichotomy.

We have a third option, which is to look at the spectacle and its players head-on, and to clearly say: *No. I know who you are, I see what you're doing, and I do not accept the contract. I will not take your poison. I will not take your bait. I will adhere to what I know is true, and that is my requirement for connection with nature and all life, via the power, nutrients, solace, and energy of the sun, water, salt, tides, ideas, trees, plants, birth itself, and the innate wisdom of my body.*

We have this choice not only throughout life as a whole, but also specifically in our experiences of pregnancy and birth. Every woman, on some level, knows how institutional birth works, and has the option to see it for what it is. Nothing is truly hidden. We have only to lift the veil of illusion and self-delusion. From our own experience of birth onward, if only in the traces and tokens of obstetric trauma that we hold in our bodies from the past, the murmuring truth of birth cannot be obscured entirely. Each actor knows their lines, and all the functionaries—nurses, doctors, and midwives—are trained within the echelons of the dark cult of medicine to continuously disclose. This is a part of what it is to be inducted into the priesthood. This is what "informed consent" *is*. It is a euphemism for the primary satanic law: the mandate of disclosure.

From the very first visit to the obstetrician's office or the midwife's clinic, the pregnant woman is repeatedly informed that she has no power in this arena, or in this relationship. She is informed that her body will be entered, violated, excavated, forced open, and cut. All of that *will* happen; this is guaranteed to us. This is delineated in every pregnancy and birth book, and on every mainstream website. It's what obstetricians prime us for from our very first visit. None of this is ever hidden.

The choice we are always given, however, is whether we contract into this arrangement or if we instead say, *no, I see what you are. I see what you are committed to doing, and what you are paid very handsomely to do. I acknowledge that you too have been captured, and that part of you believes that what you're doing is right. And I will not enter your realm. I will not participate in the drama. I will not present my body, my self, my soul, or my child to you or to this system for extraction and harvesting. No.*

ANYTHING YOU DESIRE

Whether in the context of the universe of the soul's journey, the universe of our lives on earth, the life of a cell or a particle, or the sub-universe of experience, I suspect that the basic structure of all of existence is assembled through choice in some way, and determined by consent. Consent is how we commit to the particular cosmic geography of belief that leads us into every choice-point. Consent is present in the macro and the micro of all cause and effect.

Everything exists and is available at all times. And yet how we choose to move our bodies and our attention through space is the very thing that sculpts the frieze. Yes, we get to have anything we desire, and in every instance, we decide what that is. We all "create our own reality." And we can only ever "create reality" within the ambit of the reality from which we are creating. This is the paradox.

Choice does not occur in a vacuum, nor outside of the parameters we invariably impose on the possibilities made available to us through every prior choice that led to this one. What we desire and how we choose will always be structured first by who we know ourselves to be, and the world we permit ourselves to occupy. All worlds are their own vortex of resonance and vibration.

The world of industrial birth is precisely calibrated in order to preclude, eclipse, and obliterate the kaleidoscopic, hallucinogenic, entheogenic, and intergalactic world of spontaneous, physiological, autonomous birth. Those who are selling the idea that physiological birth (or "natural" birth) can happen in a hospital are revealing their resonance with and adherence to the paradigm of the technocrat, the cyborg, and the slave.

But the truth is, you are always free. Whether you like it or not, whether you accept it or not, whether you decide to shackle yourself or not, you are free. You are always free to choose where your energy and attention reside. You are free to put yourself in a position in which your choices will be dictated to you according to a technocratic hierarchy, just as you are free to choose to become the person who enters the vortex of a world in which your choices are ordained by the limitations (and risks, and gifts) of your own body, mind, soul, nature, and God.

INTEGRATION QUESTIONS

1. Where will you be giving birth: at home, in the hospital, at a birth centre? What is your primary reason for choosing this

environment for your birth? When you sit with that choice, and feel into it, is it motivated by fear, or inspiration?

2. Who have you invited to your birth, if anyone? What are the qualities of their energy that you know will be of support to you during your birth process? Do you feel any sense of obligation to invite this person (or these people) into your birth space?

3. Look at a choice you presently have before you. What is the underlying energy and degree of ownership in the quality of your choosing? It is always helpful to ask, at any given juncture, *Am I choosing from a state of clarity, self-responsibility, and non-drama?* What is the most logical conclusion of each option you can identify as being available to you?

CHAPTER SEVEN

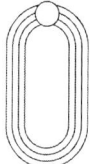

BIRTH AS SPIRITUAL TECHNOLOGY

THE GRACE OF GOD

Connecting with God and yielding to God's all-encompassing benevolence has been central to my life's path, and essential to my journey to ecstatic, blissful birth, and the reclamation—or recognition—of my power.

Who and what is God? That is for each of us to know in our own way, but I believe God to be the underlying force and energy of life, and the creator of everything in this world, and beyond. God is the entity who is only love, who exists outside of me, and who made me and all things. I believe that we are imbued with elements of God's divine energy, which exists within us always.

Through God's grace, we are given the terrible, wonderful, visionary power of choice, and we can choose to embody and express the energy of God's love and inspiration (or not) in every moment. (God also has an incredible sense of humour. In what might be the most stunning example of both God's flair for irony, and his irrefutable generosity, He has even gone so far as to give us the freedom to decide whether or not we believe in Him.)[24]

The continuous interplay between choice and surrender is part of the truly unfathomable paradox of our existence, which, despite the seeming dichotomy, is nonetheless in harmony with both relativism and divine objective morality. Relativism, the idea that there is no definitive Truth, that we all have our own truth, and that everything is comparative, conditional, and contingent upon a series of infinite variables which no one individual can ever fully grasp, suggests that we cannot rightfully judge another person, given that we can never really know all the details of a particular situation.

---

[24] Several people over the years have expressed surprise (and dismay) that I use male pronouns to refer to God, and I have even encountered some women (and men) who have presumed to correct me. There is no mistake. In order to preempt any misunderstandings, let me assure you, my thoughtful readers, that I am indeed deliberately choosing to refer to God as "He," for a number of reasons: First, I grew up in the Anglican church prior to its appropriation by the now-larger church of "woke," and while I have always understood intellectually and spiritually that God exists far outside of sex or gender, the idea of the triune God—the Father, the Son, and the Holy Ghost—is familiar and sensible to me (and in my view no way excludes or negates the power of feminine energy, the mother, or the all-encompassing matrix). Furthermore, as a recovered radical feminist, after almost a decade of embracing and fully identifying with that ideology, I now recognize that radical feminism (as with many other identity-based political movements) is utterly enmeshed in victimhood, a perpetual persecution complex, and an obsession with scapegoating the male sex and "The Patriarchy" for all the ills of the world—which is nonsense. It was my realization that choice is always available and that God Himself has given us life and agency that allowed me to crawl out of what was, quite truly, a very dark, self-defeating hole of chronic, circular, and frankly childish rage, and to claim my true creative power as a woman and a human being. I am no longer concerned with what I see as the fruitless and very much encouraged "battle of the sexes," or in arguing the merits of matriarchy vs. patriarchy (neither are interesting to me). My understanding of God is personal and intimate, and while I will probably always feel somewhat ambivalent about religion and even the Bible, I respect them both, and I don't feel qualified or inspired to follow trends to modify language for the sake of social positioning or conceit. I am certainly never going to attempt to "neutralize" the inherent sex (and sexiness) of language, a project that I see as not only futile (language is never neutral), but also arrogant and embarrassing.

Most people see this as somehow in conflict with the idea of a consistent morality. But to my mind, morality is synonymous and congruent with "natural law," the ever-present, moral structure of nature as established by God that we are pre-equipped to recognize and know as human beings. This is one of the features that differentiates us from our animal relations. I think both relativism and objective morality exist synchronously and symbiotically.

In the context of my own daily life, this means that while I cannot duly judge other people (because indeed we do all have our unique story, interpretation, and experiences) I *can* however rightfully judge my *own* behaviour and the merits of whatever choice-point is in front of me. In fact, in order to be right with God, I *must* be inclined to see my own actions clearly, and to apply an incisive willingness to discern the righteousness or depravity of whatever framework I am considering utilizing or contracting with when it comes to both the big decisions and the seemingly small ones. This is how we choose powerfully, and correctly: by acknowledging to ourselves that there is always a right and righteous path.

The idea of "creating one's own reality" has, I think, been misappropriated, in many cases as an argument against God. It is my conviction, especially after having freely chosen a blissful birth, that the creator of all things has gifted us with the power to name, to assign, and to conjure forth—in the image of the divine—through right and mindful action, which always begins with the thoughts we entertain, and the words we speak. To allow the world to be what it is—and others to be who they are—while honouring God and the power He has vested in us through choice, is an act of faith.

Especially now, those of us with fundamentally unadulterated souls are being invited to explore the process of individuation and what it means to take full responsibility for our decisions and our impact more carefully than ever before. Our capacity to refine and fortify ourselves spiritually and energetically, and to discern truth from deception is the primary distinction of this transformative age.

Each of us is a part of the visceral swamp of consciousness, and yet we are being called into full engagement with the world and with our fellow humans, our children, and our partners and families. We are being solicited to become fully participatory in the development of a vigorously boundaried energy-field and vibration via the clarification and purification of who and what we are.

Knowing how and when to yield to inevitable pressure, along with how to transmute that pressure without losing ourselves, is key. It is a rare individual who truly knows herself, loves herself, trusts herself, and who also knows that no matter what happens out there in the world, her *inner* structure is indelible. It is the rare person who is truly individuated, and in possession of unalloyed flexibility, adaptability, dextrous access to her healing power, and who can *yield to reality,* while staying true to herself, poised, and in presence.

Being in possession of a robust, fortified energy field is the opposite of brittleness. Energetic sovereignty is resonant, absorptive, and buffering—truly protective in its transparency, and clear to all by the reflection of its impact. It is in the process of consolidating our vibratory field that we learn to let go; to surrender, and to release the judgement of others, while also being able to make the choices that are correct for us and for our babies, which then keeps us in alignment with our inner compass and our soul's purpose.

This is the way to do both life and birth. It's the simplest thing in the world, and at the same time it can feel like the greatest challenge, primarily because (as we are all aware) every person is contending with multiple layers of trauma (including birth-related trauma) which can leave us with the pervasive belief that we are undeserving of the immense power, unconditional bounty, and clemency of God's grace.

We have been (and continue to be) programmed through the unnecessary desecration of birth, to fear the organic processes of life. The supreme motivating reason for this is that birth and death are the ultimate portals to connection with God and the divine parts of ourselves.

By way of the abusive rituals of industrial obstetrics and its occult ceremony of violence, the most sacred portal (birth) is sullied: we are marked by pain that isn't ours, and this pain is extracted from us. In this way, we are primed for further extraction as our lives unfold. The unhealed wounds of trauma make us exponentially more susceptible to varying forms of commodification.

The purpose of industrial obstetrics is to thwart our ultimate power-source: birth, but also death. Birth and death are, in a sense, one and the same. Birth *is* a kind of death, and death *is* a kind of birth into another realm. Both of these rites of passage have been captured by the industrial technocracy, and the overall perception of both events has been dramatically altered and controlled. We have, as a collective, been disciplined to view both birth and death as dirty, unacceptable, frightening, and as inherently *painful.*

I believe that the increasingly evident corporate, governmental and institutional urge to control and dominate nature is essentially a form of participation in and endorsement of a kind of satanic reversal. I recognize that the words "satanic" or "demonic" can come across as terminology that is very triggering or extreme for some. But I have come to believe that these terms, while intense, are actually very accurate metaphors for what I see playing out in every area of life during this particular age.

We can observe the satanic and demonic gestures most prominently in the way that our sacred rites of passage—those that are rooted in the body and nature and therefore deeply connected to what I know as God—are being contorted and inverted in a crusade against all that is holy. There is really no more potent example of this dynamic than what has been done to birth itself. From the fundamental defilement and fragmentation of the human body at its origin point has arisen a culture of simulation, pretence, and deceit.

SINGULARITY

I am by no means the only one for whom the existence of an array of portals into the folds of the tapestry of space, time, and other realms are unmistakably accessible. It is in our nature as human beings to seek out these connection points, and yet there has been a co-opting of this innate desire by darker technocratic interests, in stark contrast to what is available to us through our spontaneous, biological experiences of birth, sex, death, and the numinosum we claim in concert with the divine.

I wrote the first draft of this book in the late-spring of 2022, right at the time when CERN (the European Organization for Nuclear Research, established in 1954 in Geneva, Switzerland) was about to fire up the Large Hadron Collider (LHC) using 13.6 trillion electronvolts, the world-record expenditure of energy at one time. The LHC has been used over the past several decades to execute multiple high-energy atomic experiments using the smallest particles known to humanity. In plain language, as far as I can tell, this essentially involves taking the most fundamental elements of matter, and shooting them at the speed of light through a magnetic field to…see what happens.

CERN has been trotted out into the mainstream media here and there, for select appearances over the years, but in 2022, there was a larger ripple. Some people are terrified by the potential implications of CERNs activities, others are delighted and excited by these apparent advancements in science and technology, and still more remain utterly oblivious, or just couldn't care less. Apart from the obscene cost (in so many ways) and power usage, the experiments being done at CERN are particularly interesting to me in relation to how information about quantum computing is divulged by the media and apprehended by the public, and the potential implications of this endeavour overall, for the story of humanity.

The topic is rife for conspiracy theorizing in all directions. Many describe the experiments at CERN as the "literal" opening up of portals to other dimensions—a tearing open of the fabric of the cosmos to release into the abyss everything at once—the full erection of the tower of babel. Quite honestly, I'm not entirely sure what elements of this news story are true.[25] What I *do* believe, know, observe, however, is that the very idea of the LHC (and its possible powers) is, without a doubt, an expression of the same underlying concept that is at the heart of the growing proliferation of all forms of quantum entanglement that we are continuously consenting to and weaving into our collective and individual perceptions of reality.

For example, the prevalence of the term *nuclear family*, and its negative connotations is emblematic of this dynamic, and seems to have been brought into popular consciousness as a way to erode the relevance, momentousness, and dignity of parentage and genetic kinship, not to mention motherhood and birth explicitly. Anti-natalism, and the idea of the family as inherently destructive is one of the most pathological and twisted notions that has been spuriously linked to rationality, science, and progress.

From MRNA injections that modify the scripting of our bodies' DNA, to the macabre twistedness of surrogacy, to the dawn of human/machine interfacing and hybridization at every stage and iteration of life, to the increasingly dystopian presence of so-called "artificial intelligence" (true stupidity), we are increasingly incapable of even perceiving the

---

[25] I'm not even convinced that nuclear energy is real—chalk it up to residual skepticism thanks to NASA, the pharmaceutical industry, high school revisionist history, St. Rona, and the longstanding psychological operation of medical birth, among so many other false flags. But I also recognize that dirty money has to be laundered somehow, so why not into a giant phallic special blaster of invisible iotas?

technocratic, transhumanist encroachments into our daily lives. Indeed, I am convinced that "The Singularity" (i.e., the merging of our bodies and minds with the digital "ecosystem" *à la* futurist Ray Kurzweil) has arrived. We are bearing witness to an emerging communism of consciousness, activated by the belief that we (or rather the technology we have spawned) have a greater authority and power than God, and that we can elevate ourselves above the laws of the creator of this universe, to control the domains of biological existence. *Homo Deus.* We shall see.

The irony of course, implicit in the hubristic efforts of CERN, transhumanism, and biometric computing, is that human beings *are* the quantum field. We already possess the power to travel into and through different dimensions, and we are granted this power by way of the portals of birth, sex, life, and death—the only authentic portals to God. It is the immensity of these experiences which are only available to us through the integration of mind, body, and soul that compose the access points to full embodiment and individuation.

There is no space travel outside of the realm of consciousness. There is no immortality except that of the soul, which I think exists eternally, outside of the precincts of this world. The expressions of creativity that we are made for, and the power of creation that God has gifted us—through writing, art-making, mark-making, the creative potential of technology, and of course, procreation—involve moral questions and the drawing of moral lines in the sand. All of these moral boundaries are ours to know. We are born with the intrinsic gift to delineate and establish our own ethical limitations, and we always have a choice.

Technology, and our propensity to develop it, is bred in the bone, inherent to our fundamental makeup. Whether it's a chisel, knitting needles, a computer, dance, or the breath itself, technology is not just what we make, it is the underlying impetus and intention to create. But the most responsive, intelligent, refined, and ingenious forms of technology are those which reside within and are available to us through body and soul.

Birth itself is the preeminent technology for space and time-travel, and for accessing the chief portals to knowing, to God, connection, transcendence, and realming. We traverse light years and aeons through birth. This is part of its design. But this kind of voyaging is, for most of us, contingent upon the right conditions, which we access and create through choice.

INFINITE CHOICE

I once did a birth preparation coaching session with a beloved client who said *I would love to have a pain-free, blissful birth experience, but God will decide.* To this I replied, *No, you will decide. God has already decided that this is available for you, and for any woman, to choose.*

God—or whatever power it is that you believe is at the nucleus of each person's shockingly stratospherically complex experience of existence—has already created the parameters and the framework for us to choose. The idea that devotion or faith is a matter of simply throwing our hands up in the air and letting God "decide" is one of the most irksome, ineffectual, and frankly lazy (if not cowardly) forms of spiritual bypassing, in my opinion, and it's also an outlook that can easily slide into irresponsibility even so far as being used as an excuse for wrongdoing.

God has created the system itself that allows for infinite perspectives, "timelines," and reverberating belief-vortices which are available to be entered into freely and willingly. God has already decided that you, a unique human being, gets to be here, to play in this realm of *infinite* choice.

As you approach your birth, your choice-points (forming the "bridge of incidents" to which Neville Goddard refers) are continuously shaping the experience that you are living into. Every point along the way—each portal that we either pass through or decline—refines and whittles down the possibilities for how your upcoming birth (or any experience that you might be anticipating) plays out.

Once we arrive at the threshold of our births, there will be a layer of the experience that, on account of the choices you have already made, is now predetermined. This is the layer that has occurred at the level of the construction of self. Who have you become? Who is it that you have chosen to *be* through the structuring of this event? Who have you dedicated yourself to becoming? This may, in some ways, be conscious, but it will most likely be crafted without your full attentive awareness.

In my own case, as Helio's birth approached, I was very conscious of basically just...not being even remotely concerned about *anything*. I wasn't dwelling or fussing or feeling any anxiety at all about his birth. I wasn't even thinking about birth. I had, reflexively, adopted a form of loving dispassion and non-attachment, knowing that what we fixate upon inevitably expands in significance and prominence (whether positively or negatively). I was so accidentally relaxed about birth, and so secure in my choices, that the outcome was simply assumed.

This was surprising in some ways, given all of the apparent "complications" that I had weathered during my pregnancy: complications with my body, experiences of extreme pain, and the several weeks of panic attacks related to what were, at the time, some of the most intense feelings of existential fear I had ever endured—not so much the fear of actual, literal death, but rather the fear of obliteration, and fear of the dark pain and sorrow that I had lived through during Ignatius's birth, previously.

Yet I had approached that fear very methodically, *actively* dissolving it, and what remained felt like a benevolent indifference. By the time Helio's birth began, I wasn't actually thinking about the process at all. It was already done.

What I realise now is that the absence of focus on the event entirely was also what created the space—a looseness; an expanse of subconscious acreage; the openness of possibility—which allowed me to think differently about myself, and about my birth and my baby, and to co-create with him a new kind of connection, which permitted me to learn, ultimately, what it is to surrender.

RELIGION AND REALITY CREATION

Whether we are aware of this or not, birth and religion are intertwined, and our understanding of birth—individual and collective—has been heavily shaped by theology, religious dogma, and pop culture depictions of faith. Instead of recognizing the birth process as a gift, and honouring it as the expression, extension, and culmination of our divine sexuality that it is—the very apex of holiness—religion has been leveraged and contorted to support the notion that birth is impure or blasphemous, when the only truth in this lies in what we have imposed on birthing mothers and babies in the name of false doctrine.

Many of us are still recovering from religious misinterpretations of how birth works, what it means, and what it does to us. The idea of birth as *suffering* and as a form of retribution has been encoded into our programming, and seeps into our experience of postpartum, mothering, and beyond. *Childbirth is meant to be painful,* wrote one woman in a public online discussion on the topic. *It's a loving correctional curse from the garden. Since The Fall of man, life is given through sacrifice. There is no greater truth than our ability to overcome through Jesus, our saviour. Accept it or not.*

I don't entirely disagree with this assessment, though I suspect this woman and I might quibble over our analysis of the granular meaning of "sacrifice," "overcoming," and "acceptance." Yet I am continuously struck by the number of mothers who have internalized a very negative perspective of the experience and sensation of birth, based upon the idea that pain in birth was imposed on human women as a punishment, originating from the insubordination of Eve in the Garden of Eden.

Many people often impute (or state outright) that it may even be sacrilegious *not* to experience pain or torment while giving birth. This is, I believe, a simplistic, superficial (if not highly distorted) reading of Genesis. (Also, while I see the Bible as just as legitimate and accurate a documentation of world events as any published work of history, human women were giving birth for aeons before its composition and dissemination, and I suspect there may be aspects of God's omnipotence and omniscience that even the holiest of holy books may not have the capacity to fully articulate.)

I regard the story of Adam and Eve as an allegory for the immense power and gift of choice. When Eve and Adam fatefully disobeyed God, their loss of innocence required the assumption of responsibility for their own agency, which they and their forebears were henceforth called to enact via their God-given (and chosen) free will. The often-volatile power of judgement and discernment go hand-in-hand with the burden (or the privilege, depending on one's perspective) of bearing responsibility for subsistence, whether by toiling to tend the earth (broadly, the "work" of men) or in toiling to bear children (the "work" of women).

The iconic Old Testament story of our earliest predecessors seems to illustrate that *all* aspects of life were altered once Adam and Eve tasted of the fruit of the tree of knowledge of good and evil. Rather than being a "curse" this was merely a reflection of the reality that Eve and Adam had, through choice, departed the realm of effortless, Edenic innocence, into a new domain of accountability: freedom. Adulthood. And we, the daughters of Eve, the sons of Adam, are continuously re-learning the lessons of consequence.

The social treatment of birth (certainly within Judeo-Christian, Abrahamic culture) also reveals a number of interesting angles and layers of collective amnesia. What a coincidence that the religious tradition which (whether we like it or not) underpins all of western society is anchored by an event called "The Nativity," in which an otherwise ordinary woman is called to holiness and gives birth to her baby freely and safely in a barn with the utmost ease and a notable lack of drama. In every portrayal, sacred or profane, the birth of Jesus Christ is represented as a freebirth: transcendent, immaculate, but also utterly normal, straightforward, and absent any need for (or mention of) midwives or medical professionals.

Birth prepares us for the spiritual work of mothering. Just as birth is the portal to existence and to our most profound connection to God, it is also our initiation into motherhood, and motherhood is primarily a spiritual issue. Of course, every aspect of life is spiritual, but I know from my own experience that it is mothering that has encompassed my soul's primary curriculum.

In (and through) caring for our children, we see ourselves, we know ourselves, and we are shown what boundaries, leadership, discipline, and love truly mean. The story of Jesus and the relationship he has with his mother is full of subtle yet potent lessons and illustrations of the power and spiritual weight of motherhood. As mothers, we establish the emotional tenor of our families, and in so many tangible and intangible ways, we structure our children's relationship to choice.

This is evident in the trajectory of Jesus' life. His example of the spiritual radicality of choice and the repudiation of victimhood is, obviously, unparalleled. Jesus' volition was so comprehensive and elemental that he even chose to love the world as it is, surrendering always, but never acquiescing to despair. Whether or not you are a Christian, and whether or not you believe in a literal Jesus, or if you think Jesus was the incarnate son of God, is irrelevant.

The biblical stories of original sin and the life of Jesus, are, among many other things, representative of how powerful our minds are, as the vehicle by which our souls can access the transmutation of suffering. It's not that suffering itself is inherently virtuous (it isn't); it's not that pain is automatically virtuous (it's not). It's that suffering and pain can be portals to the ultimate power: surrender, acceptance, and gratitude to the creator of all that is, for life, in all of its complexity and magnificence.

At this stage in my own life, the beliefs I hold don't necessarily align with any particular theology, but I do consider myself to be a Christian. The Irish portion of my family were Catholic, and the English were Anglican (several branches since 1543 I have been told). I grew up within the Anglican (Episcopalian) tradition, with a smattering of Catholicism, although over the years my capacity to tolerate those institutions' hypocrisy and cowardice has waned to the degree that my interest in the church has been depleted almost entirely.

I remain somewhat nostalgic for (and attached to), the ritual and aesthetics of the high church, and in many ways, I admire those people who can still participate unflinchingly in the liturgy, and find the good in religious institutions that seem unremittingly corrupt to me. My primary mode of spiritual inquiry and knowing, is, however, at this stage, unabashedly phenomenological.

Phenomenology, as Romanian scholar Nicolae Turcan writes, is "a discipline of experience, a description of phenomena which appear to consciousness, overcoming subjective, empirical experience to reveal the structures, meanings, and profound truths of the human being's experience."[26] I have found birth to be the foremost adventure into both spiritual awakening and the landscape of human consciousness, as well as the outer limits (or limitlessness) of free will. Expanding my

---

[26] Turcan, Nicolae. 2021. "A Phenomenological Turn of Eastern Orthodox Theology." *Crossing: The INPR Journal* II (November). https://doi.org/10.21428/8766eb43.fdfad341.

understanding of self-responsibility to include my relationship with God has been central to my conceptualization of Being and birth.

Since fully accepting the idea that divine creation has granted us ultimate freedom and volition—that *every* single thing I experience is crafted from my choosing, and that any result that arises is the construct of each step that I have selected—my life has blossomed. This includes my understanding of the facts and circumstances of my own birth. I believe that participation in the universal stream of consciousness always involves an element of free will from our earliest God-given cosmic beginnings.

I believe that God shaped us to be self-determining—capable of influencing and directing the course of our lives.[27] I am a co-creator with God, by virtue of having been created in the image of the divine, in the likeness of the creator. Because of this, it is entirely up to me to choose blissful birth, blissful postpartum, blissful mothering…or not.

ABUNDANCE AND VIRTUE

Some of the complicating factors that can arise in relation to "success" or mastery in one particular domain of reality creation, especially when it comes to our understanding of morality can include:

- developing a proficiency in "manifesting" or choosing in one area which may not always easily translate to other parts of life (causing us to question ourselves, our capacity, or our deservingness), and
- misconstruing a facility for manifestation as a sign of moral virtue.

For example, many people whose behaviour is quite awful or even evil, have, evidently, cracked the money manifestation code, which has its own

---

[27] The question of belief is immensely personal and, as with every part of the material in this book, these ideas are yours to try on, to play with, to ruminate on, and to discard if they don't feel right for you or align with the tenets and teachings of your own faith tradition.

program and configuration, and which anyone, no matter their moral compass, can learn to employ. Of course, there are many deeply moral, honourable, and principled people who also happen to be immensely wealthy, but one of the most persistent and influential cultural stories is that poverty itself is a virtue, and many people subconsciously believe that to be wealthy actually requires a degree of wickedness. This is not the case at all, but the persistence of this narrative has had a powerful effect on most people's underlying beliefs about money.

Part of this misunderstanding arises as a result of overlooking some of the nuances of how manifestation works. Within the general category of affluence, for instance, there are essential distinctions between accumulating money, acquiring wealth, being prosperous, and living in the spirit of abundance.

The latter, abundance, is a responsive state of being that derives from a wellspring of true inner fecundity. True abundance involves an orientation and alignment in all of the areas of our lives: the material, the spiritual, the resonant, the creative, the relational. The ability to make money is not an indication of purity, no—but *true* abundance is transparent, and reveals its sanctity. Abundance is our eternal heirloom, and the alignment that occurs when we harness the skill and discipline of surrender is as important for coming into right-relationship with money as it is in the realm of birth.

Similarly, it is certainly possible to deliberately cultivate a spiritual condition that will allow for a blissful birth, while also being spiritually misaligned in other ways—committed to victimhood, or even devoid of love in certain other regions of our lives, and this is the case for all of us, to some extent. This is not necessarily a problem, and it's not something to worry about (so please don't).

Furthermore, while birth is part of the entire tapestry of existence, it is also a very different matter than money, or marriage, or any other territory, and comparisons can be tricky. It is important not to allow ourselves to think that choosing to correctly apply the formula that I'm sharing in this book—which will, when harnessed and implemented honestly, fully, and wholeheartedly, result in a pain-free birth experience—therefore means that we are good, or better, or more righteous than the woman whose birth is a battlefield.

Birth does, however, always change us, and the teachings in this book are an invitation not only to put these universal principles of surrender, yielding, trust, pain dissolution, self-ownership, spiritual consolidation, and energetic hygiene into practice as we welcome our babies, but to continue to carry these concepts forward into all parts of our lives, in the spirit of true and expansive abundance. But doing so is not a requirement, nor will this necessarily occur automatically. As always humility and self-awareness are key.

Manifestation can certainly be an entry-point to cultivating virtue, but virtue is not a prerequisite for manifestation. This should come as excellent news for all of us. As a friend of mine neatly pointed out, we can either choose to perceive another person's success as an injustice (especially if we happen *not* to see in them certain virtues which we might value) or as a profound relief. *Thank God I don't have to be good or perfect either, to have what they have.*

I unreservedly believe that human beings are fundamentally oriented towards love—biologically, spiritually, chemically, energetically, and in every way—and my experiences in birth have only validated this conviction. When any woman is giving birth in an environment and an atmosphere suffused with love, intimacy, and peace, her very highest self is brought forth, and the bravest, most magnificent, most honest parts of who she is will rise to the surface.

It is through the conscious construction of our resonance and Being—our spiritual state—that the possible future becomes inevitable, and that inevitability is ultimately materialized through action. The internal shifts that precipitate any physical movement in the three-dimensional world are *also* motion—energy in motion, or emotion—and when we change our understanding of birth through the action of surrender evoked in the immediacy of knowing ourselves as whole, and as powerfully, peacefully abundant in that wholeness (the inverse of superiority or spiritual egotism), who and what we fundamentally are is changed forever, and the rest of our lives will inevitably transform as well.

There are a multitude of methodologies to how we can tend to our minds and harness the power we have been granted to create through choosing and to attune to when we're in a state of either resistance or yielding, but in the end, these techniques all inevitably converge.

Learning to surrender is key. To shield ourselves precludes surrender. The steps to forging this passage to truly being in possession of an embodied knowing of surrender are both intellectual and spiritual, yet are always, in the end, rooted (and proven) in praxis—the application and testing of the system in the midst of experience itself.

RELINQUISHING SIGNIFICANCE

The non-attachment required to surrender is in many ways dependent on relinquishing our own significance,[28] in the sense that we attribute meaning (or the essence and weight of who we are) to our influence or to the force that we imagine we exert in the world, whether through our ideas, our intellectual prowess, our validation, our lovability, or our

---

[28] This notion was inspired by the idea of "importance" which Vadim Zeland explores in his book *Reality Transurfing*. I have adapted and built upon this idea, and I prefer to use the term "significance," rather than "importance," as I think the former is a bit more nuanced and specific. Essentially though, Zeland suggests that "importance arises when something is attributed excess meaning. Importance represents excess potential in pure form. In the process of eliminating importance, balanced forces create problems for the person that created it."

material impact. And this extends to how we perceive our children and their place in the universe of existence as well.

As mothers, we are constitutionally built to protect our children, to adore them, and to sacrifice enormously to enact that protection and adoration. We are hardwired for total devotion. But this integral, appropriate, biologically-driven form of care which is both selfless, yet also inextricable from a very healthy self-interest, has been contorted and instrumentalized by the forces of domination and control (especially those at play within the industrial obstetric complex).

Instead of our instinctively surrendered commitment to guardianship, mothers are now encouraged, incentivized, and pressured via cultural programming and the technologization of pregnancy and birth into adopting a self-defeating perception of what it is to nurture, rooted in a distorted, exaggerated understanding of our significance. This distortion is manifest in inverted and misguided forms of externalizing and internalizing the very ideas of "protection," and "safety."

On the one hand, we are motivated (often through coercion) to outsource the safeguarding of our babies to professionals, devices, and external false authorities. On the other hand, we are made to believe that whatever happens to our babies is our "fault." This creates many issues socially and legally, but it also warps our sense of faith, our relationship with God, and can impair our capacity to fully surrender.

Reckoning with (and discarding) this imposed, disordered dynamic has been central to my growth as a mother and has profoundly enhanced my ability to enjoy motherhood and to access my own sense of deep safety in the world, just as withdrawing myself from an adherence to significance has profoundly shifted my experience of birth.

I now know that to love myself fully is to appreciate that I have no exceptional significance at all, and this has allowed me to know more deeply than ever that I am infinitely precious and beloved by God (and by many wonderful people whom I also love). To love my children fully is to know the same is true about them. To truly honour life is to accept its transience and impermanence. We are matter, we come from *mater* (mother), but we do not "matter."[29] None of us are really all that significant in the grand scheme of things.

Because I was able to set aside the various constructs and belief vortices that I had previously hooked into through enculturation, dogma, fear-based programming, and other people's projections, I found the space to discover that there is actually no real significance to the parts of me that are dependent on identity or self-ness, or, moreover, on the specifics of my lifeline outside of the meaning that I create through my choices and how those choices contribute to the grand tapestry.

Nonetheless, I do belong here, and my children belong here, and we are safe, especially to the extent that we surrender to the process. Again, I am not suggesting in any way we should be cavalier, or casual, or apathetic at any stage of mothering, but rather the reverse: reverence, value, and surrender go hand-in-hand with recognizing our cosmic insignificance.

The peaceful abandonment of significance is, I now believe, an important aspect of the sense of ease I was able to occupy at the end of my pregnancy with Helio and as I moved through the birth portal. As you stand on the precipice of birth, I want to encourage you to play with that exquisite polarity between your profound, inexpressible value and your glorious insignificance. You are here, blessed with the shocking beauty of this experience. There is no need to put any stock in your transformation—

---

[29] "Matter | Etymology, Origin and Meaning of Matter by Etymonline." 2009. Etymonline. January 8, 2009. https://www.etymonline.com/word/matter. C. 1200, *materie*, meaning "the subject of a mental act or a course of thought, speech, or expression," from Anglo-French *matere*, Old French *matere*, meaning "subject, theme, topic; substance, content; character, education" (12c., Modern French *matière*), and directly from Latin *materia* "substance from which something is made," and also "hard inner wood of a tree." According to de Vaan and Watkins, this is from *mater* "origin, source, mother."

that part is guaranteed. There is no pressure, no obligation whatsoever. You can choose to simply flow. As Emilee Saldaya always says, *let it be easy.*

I recall a moment, when I was moving through the gateway into my birth-dance with Helio, of noticing an almost blithely accidental absence of anxiety, fixation, or force. This was fascinating to me. I was compelled by it. *Given that my old, familiar companions, tension, self-assessment, neurosis, are gone now, who am I?* My curiosity overrode my former commitments, and I just…let it go. *What can birth be for me now? How wrong can I be about who I thought I was? I must find out.*

This was also the instance in which I realized that the journey of my pregnancy, all my past pregnancies, my earlier births, my own birth, and all the many choice-points—both conspicuous and atomic—that I had navigated throughout my lifestream had brought me here, to this climax which, in accordance with the holographic fractal nature of all, was still yet another set of choice-points. This—this continuous being and becoming the woman who can trust, surrender, and allow—was being reified, confirmed, replicated, brought into the present reality and thus proven in the instantiation of experience itself.

This is who I am and
what I am
and this is how authentic beingness
works and what it is.

This is belief, intention, and
desire made manifest,
evidenced as constructed
into the realm of materiality by
the embryonic possibility
of the thought made
word, made whole, embodied.

*I am a mother,
you are my child, and
this is life: delightful.*

*You know this already—we all do—
but I'll say it again:*

Love really is the answer.

God is love.

Birth is love.

*To love ourselves and our child—
to actively love the other—
is to surrender fully to
the moment of now:*

*to trust, to allow, and to
embrace what is true.*

THE EYE OF THE SOUL

We are all here, expressing our soul's path in exactly the way that we are meant to, at all times. Each person is accompanied through life by a Guide-Self[30] or oversoul—that abiding, integral part of ourselves that is always connected to God, or Source, and that will, if ministered to, escort us toward the path of elevation, and congruence with our radiant,

---

[30] My dear editor Sophia recently informed me that within Orthodox Christian theology, this concept is known as the *nous* (νοῦς)—the part of the soul that perceives God. This is a concept that is both beautiful and, I think, quite instinctive, and is (I suspect) shared among many religious belief systems.

complete, pristine Beingness, if we so choose. There are no *wrong* choices to make in the cosmic scheme, because at every crossroad or choice-point, we are given yet another opportunity to explore the law of cause and effect.

The freedom we are offered in every moment, through every choice-point, to adopt new and different degrees and expressions of sentience, is immense. There will always be certain choices that will lead us towards a more crystalline experience of awareness and perspective that ultimately will elevate our being. There is also an endless array of choices which, conversely, arise from a lower scale of operation, or a lower octave, and which derive from, and therefore reflect and engender fear, resentment, anger, disappointment, anxiety, and other emotions which are burdened by the density of delusion and expectation.

To choose *is* to manifest, and to do so discerningly is to honour the power of God and His creation. But it's not enough to contemplate the process, or to read about others' experiences in hopes of living vicariously through them, waiting for the surrogate to prove what you hope to someday achieve once the evidence is sound enough to your liking. The relinquishing of one's sovereignty through passivity and inertia is also an act of will. I invite you to embark upon your life without reservation.

Each of us are rays of divine energy, and we all have an opportunity to arise and to ascend in coherence with the image and essence of God. We always have access to the correct choice. We always have the option of assuming presence and responsiveness to whatever form of expansion is being presented to us in a given moment.

INTEGRATION QUESTIONS

1. Think about the premise that we can create reality with our thoughts. Can you think of any time when you observed your thoughts materializing into reality? How did it happen? Did it happen intentionally or unintentionally?

2. Think about a time when you felt like reality was working against you. Looking back, can you see how those negative events constituted choice-points that led you to what you *did* want—or something even better?

3. If "manifesting" seems impossible, reflect on your personal history. When did you first accept the idea that you can't, or shouldn't, try to manifest your desires? Who, or what, taught you that? What is the worst that could happen if you chose to believe that you can?

PART TWO

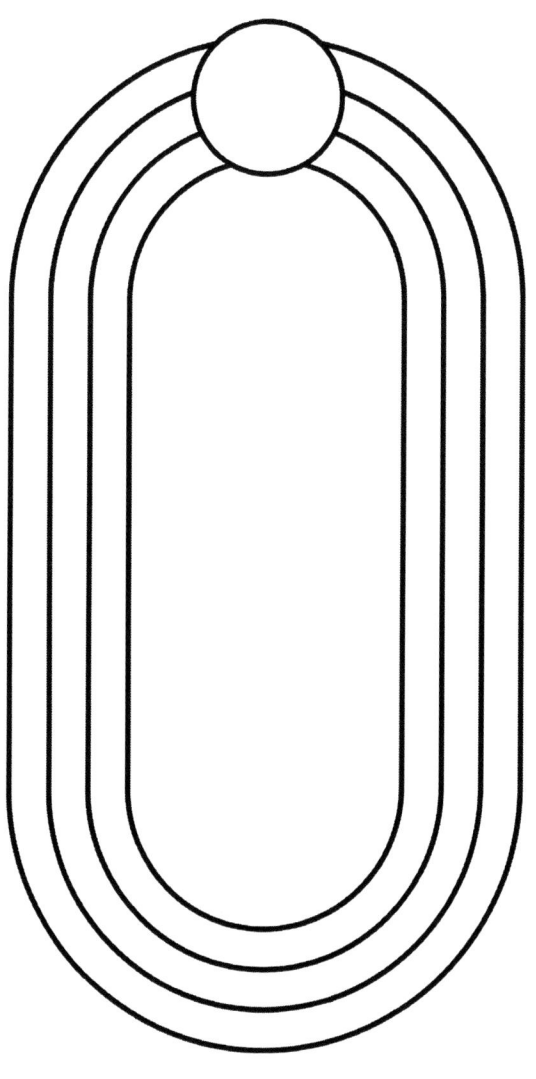

WELLSPRING

CHAPTER EIGHT

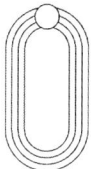

THE ULTIMATE ENTHEOGEN

KAMBÔ

Costa Rica is heaving with gringos looking for enlightenment, and I'm put off by the commodified performativity of it all. I'm not so put off, however, that I'm above participating. So when Lee and I are invited to receive an audience with an authentic indigenous shaman (oh my) who had trained for over a decade with the Amazonian Katukina tribe, I am painfully aware of playing exactly into the stereotype. We accept the offer immediately.

Through the tiny winding hamlets of Baru, Platanillo, then Tinamastes, our ancient Mitsubishi chugs, and when, before the Alfombra, the valley opens like an emerald geode, the beauty is so shocking that I have to take a breath. We turn off a side road in midtown Tinamastes and dip down into the valley, past a couple of tiny homes with muddy dooryards and chickens scratching at the threshold, and children (dirty, like ours) watching for visitors. The grove of trees opens into a field with a massive wall of jungle to the left, morning sun glistening on the grouping of small houses at the base of the plateau. It is a bewitching, fairy-tale place.

Next to the small wooden house is a larger structure, two storeys, seemingly half-built, with the front wall open to the pasture where a herd of white Brahman cows lazily graze. As we continue to drive towards the dwellings, a man comes out of the half-built structure and gestures to us to pull into the driveway.

Christos is a round fellow, wearing pants too long for his frame, thick black sport socks shoved awkwardly into his flip flops (unlike the scorching beach town where we live, it's chilly in the mountains), and a blue, sweat-stained t-shirt on which the words "Ralph Lauren Polo" are, somewhat incongruously, emblazoned. His long black hair is pulled back into a ponytail, and his broad smile is ornamented by widely-spaced white teeth. I like him immediately.

He greets us warmly, and apologizes for the state of his house which, we can see as we approach, is truly mid-construction. There are bags of plaster here and there, and the tiling is evidently fresh, given the faint scent of wet grout. Lee and I laugh and tell him that our house back in Uvita is very similar—no walls. We're right at home. Off to one side, there are two chairs set up so that those who occupy the seats can stare unfettered at the verdant paradise. In front of the two chairs are two large plastic buckets, and on the other side of the room are two single mattresses arranged side-by-side. Our unpretentious shaman invites us to sit, and pulls up a chair himself.

Christos speaks at length about his initiation into the ways of the Katukina tribe of Brazil, his birthplace, and of his indigenous heritage. He had travelled through South America in his earlier years then up into the heart, as he now knows it, of Pachamama. He views Costa Rica as the bridge between South and North America, and as an energetic conduit linking past and future, light and dark.

I don't share his background, or, necessarily, his philosophical outlook, but I am touched by the sincerity with which Christos expresses his commitment to his work as a guide and facilitator, and his belief that the medicine he works with—kambô, the collected poisonous secretions of the giant monkey frog—is intended for all people who desire it, and has been provided to us by the earth and the Creator for the healing of a multitude of rifts: psychic, interpersonal, collective, physical, and spiritual.

Christos speaks of the kambô ceremony as a deep and sacred cleansing, a process by which a person is initiated into renewed lucidity, via the shedding of toxins from both body and soul. He explains that as soon as he has administered the remedy, Lee and I will experience an immediate heat in the body that will move up to our heads, and that when he commands us to do so, we will drink a great quantity of water to mobilize the spirits and poisons we have been carrying.

We will allow the urge to vomit to overtake us, and we will purge, again, and again, throwing up and out our negative energy and any contaminants, cleansing our physical selves and our spirits, releasing it all into the buckets in front of us. He emphasizes the importance of following his instructions, and of trusting him which, I recognize in that moment, I do.

Panema, Christos explains, is, according to the Katukina people, the dark, heavy air of trauma, stilted energy, the burdens of shadow memories, and dysfunctional conditioning that we all hold inside ourselves, in some measure. The process we are about to move through will dislodge our panema, and the purging will collect the negative energy, and carry it through our bodies by the water of life. The colour and texture of the substance that we release will correlate to the specific type of panema we're letting go of: foam is anger, bile is toxicity, brown emissions indicate family or relational trauma.

Once we move through several cycles of purging, we will then travel to the mattresses on the floor in the far corner of the room, to integrate the release. Then Christos will apply sananga, a concoction made from the *Tabernaemontana undulata* shrub of South America, used primarily by the Yawanawa tribe, and this will be applied to each of our eyes. In addition to the *Tabernaemontana* shrub, sananga often contains iboga, a psychoactive alkaloid extracted from the root bark of the *Tabernanthe iboga* plant, which grows primarily in western Central Africa.

Sananga is understood to have powerful spiritual, psychological, and physical effects including eyesight enhancement, as well as having a purifying influence on our etheric vision. A single drop in each eyeball will burn intensely, we are told, but the pain will subside quickly.

Following the Sananga, Christos will dispense the rapé, a combination of various plants, tobaccos, and ash, that he will blow into each of our nostrils. The rapé binds the experience and teachings of the kambo and the Sananga, and will allow me and Lee to journey further, to process, and to consolidate, our insights.

Christos explains the risks involved in undertaking this ceremony together, as a couple. Kambô can have a profoundly clarifying effect on relationships, and while it can fasten partners even more closely together who are in alignment, the ritual also tends to augment pre-existing rifts between individuals who are not meant to be conjoined. He also warns us of the fact that kambo is widely known as a hormonal re-balancer, and can have a powerful effect on fertility, opening the meridians of the body in preparation for welcoming new life. He mentions the many "kambo-babies" that have been born following such ceremonies, and we assure him that we are prepared for whatever (or whomever) comes.

Butterflies flit in and out of the room as the final preparations are made. I feel fear. I am eager to defer to the experience, but also somewhat terrified of what I might expose of myself, or somehow fail to reveal. Finally, Lee and I are asked to set our intentions, and to sit side-by-side on the two chairs facing the tangle of palms, bougainvillea, and birds of paradise that frame the field beyond and the luxuriant forest wall.

Using fire, a piece of dried vine, and quick, decisive motions, Christos burns seven small linear points into Lee's shoulder, pulling masculine energy from Father Sky, and he does the same to the back of my calves, invoking the feminine energy of Mother Earth. I flinch from the shock of the burn. We are now instructed to drink as Christos expertly scrapes off the thin layer of scab that immediately forms on our skin, and introduces the poison to each abrasion.

Initially, the sensation is cool,
but within seconds,
scalding.

Breathe, says Christos.

Breathe and drink.

Suddenly, I am shaking
      ablaze
venom coursing swiftly through my body.

Drink more, he says again, and
I drink, spilling water
      over my shirt
      my face
      my head
          pounding, my throat closing
pounding

    Drink it all.

My belly is distended.
The discomfort—terror
—is stunning,

paralyzing,
    now agony.

Fever dream.

Lee is next to me, puking
    explosively,
        lustily.

A voice — Christos' — rings out
    a driving chant:

OH KAMBÔ
OH KAMBÔ OH
OH, KAMBÔ OH OH.

The room begins to spin and undulate.
    I have the urge appalling
      to throw up   nothing

Now I am outside
    outside my body, but also
    desperate, trying
to hold on.

The song is louder now
    churning,
      propulsive

OH KAMBÔ,
OH OH KAMBÔ OH

Suddenly horror — *what the fuck is happening* —

       I succumb to pure
            animal
                frenzy
       the heave overtakes me,
            I vomit again
            and again.

Coming up for air, Christos is there
commanding me once more, loudly, lovingly,
       DRINK MORE and
            I drink
     and purge and
         drink and purge and
             drink and purge again, to the
           rhythmic
           hymn
           emphatic

OH KAMBÔ OH
KAMBÔ OH
OH KAMBÔ
OH

Moaning weeping compulsively babbling
        shaking
            torn apart, depleted,
                open
I give in
        to pure sensation.

Another wave of water washes
        through then
            out of my body

PORTAL

                into the
red plastic bucket.

Tattered, demolished, wrung out,
        I wilt and slacken,
                head between my knees.

Ragdoll.

The darkness parts.

I feel Christos near me, noticing that
he is now wiping at my row of circular blisters,
scraping the venom from my skin.

Panting, still shaking, I stumble to the mattress.
Lee is there, and
                I collapse into the relief of
                completion.

I have no sense of how long I sleep,
but I wake to Christos' presence.

He asks if I'm ready for the Sananga,
but it's not really a question.

Obligingly, I pull both of my lower lids
down as advised.

In quick succession Christos drops
the liquid into my eyes.

The pain is excruciating,

    horrifying.
        Breathe,
says Christos patiently.

Instead, I issue a shrill scream.

Breathe.

Now, despite my disbelief
that such a thing is possible
under these
newly horrific circumstances,
I take a breath in desperation,
hazily aware of Lee
next to me, until he calls
out in pain.

Within a few seconds,
the inferno mellows, and I rise
up into my own mind,
circle my third eye,
travel
out through my
crown into the light of
pure
elemental
consciousness.

Now for the rapé,
      murmurs Christos softly.

I sit up, far beyond disorientation   resigned.

PORTAL

Christos guides us: one deep breath in, then out, as he positions the
bone tepi—the long pipe-like instrument—into my right nostril, and
blows.

I careen into immediate blackness
        Airless hyperventilation   panic.

Christos repeats his simple mantra
    Breathe
and I remember that I can.

I take a pitiful gulp as he situates the tepi
again, in my left nostril now, and
    blasts
        my awareness
            to smithereens.

I am enveloped in warm darkness.

    Stars.

    The world
    is spinning.

I am
a star moving through
    infinite space.

Someone lifts me
    up
    drapes my body
    over
    another bucket.

Yolande Norris-Clark

I'm salivating, can't stop.
black liquid streaming
        From my orifices
            mucous
                effluvium.

Lee cries
out in shock
        again.

I'm handed paper
        towel, told to blow
one nostril at a time, to spit
out the acrid substance that has
travelled to the back of my throat.

I fall
        backwards into
            deep reverie.

My mind is a dark pool.

I see flickers of white light, then
        small glowing spheres.

Pebbles drop into the field
        lake of fire
            concentric circles
                rippling outward

My eight children,
        their original faces

PORTAL

hover in essential form.

Now, a persistent golden orb
       in the solar system of perception
           appears:
           playful   oscillating.

       the spirit of our new child making himself known.

I awaken, sit up,   look out
at the shimmering
       pulsing landscape.

A heron lengthens and swoops
       elegantly
           across the sky.

I am humbled, alive,
       and very still.

The sun is still high as Lee and I finally make our way out to the truck, and back up to the dirt lane that leads to the single lane mountain road. When we reach the main intersection, we see a small cafe directly in front of us.

Neither of us had noticed it earlier that morning, but as we draw closer, I catch sight of a man standing outside—gangly, snaggle-toothed, jangling with beads and amulets, and somehow appropriately bearded—and I am at once repulsed and intrigued. I insist that Lee stop so we can hop out and figure out what this guy is about.

He describes himself as a mystic, but I can see immediately that he is, in fact, a dark wizard. I am in no way beglamoured, but I am curious, and in the swirl of this stage of my season of seeking, I sense that the particular flavour of danger he represents is worth the price of entry. When he mentions that he leads 5-MeO-DMT trips, Lee and I, again, accept.

BUFO

A few days later, we drive back up through the cloud forest to Tinamastes with a sense of excitement, but also with some measure of trepidation and even dread. Following convoluted instructions, we enter through a blue gate at the road, then proceed into the jungle. The dark wizard himself meets us outside a cerulean roundhouse and ushers us into his lair.

This place is the quintessential psychonaut's pad: a large circular living room is decorated with Indian mandala cloths hung on the walls, and the furniture is covered in Ikat and paisley prints. Several mattresses lie pushed together in the centre of the floor. It is surprisingly clean, especially given that every surface is cluttered with psychedelic paraphernalia, antiques, oddments, and art, all collected, the wizard explains, from his various travels through the Amazon, and the counterculture.

We are introduced to Theodore, the wizard's assistant, a sweet young man who exudes a kind and rather innocent energy—highly contrasting with the wizard's magus quality. Both men sit us down to explain the parameters of the ceremony and, broadly, what we might expect.

Unlike Ayahuasca, which is often a twelve- to twenty-four-hour-long marathon excursion, 5-MeO-DMT (whether consumed by inhaling the vapour of the dried secretion from the parotid glands of the Sonoran Desert toad—*Bufo Alvarius*—or taken in the form of the lab-synthetized, pure molecule) lasts for only seven to fifteen earth-minutes, and yet the experience can be one of infinite time, or the shattering of the construct of time altogether.

PORTAL

The dark wizard has a little bit of Mad Maude the Toad[31] about him: a trickster figure and, maybe, in the right—or wrong—circumstances, a bad guy, although he also has a sincere, child-like quality as well—an exuberance and enthusiasm—despite being in his sixties. He is perhaps a strange chaperone for this kind of expedition, but Lee and I stride into it, full of hubris, ready (or so we think) for the veil of our realities to be pierced, if not shredded into ribbons

I travel first. As I have been instructed, I take a single vigorous inspiration from a cylindrical atomizer. The billowing mist is cloying, almost sweet. I lie back in the centre of the room, arms open. *This really isn't so...*

      and then I dissolve, liquified.

Gone is perception
gone is the word.

Vision, light, dark, matter,
all dissolved, roaring into—out of—
      dis in te g r a t i o n.

    Terror.

---

[31] One of my favourite books as a very young child was English author-illustrator Jim Smith's *The Frog Band and Durrington Dormouse* which opens with poor Durrington fleeing a press gang. After a harrowing chase into the night, Durrington (sopping wet and exhausted) takes shelter in a grotto in the woods where, out of the darkness, a creature extends to him a gnarled and warty hand clasping a pewter goblet full of a bubbling green liquid and says, with terrible ominousness, "'Tis only me, Mad Maude the Toad. Take a drink of this. It will give you a good night's rest..." When, naturally, Durrington wakes up a hundred years into the future, hijinks ensue.

Please please please don't let me die, don't let me go, don't let me slip out into the white field.

I cling to my flesh,
      claw at my breasts. *Body*
          don't go,
             don't
                leave.

The
fragmentation   is
    Inevitable   the inevitable is
      shearing   away

There is no space
    or seeing
    perceiving
    hearing.

There is no
    no, or
      there,
no room, no   world.   *Wait,*

I can hate this.
I can hate this back into the real.
I can resist this enough to be me.
    I can want enough and be enough
        to make this mine again. I will steal it
            back with the rage and fight that is my Self…

    So much pain.
    So much terrible pain.

PORTAL

      Blades of shrieking viscous, splintered demolition. *Sweetheart.*

Wailing maelstrom.

Bright nothing
lustrous crinkling into the loop of infinite   space,
      dividing,
           proliferating,
                slipping open,
                     telescoping,
                        condensing and pulsating.

Evisceration.

Ebbing flowing throb,   presence   absence
      bending amaranthine   f r a c t a l   *yes* or
maybe,   dripping between
         warp   and   weft   …*oh wait.*

      You [this] are [is] not a   *self*
        or a thought
        or a body.

Here is the shimmering All.

Wake up.   *Wake up and die now.*

The presence of my father   the presence of God
    the dark wizard standing over me.

    You're almost through.

Now untamed brutal euphoria—crushing   diaphanous

orgasm beyond orgasm into
     sheer   ecstasy, sheer
     detonating
     explosive
     love
     and the margins of the world are   annihilated
reinstated, and

I   am   bliss
     reborn into the crystalline
         preciousness   loved
         lovable
         dear and part of
everything
     made of God

There is nothing
to ever be afraid of.

I behold Lee having his experience and I see him leave his body too. In the witnessing of my love—my divine life partner and the father of our children—in so raw and vulnerable a state, there is something here beyond even sex and the intimacy of sex that allows me to also see that the origin of everything *is* sex and orgasm, but not in the way that most of us are usually given to understand those forces.

When Lee drifts back into the world, I join him on the mattress, and we are both given a closing dose, together this time. We seize each other, melting—fully clothed, utterly chaste—and the spirits of our children alight, descend, and touch down again, for just a moment.

PORTAL

XANTHE

Our daughter Xanthe, who is almost seven years old as I write this passage, is a shining, endless summer of a girl.

It seems like a lifetime ago that I discovered I was pregnant with our fifth child—the baby who would burst forth upon the world following a two-hour-long birth process in a euphoric storm of coruscation, whom we would call Xanthe Evelyn Fidel.

Lee and I were going through a very difficult period in our marriage and in our individual lives when our second daughter was conceived. The discovery of my pregnancy was a crisis and a turning point that provoked in me a powerful reckoning with myself, God, and a reappraisal of what I thought were my most fundamental values.

For two days, at around six weeks' gestation, I considered killing the baby. Lee encouraged me to do so. This, in retrospect, and given my present views on the meaning of life (not to mention my and Lee's boundless adoration for our brilliant daughter) is a terrible thought. But I also hold deep compassion for myself at that time, and for Lee, and for any woman who has considered or carried out the same irrevocable and conclusive course of action that I was contemplating (and which, at one point many years before, I did consummate).

A significant aspect of the motivation for my fatalistic ideation was that I felt I wasn't prepared or healthy enough to bring the child into the world. I was questioning my mothering, my life, my relationship, my body, and my capacity in every way, and I had created a story that the baby was likely already compromised, or harmed by my state of being. So I resolved one evening to follow through with the termination.

I had some misoprostol[32] pills in my possession, and I made preparations to take them, but as I held them in my hand, I started to cry, and I couldn't stop. I became hysterical. I went over to our sofa, and I experienced an emotional release so intense and wrenching that I exhausted myself, and fell into a deep sleep. That night, I had one of the most crystalline and illuminating episodes of clairvoyance and claircognizance, via lucid dreaming, of my life.

In the dream, which seemed more substantive and legitimate than waking life, I found myself in a marble corridor, at the end of which was a large white marble elevator. I entered, and the elevator took me up several storeys, then opened into a gleaming white marble foyer. At the end of the room was a marble desk. I walked forward, and sitting behind the desk was a figure that I immediately recognized as God, or as a representation or representative of God. The figure—a man—looked up at me and said, simply (using the following verbiage exactly), *Your baby is delighted to be coming. They are meant to be here. And I can assure you, their dendritic spines are very well-articulated. You will call the child Fidel.*

I was thus dismissed, and I descended back down to earth in the white marble elevator. I woke up with the dream preserved in pristine detail in my mind's eye. I was also perfectly calm, and serenely happy. I had been entirely relieved of any fear, concern, or ambivalence as to whether or not this pregnancy was meant to be, and there was no remaining tendril of potential that I would or could "terminate" this fetus (or that I would ever entertain the thought of abortion ever again, under any circumstances).

But I was intensely curious about one aspect of the dream: I was sure, and *am* sure, that I had never encountered the term "dendritic spine" before in this life. I immediately researched the phrase, and discovered, for the first time, that "dendritic spine" is a term used to indicate the small protrusions present in large numbers on the surface of "dendrites," the

---

[32] Misoprostol is a pharmaceutical abortifacient.

part of each nerve cell in the brain that triggers other nerve cells, and which gives and receives crucial information—the electrified communication network of the cerebrum.

On the surface of these dendrites are "spines" through which, according to one paper on the topic,

> [a] majority of excitatory synapses are formed. Dendritic spines typically have a mushroom-like morphology, with a spherical head that contains the postsynaptic density and a stalk that connects the head to the dendritic shaft. Spines exhibit remarkable morphological plasticity during development as well as in the adult brain. It has been speculated that the morphological plasticity of dendritic spines is important for learning and memory, and spine morphological abnormalities characterize neurological disorders such as mental retardation and schizophrenia.[33]

The experience of receiving this information via a visitation from God, in addition to the many aspects of its marvelousness, has confirmed to me that God is uproariously, endearingly funny. Especially given my stubborn distaste for science (or rather, for the arrogance of those who use science to peddle propaganda, or to uphold the notion that the scientific method is the only valid basis for assessing reality or rational thought), the fact that the mystical message that my baby had been so purposefully chosen and divinely created and that she was magnificent, strong, brilliant, and in possession of a fully dialed-in and "articulated" organic electrical system was being delivered to me through an ethereal vision by a man in a literal white coat, speaking the academic language of brain chemistry still strikes me as incredible funny. Touché, God, touché.

---

[33] Irie, Fujio, and Y. L. Yamaguchi. 2009. "Eph Receptor Signaling and Spine Morphology." In *Elsevier EBooks*, 1141-45. https://doi.org/10.1016/b978-008045046-9.01799-x.

It was years later that I began reading about quantum origination, regression, and soul-retrieval, and while I'm still not entirely sure what I think about past lives or soul-journeying, I find it fascinating. Somehow, the more my fundamental faith in God grows, the more at ease I am with not-knowing the specifics of our origins or destinies after life, and yet the more open I am to exposing myself to various theories on the subject.

Apparently, it is at around forty-nine days after conception that the pineal gland of a preborn baby forms fully and begins to excrete small amounts of DMT. According to *The Tibetan Book of the Dead,* this is also the time at which a child's soul enters its body. But I wonder if this is always the case, or if we have some capacity to realm, or to ghost, or to slough off the soul and leave and return at various stages following conception, or before. I do know that I have felt my children's presence powerfully in a multitude of ways, at every phase of their beingness, including at the moment of orgasmic cellular collision, in union with their father.

EGO ELEGY

The term *entheogen,* coined in the late 1970s by Jonathan Ott (an ethnobotanist who specialized in the use of medicinal, ceremonial, and psychedelic plants and substances) is a portmanteau of two words from ancient Greek: *entheos,*[34] an adjective which means "full of, possessed by, or inspired by god,"[35] and *genesthai,*[36] a verb which means "to become," forming the contemporary designation that is now widely used to indicate any substance that elicits in the human being an experience of non-duality, or a sense of total integration with all of existence.

---

[34] ἔνθεος

[35] Upon the recommendation of my brilliant editor and theological consultant Sophia Zaferes, "god" in this case is written in lowercase, given the context of the pantheism of ancient Greece.

[36] γενέσθαι

5-methoxy-N,N-dimethyltryptamine, or 5-MeO-DMT is considered to be the foremost entheogen and was christened "the God molecule" by clinical psychiatrist Rick Strassman. Strassman has studied and written extensively on both "the spirit molecule," which refers to NmDMT (the active ingredient in ayahuasca) and 5-MeO-DMT, which is seen as exponentially more powerful than NmDMT, and is widely acknowledged for temporarily repatriating the explorer across the cosmic boundary of the earth plane, through the realm of the spirits entirely, beyond the conceptual firmament, into the inchoate domain of God.

Psychoactive drugs—used in various contexts within what I see as a sort of gradation between recreational, reverential, and therapeutic—have certainly been a constitutive element in my ongoing process of awakening. For me, the crossing into abstraction and disintegration that 5-MeO precipitated was terrifying and ecstatic, and shockingly similar to birth. Consuming exogenous 5-MeO-DMT specifically, confirmed what I have, on some plane of my consciousness, always known: that God and eternity can never be thwarted, or rejected, or absented from any part of existence or non-existence.

Like birth, my journey on 5-MeO-DMT was a kind of death: dying to my past self, and to the very notion of self entirely. The induction obliterated my formerly held fantasy of separateness and isolation, giving me access to a state of consciousness that I had felt flickers of in my previous births (and psychonautic explorations), but had been too afraid of diving into fully…but it also reconfirmed what I know is the preciousness of our capacity, and obligation even, to claim differentiation and individuation in this human form.

In specific terms, 5-MeO allowed me to remember the following direct access points to being:

- unafraid of death
- unafraid of birth

- unafraid of fear
- unafraid to claim and adore the value and rarity of life in every form, without undue attachment or fetishization
- familiar with how to choose to transmute pain—especially given that what I felt, despite no physical harm being done to my body, was the most torturous, grievous, searing pain imaginable
- re-accustomed to time-space travel, non-locality, or "realming," as our sweet Cosmo describes the practice
- intimate with surrender (and resistance)
- far less angry and less apt to take things personally (I still get enraged, of course, but the length of time between the dissipation of rage and forgiveness/reharmonization is remarkably curtailed; please note that this might not really mean much comparatively, but for me personally it's quite a significant thing)
- almost entirely disinterested and non-invested in the frivolous theatrics of world politics
- cognizant that we are always connected to God and that God is Love
- aware of past experiences as a quantum field, and attuned to the knowing that I have encountered this world before, in some way
- in possession of the profound truth that orgasm is the "big bang," the origin of species, and is indelibly tied to Love—while holding a strong concurrent sense of boundaried disavowal of the distortions of sexual violation and obscenity
- deeply connected to the total coherence of God's sublime omniscient love, and my essential place in the unified whole of existence, while also knowing and fully appreciating the importance of my God-gifted ability to discriminate between good and evil.

5-MeO-DMT also gave me an entirely renewed understanding of, and facility for, energy-work and energy healing. I was reminded by this experience that the tendrils of electricity I intuitively move through my body when I'm transmitting the soothing frequency of restoration to one of my kids is similar to the way the Kundalini spiral is often described: A laser focus of energy, summoned without effort—pliable but delicate, gossamer yet eternal, a subtle similitude of the way that energy moves and spirals during an orgasmic experience.

I am very grateful to have had these experiences of 5-MeO along with all of my other various psychedelic trips, even the especially awful ones. The stages of remembering our divine origins can occur in a multitude of ways. For many of us the process of reclamation can be elusive and immensely challenging especially when we lack culturally incorporated initiatory rites enacted to bring to the centre of our awareness our steadfast relationship and perpetual integration with God. For so many of us, this absence of ceremony in the context of multiple and compounding examples of cultural desolation—not least of which is the deliberate despoiling of birth's biological orchestration—is corrosive.

For some women, the remembering and reclamation occurs during birth itself. But I also know that for others, the strata of conditioning, fear, anxiety, dysfunction, and neurosis may be so intense that external stimulation or substances can serve, in a positive way, to unfasten certain forms of patterning, and to help us to see (perhaps idiosyncratically) that the state of ever-present connection with the sacred (which we often only recognize within those exceptional numinous experiences of non-duality) are never actually out of reach.

I am also very aware of the potential perils of taking entheogenic substances, one being that the use of spiritual "medicines" can devolve into spiritual bypassing: tripping in order to avoid the material world, or inadvertently establishing an emotionally addictive habit of continuously sitting in ceremony to evade the responsibilities of deeper healing. I fully acknowledge that there can be a temptation to see drugs as a "jumpstart" to spiritual awakening, but I also believe, as I have alluded to previously, that this may be its own meta-illusion. There really isn't any "jumpstart" available for anyone, and every path we walk in life is…the path we walk, punctuated as always, with peaks, valleys, and obstacles along the way.

The threat of demonic possession or incursion is another concern that many people specifically associate with the consumption of psychotropic substances. This too is a significant matter—one I don't want to dismiss—and an enormously complex topic. And yet, it is also true that every substance changes our physiology and our brains, and has an effect on the state of our souls. In my experience (and by my observation), the spiritual detriments of alcohol are often far greater than psychedelics, for example, although booze, too, is a charged and gnarly topic, one that cannot be judged in simple, moralistic terms. The alchemy of fermentation has been present in every culture across time and remains an important aspect of the sacramental rituals of many faith traditions.

I have found that over the years my interest in (and my sense of the correctness and ethics of) consuming certain compounds, plants—or foods, for that matter—has fluctuated based on my own changing circumstances and state of being. In the end, every substance, whether unaltered or concocted from components made available to human beings by God, has a rightful place in the world. It is for each of us to determine the correct time and place for these elixirs in our own lives.

THE SPIRITUAL POLITICS OF DMT

Psychonautic travel has certainly had a hand in unfastening several of my formerly held stories and commitments. But I don't want to suggest that the orgasmic, blissful birth of Helio, or the expanded octaves of awareness, sensation, and consciousness that I accessed through his birth were only made possible as a result of my consumption of extrinsic drugs beforehand. In my view, entheogens are best imbibed (if at all) as a brief reminder of our indigenous capacity to realm, a power that we all possess. And, taking 5-MeO *did* shatter me—the story of me—in ways that I was able to very potently apply to birth, and specifically to choosing orgasmic, ecstatic birth.

Exercising our ability to produce certain states of mind and being, through full embodiment and the total embrace of intrinsically liminal transitions, actually builds our spiritual intelligence and integrity. We are made for this—for birth, sex, and death—and there are ways in which we can better orient ourselves to yield to and receive the lessons of spiritual dissolution offered to us through birth.

In fact, one of the most profound revelations from my experiences with 5-MeO-DMT (and the potent purification of kambô) is just how abundantly available this kind of journeying is to those of us who can—or who will—recollect, that birth (along with sex and death) is the richest foundation for this form of activation and awakening, precisely because it is during organic experiences of expanded awareness that our bodies are designed to create and release all forms of DMT endogenously, within the brain's pineal gland.

The autonomic secretion of DMT is perhaps the most interesting and significant component involved in the alchemical fusion of substances that are produced by various glands in the body in a domino effect during birth. One study has shown that mice dosed with 5-MeO-DMT exhibited greater neurological cell proliferation and more complex dendritic morphology[37] than the animals that did not receive this influx. If it is indeed the case that DMT is related to the architecture and chemistry of our mystical and metaphysical intelligence, I can't help but interpret all

---

[37] Dendrites are the branched protoplasmic extensions of a nerve cell that propagate the electrochemical stimulation received from other neural cells to the cell body, or soma, of the neuron from which the dendrites project.

the ways that we are conditioned to fear birth, and to loathe it, as an organised assault on our spiritual nucleus.

Without a doubt, there is a deeper, darker logic to the concerted efforts that have gone into desecrating birth than simply financial profit. A core component of the inverted demonic economy of human energy extraction is the necessity of inhibiting our capacity to know ourselves as sovereign and whole. The more we can be convinced that we are dependent on tyrannical systems of mental governance for survival (on all levels) and that our bodies are but an arrangement of capricious pieces of "wetware" along with our "hackable[38]" brains, the more easily we can be persuaded to offer ourselves up for the mining of our sentience, which is precisely what occurs when we inadvertently betray our inner knowing through learned self-destruction, cowardice, cruelty, and betrayal. Trauma drives all of this, and the original pattern and imprint is imparted during birth. When mothers and children are born into torture, disintegration, and paralysis (of any kind), our flourishing as individuals and as a species (or whatever humans are—a class unto ourselves) is inevitably affected.

According to "the science," most (if not all) of the pharmaceutical stimulants and analgesics so casually employed within obstetrics *do* have a long-term effect on the neurological structure of our brains. Pitocin (another name for Syntocinon, a synthetic, counterfeit version of oxytocin, the hormone of love, adoration, and bonding) has been studied extensively, and researchers such as Dr. Michel Odent and Dr. Sarah Buckley (among others) have pointed out that there is significant evidence suggesting that the effects of Pitocin at birth can damage our natural oxytocin receptors, and therefore alter our baseline capacity to experience full attachment and empathy throughout a lifetime (and that its effects may even be detrimental intergenerationally).

---

[38] As WEF sycophant Yuval Noah Harari has termed it.

My strong (and totally speculative) suspicion is that Pitocin not only destroys oxytocin receptors but that it also injures the function of the pineal gland, and therefore inhibits the production of DMT, achieving extensive spiritual devastation through deliberate pharmaceutical engineering. Spiritual alienation in particular is one of the central reasons why all aspects of birth—the physical, spiritual, psychic, sexual, and emotional—are so intentionally demolished by the destructive machinations of industrial obstetric sabotage and abuse.

The inherently sexual nature of birth manifestly reveals that the many forms of violation inflicted on mothers and babies are also constitutionally sexual in essence, and this also relates specifically to DMT. My life experiences of non-duality thus far have occurred in the context of the use of 5-MeO-DMT, but also during birth and orgasm, which naturally elicit the production and excretion of this compound.

As I have been reiterating for over twenty years, the industrial obstetric system is not "broken," and never was. It is not an inadvertent blunder that the sacred holiness of birth has been turned inside-out, despoiled, and ravaged. It is not a mistake that mothers and babies are routinely mistreated during birth, our bodies violated, and our souls wounded. The medicalization of birth has been meticulously, methodically designed to achieve the precise outcomes that we see today: widespread subservience to false authority, victim-consciousness, a propensity for self-harm, and spiritual alienation. And the distorted field of midwifery is as complicit with this agenda as is the medico-pharmaceutical complex.

What I also suspect (or rather, what I know) is that part of the devious soul-extraction program involves convincing us that we are doomed by our woundings, which is simply not true. We are in no way condemned or permanently damaged by what are nonetheless the very real traumas and injuries of primal origin that most (or all) of us undergo. In fact, we always have the potential to heal from every form of dis-ease.

The human being is defined by our incredible, irrepressible orientation toward regeneration and resurrection. Given even the slightest alignment with biological law and instinct (especially when we can avoid succumbing to the fantastically counterproductive and inhibitory "treatments" offered by allopathy), healing is always inevitable and ongoing. And at times, the full resolution of healing involves the death of the body.

FEAST OF LOVE

Since Helio's arrival, the ease with which I can access the capacity to realm has been amplified in every way. I have reached previously-unknown pinnacles of sexual bliss in union with my husband, I have a far deeper sense of connection with the natural world, my dreams are consistently vivid, inklings of clairsentience are ever-present, and I feel an enhanced intimacy with God, among many other observations.

I have reflected back on the various instances in which I have briefly known the rhapsodic non-dual decomposition of the ego in conjunction with realming and DMT (both exogenous and endogenous), and two consistent features have emerged as true:

The first is this mind-bendingly paradoxical fact: in every instance of experiencing a dissolution of self and a displacement of consciousness into the cosmos, from taking 5-MeO, to holy sexual ecstasy, to blissful birth, I have had to *actively choose* to abandon all that I think I am and to deliberately surrender. What I have found is that surrender, submerging into the numinosum, is not an entirely automatic process. Deliberation and choice are always core elements to yielding. I have had to decide, to elect, to allow my identity—the idea that I have of my Self—to be stripped away, which might seemingly preclude choice, but which emphatically (perhaps surprisingly) does not.

My second central observation is that becoming alive to our consonance with God through the death of the ego is inherently intertwined with the bliss of orgasmic transcendence through God-connected states like birth, death, and sex as a kind of "everything bagel" of love—*eros, agape, philia,* and *storgi*[39] intermixed.

What I know (but may never have the skill to properly articulate, although here I am giving it my all) is that choice and surrender, creation and dissolution, birth and death, are elliptical, infinite loops of energy, and that electing—choosing—to move through the birth portal in bliss is so much more than simply wanting to avoid pain.

The living body is the most sensitive and glorious conductor of energy in existence, and the most potent interface with the divine. This has always been the purpose of birth: we are created to experience crescendos of spiritual sensitivity and perception during which we become direct conduits to God, with all portals of awareness open and receiving. In fact, we have the power to invoke those states of transcendence at any time at all, and birth can be—is *designed* to be—the training ground for honing this power.

Birth is inherently psychedelic, inherently primeval, inherently transcendent, inherently God-connected. We are never not in the presence of God. And the more we are willing to choose to surrender to the here, the now, the good, the boundless, and the everlasting wonder of what we are—motes of light, passing through—the more we can continue to effortlessly generate that energy of love, pleasure, intimacy, responsibility, and choice. All of these are practices and frequencies, inextricable one from another.

---

[39] Ἀγάπη, ἔρως, φιλία, στοργή: love is one, but these are the four main articulations of the multidimensionality of Love within the ancient Greek framework (the basis of Western philosophical thought), which I have found to be beneficial given our limited vocabulary for love in the English language.

INTEGRATION QUESTIONS

1. What are your personal experiences with entheogens (if any), and what it was like to surrender (or not) to an entheogenic substance? What did you learn from it?

2. Do you believe that you can access that intensity of psychedelic experience *without* taking an extrinsic substance?

3. Have you ever given your power away by seeking spiritual "highs" from drugs, as opposed to finding expansion through inner work? If so, what positive lesson did you glean from this experience?

CHAPTER NINE

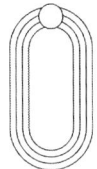

PILGRIMAGE

MOTHER, NATURE

Pregnancy is a vortex of its own.

Intercession,
      visitation,
            possession.

Exquisite immersion
      shimmering love.

Becoming pregnant is
      immolation and
           penance.

An irrevocable life sentence, a
          dropped   thread.

Pregnancy is
the end of it all,

PORTAL

  the dawning of devotion,
    the beginning of everything.

Focus.

Now that you have multiplied,
   where have you gone?

Rash, reckless, reverential,
   the pregnant You, is
    an installation
    a work of art.

Masterpiece.
Tour de force.

Concrete poetry.

Idiom.

Alien.

Nothing doing.
A dime a dozen.
Replicant.

Lazy, wallowing,
  pitiful
   stagnant.
Hurry up, it's time.[40]

---

[40] I wrote this in a bit of a fugue state, and then realized I had accidentally referenced T.S. Eliot's *The Waste Land* (which I read in high school), and which

Pregnancy will bowl you over at its insistence.
It will wash you clean, its torrential
gale rushing always onward, ineluctable,
compulsive, heedless of protest,
negotiation, or entreaty.

plodding, ponderous, unrelenting

Ungovernable.

While pregnant, you belong to everything.

Leaking,
    seeping,
        beset,
            besieged,
    freakish,
        seeking,
            weeping,
    indiscrete,
        yet ever regal,
pregnancy will keep you
    cloistered   and   cleaved.

You are the inlet,
and the charge.

---

includes the line *Hurry up please, it's time*, also echoed in the title of Anne Sexton's pain-soaked, rage-tinged, irreverent poem of the same name (which I also read as a teenager) in which she writes, *Once upon a time we were all born, / popped out like jelly rolls / forgetting our fishdom, / the pleasuring seas, / the country of comfort, / spanked into the oxygens of death, / Good morning life, we say when we wake, / hail mary coffee toast / and we Americans take juice, / a liquid sun going down. / Good morning life. / To wake up is to be born.*

PORTAL

The freight and the tariff.
You can never leave,
    until first
        departed from.

Consecration.

To become pregnant
    is to enter the hinterland.

The holy land.

You are the fountainhead,
    the seedbed
    the terrain and
    the soil
        itself.

Hallowed,
magnificent,
    inscribed in flesh

You, woman, are
    the incarnate word
    the eternal refrain.

Sacred Mother.

Yolande Norris-Clark

ANNUNCIATION

One of the many repercussions of having been born into an atmosphere of violence and tension, then immediately separated from my mother and kept in isolation, is that I have frequently felt a sense of discomfort with being loved or accepting my lovability. This has manifested in a certain prickliness, and an unconscious tendency towards avoiding vulnerability, often expressed as skepticism, guardedness, armouring, and (I'm ashamed to admit) what sometimes comes across as disdain and superiority. Preemptive disgust has been a trusty shield.

I love humanity—to the point of heartache—and I have devoted my life to service. But outside my handful of dear friends, and my beloved husband and children who are my clan and my home, I am a very private and somewhat insular person.

I have struggled with succumbing to the promise of abiding love, the acceptance of everyday miracles, and the vulnerability of conscious faith. Prior to what I think of as my experience of annunciation—of having been visited by the energy of God, who answered my prayer and granted to me and Lee the conception of our baby Helio—I had resigned myself to the reality that I could never embark on birth as anything other than a battle.

Accepting the fulfillment of my clear, humble, steadfast request of God was itself a confirmation of my faith. I realized that I was being offered an invitation to embrace the answered prayer for the child whose spirit had been disclosed to me (and Lee) so intimately, well before the apposition and adhesion of expatriate cells within my womb. I had done nothing but meekly ask for this baby, and then entered into loving communion with my husband. The rest of it—the organization of the infinite, fractalate details of the composition of pregnancy—was thanks entirely to the mastery of the grand, divine design of life. My own newfound receptivity was a testament to the eternal presence of God and of divine provision and nurturance ever-manifest within creation.

PORTAL

Conception itself is a gateway, and pregnancy is a spiritual quest. As the child within me—unquestioningly alive from the first moment—underwent his endless differentiation in my body, from germinal matter to ectoderm, mesoderm, and microscopic circulatory system, I felt a melting tenderness. I moved through multiple cycles of release, shedding layers of old loyalties, and pledges, and I found myself crafting a new commitment to the tentative sense of possibility—the possibility that maybe birth never had to be the way I had always chosen for it to be, by habit, assumption, and belief.

Yet despite the fact that our child had been conceived in full desire and awareness, as soon as I knew I was indeed pregnant, I was flooded with doubt. The waves of fear rolled in again and again. I had to remind myself repeatedly that beyond the physical world, this child was meant to come through me. I had been chosen once again, and I had the choice to accept this vocation, or to resist.

As my pregnancy progressed, my defences cracked, and the light flooded in. Eventually my armour corroded from the inside out, and I cast it off, exposed, finally willing to allow for an entirely new kind of transformation. When I finally chose to commit to that invitation to be reconstructed through my acquiescence in faith, I gained the capacity to effortlessly weave into existence, moment to moment, a birth that was pure bliss, total ecstasy, and entirely pain-free—and to do so effortlessly.

I have since come to know that this formula—the formula I am sharing in the pages that follow—is applicable to every area of our lives, be it self-healing, abundance, security, love, mothering, or anything else we may desire.

I have also come to know that it is possible for *all* women to achieve this for their births, and to then take this knowing into all other areas of their lives, and to craft the reality of their dreams.

(Note: Please remember that nothing in this book constitutes medical advice of any kind. I am not a medical practitioner nor is this book about birth as a medical experience. The following pages include some very general descriptions of theoretical emergency scenarios. Always consult with your own intuition and those you trust if you have any questions about your health. If you are seeking a medicalized experience, you will want to turn to a licensed, accredited medical professional. You are responsible for your health and wellbeing, during pregnancy and otherwise.)

LIVESTOCK MANAGEMENT

From the first visit with a midwife or family doctor to "confirm" our pregnancy, and even well before our official entry into the system beginning with the externalization of instinct via the pregnancy test, the industrial obstetric ordeal of so-called "prenatal care" is a hazing process that prepares pregnant women for the initiation ceremony of institutional birth. Everything that comprises medicalized "prenatal care," from each discrete technique and maneuver to the very paradigm itself, is an industrial livestock management system. There is very little (if any) evidence that anything offered within the industrial system is actually beneficial. At its core, the objectives of the obstetrics program are primarily obedience, discipline, compliance and control.

It makes no difference if this program is delivered by a doctor in a white coat, or by a midwife well-versed in the use of tone and subtlety to pressure a mother into submitting to the very same rituals and procedures that are standard medical fare (while framing this obstetric replica as "holistic" and "empowering"). All branches of industrial obstetrics are designed to fracture a mother's connection with her baby, fragment her sense of Self, cripple her instincts, and reinforce her subservience to the medical hierarchy.

I have never encountered a medical professional who understands much of anything about how birth really works (or, for that matter, who has even witnessed a "normal," spontaneous, unfettered birth), or how to truly support a mother's flourishing through pregnancy. Sadly, midwives are often among the most dangerous, ignorant, and abusive of practitioners, especially given the widespread delusion, martyrdom mindset, superiority, and false dichotomies and distinctions rampant within that profession.

The vast majority of the women (and, bizarrely, the men) who call themselves midwives have been educated within the institutional medical model, by instructors who are themselves medical operatives, and go on to become licensed and regulated by state-controlled medical organizations. This means that they do not work for mothers directly, and are unable, by definition, to uphold a birthing woman's authority. We cannot serve two masters. The regulation of midwifery represents an inherent, inarguable conflict of interest.

Many (if not most) of the women I have served in my practice over the past fifteen years have been profoundly traumatized by their previous encounters with midwives, who initially presented themselves as "natural," (and even in some cases as "independent," while nonetheless carrying a license) and willing to support what is referred to as "physiological birth." In the end, however, they still delivered the classic bait-and-switch, usually in the form of a "reason," revealed within days of a mother's birth (and sometimes during her birth)—based upon the parameters of the midwife's practise "guidelines"—for suddenly withdrawing her support, suggesting a transfer, or inflicting upon the mother counterproductive acts of humiliation and violation under the pretext of heroism.

Based on decades of experience, observation, and direct work with mothers and babies, I have concluded that if there *is* any real relationship whatsoever between standard "prenatal care" operations and maternal-infant outcomes, it is most likely—or most often—a negative one.

Whether in the form of surveillance or extraction, every practice within the medical model is predicated on the assumption of dysfunction, the catastrophizing of normal physiological variations, and the imposition of control through fear, infantilization, and intimidation.

No woman deserves to be condescended to, treated like a child, or sexually assaulted, yet these behaviours are standardized, codified, and seen as completely normal aspects of impending motherhood. No woman has an obligation to capitulate to this, and you have every right to withdraw your presence, your energy, and your consent from this system at any time by simply removing yourself from that world, if you choose to. As we discussed in Chapter Six, however, it is also important to realise that obstetrics is, contemporaneously, a language, a landscape, and a world of manipulation. Once you willingly enter that world, it can be very tricky to extricate yourself, and the more time you spend there, the riskier and more daunting a departure from that sphere of influence can become.

And yet, you *can* wrest yourself from medical management. Many women do. The most powerful, positive, life-affirming, freeing, and health-promoting choice I have ever made in my life was to remove myself entirely from the industrial obstetric apparatus (and from allopathic medicine altogether).

WILD PREGNANCY

I have chosen to experience my pregnancies and births as normal biological events that transpire from the ongoing current of my life. The conception, gestation, and emergence of my children arises from the medium of my day-to-day existence. I never seek out professional assistance or input when it comes to any other aspect of my biology—not even healing—therefore it would be contradictory to my values for me to outsource my responsibility in procreation.

I named this consciously spontaneous approach to allowing maternity to unfold as the normal biological event that it is, *wild pregnancy*. This is, perhaps, a simplistic term, but pregnancy does have an ineludible wildness to it. Despite the best efforts of science and progress, and maybe even in spite of ourselves, I remain confident that life, so brazenly represented by the lush, disobedient abundance of our overflowing pregnant bodies, will never be tamed.

Of course, none of us are entirely wild—we are all invariably domesticated to a certain extent. Over the years I have encountered a number of quibbles and criticisms of the phrase *wild pregnancy*, including the notion that the concept and the terminology are "extreme," and that there is a somehow better, more measured, "middle way" that one should strive for. But this idea seems to be based upon the assumption that what I have to say about birth is somehow dictatorial or prescriptive, which is not the case at all.

I am interested only in offering an example—a story—of what is possible, based upon the insights gleaned from walking my own path. I have no investment in my example being followed, nor am I interested in offering advice, establishing a credo, or developing dogma. The suggestion that there is any kind of defined, objective "middle path" is, to my mind, just as overbearing and restrictive as the notion that women "should" freebirth, or "should" give birth in a hospital. There is no "middle way," because the "middle" and the margins are different for everyone.

The more I have embraced the power I possess to claim the full expression of my biology (as is the indelible right of every woman and man) and the indigeneity and sovereignty that is my birthright, the more freedom, joy, and insight I have found in the flow of my life-stream. And as I have grown and matured as a mother, a birth-giver, and a birthkeeper, I have continued to refine my personal definition of wildness. That definition shifts ongoingly as I learn and expand, and none of this has anything whatsoever to do with public perception, or seeking flattery, validation, or acknowledgement.

I unwaveringly admit that I do not trust doctors, nurses, or midwives, nor their studies, potions, injections, medications, or tests—I simply don't trust "the science" at all. Yet the real reason that I choose wild pregnancy is because I want to—and also because I *do* trust the process of life and death, the vagaries of nature, and the unerring, insistent commitment of my body (like all bodies) to reveal to me what is true. I trust in my own devotion to listen, and to allow.

There is no objective "safety." There is no "safe option." There is only choosing the kind of risk you're willing to take, in alignment with who you are, what you value, and what you know to be true. Every choice increases or intensifies risk in some directions and diminishes risk in others.

There is no test or diagnostic procedure that is capable of giving me any information about my health or the health of my child that could ever rival pure sensation, full embodiment, and the all-encompassing sentience of total aliveness. There is no digital surveillance device or blood test that can offer me greater insight than my own capacity for attunement, perception, and resonance. There is no technology more sophisticated than the human being. The body itself is the most responsive instrument. Your body—your heart—is the nucleus of the expression, emission, transmission, and absorption of all forms of energy available to you in this lifetime.[41]

Just as I am miraculously capable of becoming pregnant without instruction or examination, my children have likewise all grown effortlessly in my womb with no guidance, advice, or outside management from anyone (not even myself). The purpose of medical investigation, testing, and diagnostics is to look for problems, and then to find them,

---

[41] Norris-Clark, Yolande. 2022. "My Favourite Bioresonance Device." *Substack*, May 20, 2022. https://yolandenorrisclark.substack.com/p/my-favourite-bioresonance-device.

regardless of the potentially inciting impacts of that investigation; regardless of whether or not there are even any symptoms, yet every symptom is simply a message from your body, showing you the consequence of your choices and the nature of reality.

I am the sole authority and the only "expert" when it comes to my and my baby's well-being, and that "expertise" is implicit and instinctive. At no point during any of my pregnancies have I felt the need to measure, assess, monitor, document, or scrutinize my own body or my baby's as we grow and change together.

I *am* my baby. My baby is me. We are creating each other, with and through God, and we exist in symbiotic relationship at all times. I feel no temptation to displace the sacred intimacy of pregnancy in any way. No one has greater authority, wisdom, or cognizance than I do about myself, or my child. And the same can be true for you.

What is your body telling you?

What is your baby telling you?

Are you prepared to listen?

KEYS TO FREEDOM

Regardless of the larger contextual choices you happen to make during your pregnancy, all of which will inform the set and setting of your birth, such as which world you decide to occupy (whether the vortex of allopathy, or the universe of sovereign birth), the individuals you select as your inner circle and support network, or the practices and habits you cultivate, you may encounter people along the way who disapprove of, scorn, reject, or criticize those choices.

If this occurs, please know that true freedom lies within the capacity to follow our own internal authority, without being unduly pressured, persuaded, influenced, or compelled by the opinions of others.

Without a doubt, we are biologically designed to seek support and protection from those we feel closest to—especially as mothers—and for this reason, it can seem particularly challenging during pregnancy to claim the liberation that is ours when many of the people around us (often the people we love and otherwise trust the most) may be deeply afraid of birth, and profoundly uncomfortable with the unknown.

Many mothers will encounter friends, family members, acquaintances, and even strangers, who project their fear and discomfort onto them, particularly when they have chosen a path that diverges from the mainstream. While this can feel disconcerting, it can also serve as a very useful barometer of our own values, priorities, and true desires.

Before taking any kind of leap, whether it's making a life-altering decision to enter (or leave) a particular world, accepting a protocol, procedure, or operation, or contracting into any relationship via consent, there are two important sets of questions to ask oneself:

(a) What are the most logical potential outcomes of making this choice (or not), and by extension, which of those logical potential outcomes can I live with (or not)?

(b) How might I feel if someone criticizes, judges, or condemns me for this choice?

The first is fairly obvious—it is always wise to explore all the potentialities of a given decision as thoroughly as we can, and to interrogate our own long-term motivations and interests.

But the second offers a more subtle nuance. When we feel triggered, offended, upset, hurt, or attacked by someone else's opinion of our personal choices, we are experiencing the revelatory proof that we ourselves are not fully at peace with the decision we made.

The very fact of our own activation in response to questioning, criticism, or the airing of a contradictory perspective when we have willingly shared our selected path with another (thus, by definition opening ourselves up to the possibility and even likelihood of differentiation) demonstrates that *we* lack a foundation of conviction or power in our choice.

Furthermore, the existence of even a hint of outrage, insult, discomfort, annoyance, anger on our part—any form of resistance at all to another person's conflicting viewpoint regarding a life-choice that we have made, is the evidence itself that our own energy vortex is oscillating at a concomitant frequency to that of the critic, the doubter, or the one by whom we feel disparaged or threatened.

The truth of the other is mirrored to us in our resistance to it. Any degree of resistance indicates an existing energetic covenant with the very thing to which we stand in opposition. In this way, the feeling of resistance is a gift: a revelation.

It is only when we ourselves are struggling with the choices we've made, and with the inevitable fact that we are responsible for those choices (and their logical outcomes), that we could possibly be bothered by what others think. Affront and indignation are expressions of impotence, denial, and infantilization.

There are countless instances in my own life when I have been given the opportunity to unravel and reassess my continued commitments to victimhood, outrage, and anger. The evidence of growth, however, lies in those areas that no longer hold any kind of charge or activation.

During my early years of mothering, I was incessantly outraged by what I saw as the impertinence, ignorance, and disrespect of people on the sidelines. How dare they question my authority and my better judgement? How dare they presume to comment on my experience? I was quite adorable in my indignation.

At this stage in my life, however, not only am I unaffected by the criticisms of others when it comes to how I approach pregnancy, birth, or mothering (or the health decisions I make for my children), but I tend not even to have the experience of encountering censure, or disparagement, for the most part.

That's not because other people no longer judge me, disagree with me, condemn me, or express antipathy and hostility towards me—they do, probably more often than ever, simply because my audience has grown. The difference, though, is that those comments and criticisms simply do not enter my personal vortex of energy. I don't notice them, I don't care about them, they simply do not exist for me.

It did take time, perspective, learning, and experience for me to come to this point, and despite my confidence about birth and mothering, there are lots of other areas that still "trigger" me, but I am comforted by the knowledge that, like everything, our susceptibility to being judged or denounced can only ever really be determined by our energetic consent.

It is *always* the case that, no matter what you do or don't do in life, some people will hate you, resent you, find you annoying, find you irrelevant, find you unattractive, disagree with you, or be jealous of you—always, no matter what.

If you do anything at all that is even remotely significant, or powerful, or influential, the number of such people will grow exponentially, and they'll get louder about their feelings. This is not personal. It's just a math equation.

PORTAL

If you allow your fear of others disagreeing with you or hating you to have *any* influence on what you do, how you do it, or the degree to which you do it, you are in reality only handicapping yourself in an effort to prevent a reality that *already exists* and that will always exist.

Because even if you say and do nothing at all (ever) those people who can't stand you will still be out there. Limiting yourself in an attempt to shape how others perceive you is always an exercise in futility.

When we can move beyond reactivity, and self-censorship, we are free.

PRACTICE

If anyone had asked me, during my pregnancy with Helio—the pregnancy that led to my ninth birth—what I was doing to "create," "manifest," or choose a blissful birth experience, not to mention the orgasmic, almost-silent, ecstatic birth that I ended up with, I probably would have been taken aback by the question. Helio's gestation was, on the surface, one of the least intentional, least evidently sacred, and least peaceful pregnancies I have experienced. Truthfully, my life was a totally chaotic mess at the time.

I share this in hopes of reassuring you: if you are presently pregnant, and you find yourself feeling dismayed, guilty, or disappointed in yourself; questioning whether or not you are sufficiently spiritually attuned, or if you have really been doing the things that you're "supposed" to do to prepare for a "spiritual" birth experience, don't despair. You may even be reading this book out of a sense of duty or obligation. I hope that's not the case, and that at the very least, you're enjoying the ride (this book and your pregnancy), but if you have even had a passing thought that you "should" be approaching your birth with a particular methodology, degree of academic rigour, or special process, please stop.

You can't mess this up. In every way, you are worthy, and everything I have tasted belongs to you too.

Our experience of pregnancy matters deeply, as does the way we care for ourselves and our babies, before and after birth. However, I don't want any woman thinking fatalistically, or giving up on herself and the idea of birthing in bliss simply because she feels she has somehow failed to do the "right" pregnancy rituals. That's not how any of this works. Health, overall, is informed by innumerable factors, not the least of which is our belief about our own resilience.

One thing that excites me about having had the most transcendently blissful birth after a pregnancy which, in many ways, was quite awful, is that this proves to me even more potently that the most profound shifts which contribute to the outcome of birth may be occurring internally, yet may not be revealed to us until the moment of culmination. Our deepest desires might initially be hidden from our conscious awareness—and may even be obscured by all those surface wants and good intentions until the moment of transformative action in which we are unveiled to ourselves, in our naked truth.

My own deepest desire, disclosed in what I created my most recent birth to be, hadn't really crossed my mind in much of a conscious, coherent way until my waters released, when I was presented with what was immediately clear to me as a significant choice-point. I see now, looking back, that I did indeed create this birth. I did so to some extent in that moment of awareness, when the floodgates opened, but also through imperceptibly having become a woman who could harness pain and access a *beingness* and fulfillment through birth as the technology that it is, in a surprisingly circuitous, meandering way, over all the years, seasons, and choices that came before.

This was a humbling and profound realization because, like so many of us, I had been conditioned to view spiritual advancement and distillation (or skill and refinement, depending on how one perceives it) as something that comes, more or less, via the linear implementation of specific practices, as opposed to *the* practice, or praxis, of life. I know now that it is both—and all of the above. Practice in the form of ritual, repetition, and rhythm *is* important, and there are times in our lives when practice and ritual come to us in ways that are recognizable as such—formatted and formalized. But this is not always the case.

There is a place for codified technique, absolutely. I have, over the years, engaged in various formal systems as a seeker. I practiced yoga for a long time in my twenties, and I was very into ecstatic dance. Church has been important to me at different times, and for a while I was a practitioner of Zen Buddhism. I have meditated according to a multitude of traditions, embraced and released (and then re-claimed, in some cases) a range of spiritual practices. The energy with which I undertook most of these disciplines was largely that of striving, endeavouring, aspiring, searching, wanting; I was also driven in many ways by shame and regret—a kind of trauma-informed spiritual quest.

As we get older and, hopefully, wiser, we recognize that literally every act and habit in our lives *is* the practice. Anything in life that we engage in—from getting out of bed, basic self-care, the way we prepare our food and attend to our nourishment, to weeding the garden, reading stories to our kids, and brushing our kids' teeth—is the *primary* practice, and maybe the only truly authentic practice; the stuff of life.

Yes, carving out time to create a space of ritual observance can be immensely beneficial, but even *more* potent is attending to the day-to-day with the same kind of reverence and devotion that we might bring to prayer, or to formalized movement or meditation. This also doesn't always happen, and that's okay too.

At this point in my life, I am aware that the time I invested in formal, ritual practices over the years has benefited me greatly. But before Helio's birth

I still carried a sense of directly equating how *correctly* I engaged in practices that would ostensibly bring me peace, centredness, non-attachment, non-duality, etc. with the capacity that I had for being a person that could *do* peace and centredness, non-attachment, non-duality, integration, and pleasure—as though these are states that we actually have to acquire, declare, and even fight for, rather than qualities that are always ours to reclaim and embody. In fact, we all, with the merest internal inflection, have the ability to simply *become* those states of being.

Whether or not we are capable of making that slight shift in articulation that precipitates transformation, however, as minute as it is (not to mention whether or not we actually *will*), is a very different story. As we have discussed, capacity is built through belief, created by internal dialogue, and our internal dialogue follows our imagination.

So, while it seemed as though my pregnancy with Helio was even less structured, less attentive to wellness, less spiritually disciplined, less aligned, messier, and far more stressed than my previous pregnancies—and although what one might infer from this is that I would have been far *less* likely to experience an easy birth (let alone a pleasurable, blissful, orgasmic one)—I can recognize in retrospect that there were things I did intuitively during that pregnancy which, at the time, seemed insignificant to me, but which I see now were actually profound moments of transmission and integration brought forth through a kind of consolidation of both instinct and imagination.

As always, belief is everything, and the choice and responsibility is ours. Some of the sickest people I've ever known have been those who are the most devoted to specific wellness diets, plant medicine ceremony, EMF-mitigation strategies, yoga, working out, meditation, Pilates, toxin-free lifestyles, dieta, therapy, linen tunics, shilajit, and on and on. Meanwhile, some of the healthiest, and most integrated people I have ever known, pay very little attention to the specifics of what they eat, or the kind of purification process their water goes through before it's considered drinkable.

With this insight, I also now know that it is possible to surrender to pregnancy with what is at once a sense of fluency, gentleness, consciousness, and ritual, in a way that is easeful and uncontrived, and to truly care for ourselves and our babies prenatally, in accordance with the deepest truth of what it is to be fully nurtured.

During pregnancy, there *is* a balance to be found, between nature and nurture, regimen and flow, method and madness, even. That balance is for you to discover, primarily through trial and error, but also by sharing with, observing, and witnessing those who have come before, noting their results, listening to their stories, and allowing their wisdom to filter through your own instinctive knowing.

SEXUAL AWAKENING

Our past sexual experiences are always part of our present sexuality, and any form of sexual trauma we might be carrying is significant to the birth process. Nurturing, healing, and consciously attending to our sexuality—during pregnancy especially—is an immensely important part of choosing a blissful birth. This will look very different for different women, depending on the nature of their intimate relationship with their partner and the texture of the relationship they have with themselves and their sexuality in general.

As we touched on in Chapter Two, sexual trauma (like birth trauma) is ubiquitous, because birth trauma *is* sexual trauma. Sexuality and pleasure are on a continuum that spans every part of our lives—there is really no demarcation between our sexual selves and our every action, response, task, or expression.

Life is sexual, and sexuality is aliveness, which, sadly, is still an immensely confronting idea for many people, especially those who are rightfully concerned about the sexual exploitation and abuse of children, and the increasingly socially-sanctioned erosion and violation of their minds on the part of corrupt media and government (all of which is, I believe, one of the most significant social and political issues of our time). A great many individuals are more confused than ever about how to reconcile the fact that we are, inarguably, sexual beings from the moment of conception, with the importance of ensuring that our children's innocence is sheltered and sustained appropriately.

In my view, it is only when we can acknowledge and truly honour the innate and omnipresent erotic charge that powers all of life, that we will ever, as a society or as individual parents, be capable of safeguarding our children from sexual predation, or maintaining integral and healthy boundaries around our own sexuality while modelling that for our kids.

In every moment of our lives, we are, at a certain octave, expressing our sexuality—even repression is a form of sexual communication. Embodiment itself is inherently sexual. Since becoming a mother, I have become far more skilled in my capacity to perceive and know my sexual self, and also to conjure what is most often described as a "Kundalini unwinding," or a coiling and uncoiling of sexual electricity as a form of energetic summoning.

This harnessing of generative ardour can occur in response to numerous contexts and situations in life, and in a multitude of ways that are not at all explicit, and certainly not inappropriate. For example, energetic healing, realming, and even eating food, involve the transmission of animating energy that can originate, or be felt in the pelvic area and yoni—without in any way involving the arousal of overt sexual desire.

Learning to attune to these forms of sensitivity has much to do with opening oneself to the process of healing, and overall maturation, which is a lifelong endeavour. I am very much still in the midst of healing the trauma from my own birth, my childhood, and my ancestral wounds (a process which will continue to unfold for the duration of my life), all of which is inseparably related to how I have ripened and mellowed over the years, becoming more comfortable with myself and who I am, in all ways, including sexually.

I can't say that I have ever really engaged in specific practices designed or orchestrated for sexual healing or connection, but one of the most fundamental sources of authentic healing in every direction (while also being an origin point for sexual growth, not to mention bliss in birth) has been the ever-deepening sense of safety and intimacy I have in my marriage.

My husband Lee and I have been together for seventeen years now, and we have been devoted, faithful, and monogamous throughout that time. It has taken me almost two decades to develop the level of trust I feel in myself and my body through the affinity, respect, and tenderness created within the container of our marriage. Energetic hygiene has been a crucial component to this.

I experienced a lot of sexual trauma as a young person, and the influence of porn and porn culture, especially, on my conceptualization of sex and my own body was very toxic. It's really only in recent years, after decades of purification through holy, loving sex, in a relationship devoid of pornography, pain, or prurience, that I have felt a distinct—and remarkable—augmentation in my capacity for galactic realming through orgasm. Since Helio's birth, my ability to access pleasure, transcendence, and to voyage via orgasm during sex has grown exponentially.

In prioritizing sexuality in our marriage, a flourishing of sexual healing and growth has ensued. Lee and I have never found that having children, or parenting in general, has hampered our ability to be intimate, and it has certainly not negatively impacted our desire, or the erotic charge we feel for each other—very much the opposite, in fact. But it's also true that consciously nurturing one's sexuality and sexual relationship is self-propelling. Sex is a habit as much as a practice, and sex itself is a sexual accelerant. Birth too—as sexual as it is, as the culmination of sexual union—is a foundational influence on our sexuality and sexual relationships.

Birth and motherhood are the apex of sexual power. It is through birth that our sexuality comes to fruition. It cannot be overstated that birth is sexual, birth is sex, birth is orgasm, and birth is also the most intimate and vulnerable experience of life. Birth and sexuality are the same, and they are sacred.

Paradoxically, adhering to the devotional path of sexual intimacy in relationship, and valuing sex as a form of prayer and worship, and as a source of joy, safety, and trust, has also allowed me and Lee to downgrade the significance of sex in our relationship, in a sense (just as we discussed the idea of "significance" in terms of the self, identity, and mothering in Chapter Seven). Sex is absolutely a priority in our lives, and yet for this reason, we also don't need to think or talk about it that much at all.

We don't plan for it or make a big deal about it. We just have it, and enjoy it, several times a week, as often as we did when we first met almost twenty years ago, albeit with far more passion and ecstasy than ever.

NOURISHMENT

I am aware that nutrition is generally identified as one of the most important aspects of prenatal health. But I have come to the conclusion that our choice of foods is far less significant than the energy and spirit with which we take in nourishment of all forms, including from the foods we consume. Anxiety, guilt, shame, and stress are, in my view, far more detrimental to health than any form of comestible that has been deemed sub-par or "toxic."

I certainly enjoy good food, and I also feel inspired to fuel my body with foods that I know to be wholesome and beneficial. I prioritize high-quality protein in the form of pasture-raised animal products, especially beef, lamb, chicken, eggs, and raw dairy (raw milk kefir being one my favourite staples), along with aromatic herbs and sea salt as seasoning.

I eat simply. Now that my family and I live in the tropics, we are blessed with an abundance of local fruits that grow year-round, and I do my best to seek out organically grown produce whenever possible (I especially love lacto-fermented vegetables like kimchi and sauerkraut). We keep chickens for eggs and meat, and while pork is not my preferred food, we have a family pig, and at home I cook exclusively with raw handmade butter, tallow, or lard. I avoid seed oils, grains, and industrially preserved and packaged foods, and I focus on the most nutrient dense options.

I do eat out occasionally, and I graciously accept food from friends without fear or questioning. I no longer even consider allowing myself to worry about leptins, gluten, toxins or pesticides. I am safe in the knowledge that my body and mind are powerful and integral enough to absorb nutrition from anything (or to generate it seemingly from nothing) and to release whatever doesn't serve me. Our bodies contain every possible element, mineral, and substance on earth, and our consciousness can always amplify whatever we require to thrive.

As a birth consultant and guide, I have supported mothers who have gestated their babies on cola and potato chips, and witnessed them give birth to vigorous, healthy children. Conversely, I have supported clients with impeccable diets and habits, who have given birth very early ("prematurely") to babies with considerable developmental distinctions and health issues. This is not to suggest that nutrition doesn't matter, only that nutrition is more layered and complex than simply food. There is no easy calculus, and there are no guarantees.

Of course, genetics, environmental factors, lineage, family history, trauma, and biological conflicts play into all of this, and our past, along with our conscious and subconscious beliefs, is always distilled through the lens of our own perception. It is my conviction overall that how we behold what we eat is far more powerful than the basic constituents of the food itself.

The human organism is self-healing and self-cleansing, and the more we can allow ourselves to trust the inherent genius of our biological design, the better we will feel, the healthier we will be, and, funnily enough, the more we will find that we then tend to honour ourselves with optimal, "correct" choices far more often.

From time to time, the "correct" choice is to accept the chemical-laden cheezie from the floor that my three-year-old has just offered me, after having been gifted the bag (by the impoverished family down the road) out of true neighbourliness and love. I *want* that cheezie in my system, imbued as it is with the chain reaction of deep generosity and care. The materiality of it, at that point, is irrelevant.

One of the most transformative health practices of all is the act of blessing of our food before we eat, no matter what it is (and this may be even more important if what we are about to consume is perhaps not quite as fresh or biodynamic as it could be). Offering a prayer of thanksgiving—even silently—has, like every conscious thought-form, an impact on the physical structure of every atom of the object on which the blessing is focused. There is no better time than pregnancy to bring the power of benediction into one's daily rhythm and practice in as many ways as possible, and in the context of family, I think establishing an ongoing ritual of saying grace is a cornerstone of wellness and spiritual cohesion.

My beliefs, convictions, and perspectives about food and nourishment have changed tremendously over the years, and (as is often the case) my older children have borne the brunt of my immature apprehensions and anxieties. This is not a problem either (as we can heal from anything), but I do see that the children of mine onto whom I projected the most concern, worry, and attempted control over food, are also the ones who have tended to have more oral health issues and dental caries.[42]

THE SEAT OF THE SOUL

Most humans today are, to an extent, calcified—ossified, and case-hardened. We have been "hardened-off" by the distortions and inversions of our conditioning, and I see this as a process that occurs not just through the traumas and challenges of birth as we enter this life, but from pre-existence or even the past-life of the soul (in whatever form that might take) and (of course) via intergenerational cellular experiences and memories.

The concept of "calcification" is, interestingly, very present in the medicalized world of pregnancy and birth. We frequently hear of "calcifications" of the placenta, although I have never known this to be a problem for any of my clients, even those who have given birth at forty-three and forty-four weeks of gestation. (Incidentally, all of my own nine babies—save Helio—were born between forty-three and forty-four weeks, and all have had gloriously healthy placentas.)

The pineal gland—also known as the "third eye," (and referred to by Rene Descartes as "the seat of the soul" and site of rational thought) has long been a feature of so-called "New Age" discourse, specifically in reference to the subject of the calcification or corruption of the pineal. In recent years however, the topic has infiltrated the mainstream, and there is a growing awareness of the importance of the function and vitality of this

---

[42] In 2008, I was introduced by my mother to the work of Dr. Ryke Geert Hamer and his discovery of the Five Biological Laws. My study of Hamer's principles have had a considerable influence on my continuously-growing understanding and mastery in the realm of self-healing.

tiny adrenal gland, the size of a grain of rice, located at the very core our brains.

The pineal gland is essential for the regulation of our circadian rhythms, the production and excretion of melatonin, the balance of serotonin, the operation of the hypothalamus, and other chemical physiological systems that intertwine with our internal spiritual and extra-sensory perception. This diminutive yet immensely powerful structure is also increasingly recognized as a locus of activation for our capacity to expand and transpose our consciousness—the control deck that mediates the world of the ineffable, the mystical, the spiritual, and our physical reality.

There is some emerging "scientific" research available on the topic of pineal gland calcification,[43] and while I don't really care about science (I find science to be the least relevant or interesting epistemological approach to knowing available) I do find it fascinating to note the convergence of "alternative" thought and the purported objectivity of science, and to observe the scientific treatment of topics that inevitably spill over into the phenomenological and the sacred. Regardless of the credence science is willing (or not) to grant the notion of pineal calcification, I see the implications of the theory evidenced in plain sight all around me: a culture of spiritual lack, self-abnegation, dissociation, existential trauma, and much more.

It is believed that human beings whose pineal glands are healthy and activated have abundant access to their natural capacity to tune into altered states of being and to communicate with their guide-selves and with the spiritual realm. What this indicates to me is that, in essence, human beings are designed—divinely designed—to retain the ability throughout our lives to intuit the visitation of concepts, ideas, and realms that exist outside of the material. We are also, I believe, architected with

---

[43] Nall, Rachel. 2020. "Decalcifying Your Pineal Gland: Does It Work?" Healthline. May 26, 2020. https://www.healthline.com/health/decalcify-pineal-gland#symptoms.

the power to communicate with each other and ourselves on a number of (possibly infinite) planes of reality and existence.

For many people, this may sound preposterous or improbable, but I think the widespread dubiousness (and cynicism even) regarding the pineal gland, is simply more evidence that we do in fact reside in a world in which the majority of the population unknowingly struggles with a major brain injury as a result of multiple assaults on the potency and performance of this remarkable organ. Not least among the objects of these assaults is birth itself, which has the power to either illuminate and mobilize ideal pineal function or, through the administration of street drugs, ritual abuse, obstetric rape, and assault, can drastically dull its operation and effectiveness.

After birth, the onslaught on the human mechanism for soul/spirit interfacing continues from multiple directions, in a multitude of forms, and includes variations of trauma that may not be recognizable for most people. This includes spiritual trauma by way of parental or caregiver abuse, authoritarian and governmental mind-control, but also via poisoning, and direct physical harm. The latter damage is inflicted by, among other things, certain forms of frequency weaponry, like ultrasound,[44] the primary purpose of which is to sever our connection with the sacred, the intuitive, and the ephemeral, and to preemptively rupture our primordial bond as mothers with our unborn children. (I never expose my babies to ultrasound, including by way of the doppler, which might seem innocuous, but is not.)

---

[44] Ultrasound consists of high-frequency soundwaves that are widely and objectively known to damage mammalian cells and tissue, and have been correlated in numerous animal studies with miscarriage, low birthweight, stillbirth, organ damage, and autism-like behavioural modifications. It has never been proven safe, nor shown to statistically improve outcomes. To explore this topic further, please reference *The Complete Guide to Freebirth* as well as my other podcasts and written works on the topic.

You may at this point be wondering about the condition of your own pineal gland, and how to know if it has been negatively affected by the barrage of potentially damaging inputs from our postmodern existence. I think we can assume, especially as adults, that our pineal glands have suffered from at least *some* measure of calcification, which tends to occur over time, especially when one is immersed in a society like ours. In my admittedly biased view, one of the most immediately obvious markers for determining if a person's pineal gland is damaged is whether or not they deny the presence of God, the holy, or the soul.

Atheism and nihilism abound, as does trenchant ego-identification. Individuals who are perpetually laconic, angry, or narcissistic, or who struggle with a sense of detachment from their bodies, self-loathing, a disordered relationship with nourishment, or disinterest in other people and the world around them except for the purposes of manipulation and control, are, I suspect, likely suffering from this kind of disability. Unfortunately, many habits that are indicative of preexisting pineal impairment, like a fixation on or obsession with screens, video games, pornography, alcohol, cruelty, and many other forms of antisocial and asocial behaviour, can perpetuate and engender further harm to our spiritual core.

And, as always, we possess an almost endless (and highly underestimated) capacity to heal from anything. It is absolutely possible to decalcify the pineal gland, and endeavouring to do so has far-reaching and positive consequences. It's also important to note that fear, shame, and self-loathing are perhaps the patterns of thought that are most damaging and inhibitory, whereas positivity, joy, and a delight in self-healing are the most powerful feedback mechanisms. Any experience that brings us into right-relationship with pleasure, love, internal knowing, and God-connection will have a concomitantly positive effect on self-healing and pineal decalcification.

In practical terms, the more we can adjust our habits to live in accordance with the movement of the sun as it transits over the earth plane—rising with the sun's advent, and sleeping at its setting, and receiving its nourishment at its apogee—the more our pineal gland will thrive.

Simply re-setting our habits to actively energize and spark the pineal gland into reactivation can make a radical difference to our wellbeing, and even the most preliminary motion in this direction will result in an immediate augmentation in your intuition, your ability to relate to and unite with other people, and this invigorating loop will reverberate throughout your entire life. It is especially important during pregnancy to practice spiritual and energetic hygiene, and to claim the joy and freedom inherent in self-discipline, and the only authentic way to access this is first by embracing self-love.

Because mind and body are one, the same practices that heal the pineal gland are also practices that will lead to good health in every region of the body and mind. Other forms of life-affirming play (like sound-healing, meditation, movement, dance, breath-work, toning, and spending ample time outside) bring blood flow and vivification to every cell, and contribute to the healing and cleansing of the pineal gland. The more you engage in these practices with a sense of levity, the more quickly you will become accustomed to—and comfortable with—exercising your ability to tune in to pleasure, other realms and dimensions, and our everlasting God-connected upper selves.

All of this facilitates the body's production of DMT, which then in turn increases DMT, often in amounts significant enough to produce noticeably psychedelic effects—no extrinsic input necessary. It is amazing what our bodies can do when we choose to be aware of our capacity and when we become willing to know that we are always healing.

Yolande Norris-Clark

THE SHAPE OF WATER

We are water. From the ecstatic cloudburst of conception, to our amphibious existence in the aqueous environment of the womb, to the deluge of emergence, and onward through the lush, irresistible exuberance of babyhood, the porous bloom of youth, and the gorgeous autumnal delicacy that occurs when we elect to succumb to the desiccation of age…every human passage is powered, punctuated, and defined by water, or its absence. Arousal, emotion, exertion, excretion, dehydration, sweat, blood, tears: the human life-stream is the story of water. Water is life.[45]

Community water fluoridation is an excellent example of how government institutions and supposed "health" organizations are actually enacting policies, mandates, and public health directives that are, at their core, satanically motivated, and which have a directly deleterious effect on pineal function and spiritual sight. Fluoride is one of the most harmful neurotoxins, and its widespread implementation is probably one of the most effective ways to undermine the ethereal cognizance and intellectual function of large swathes of the population.

In many jurisdictions, fluoride is added to the public water supply and in certain countries, especially those in which the only potable water is in bottled form (notably throughout Central America, where I live), fluoride is incorporated into almost every kind of commercial "purified" drinking water, most of which is bottled and "owned" by some of the largest and most economically powerful multinational corporations in the world.

---

[45] Water Is Life: The Rise of the Mní Wičóni Movement." 2017. Cultural Survival. March 3, 2017. https://www.culturalsurvival.org/publications/cultural-survival-quarterly/water-life-rise-mni-wiconi-movement. This is both a truism and a phrase that has become a maxim following its adoption as a slogan and rallying cry of the Standing Rock Sioux and sister tribes, during a large-scale protest against the corporate construction of a 1100-mile oil pipeline spanning indigenous territory from North Dakota to Illinois. "Never again," they vowed. "Water is life. Mní Wičóni. This is all we have left—our river, and the lands you didn't take last time."

Fluoride is also added to salt in Central America and elsewhere, as well as to industrially packaged milk, among many other staple products. In other words, the majority of people living in the so-called "third world" are being heavily dosed with fluoride on a daily basis, through the most elemental provisions upon which they depend for basic survival.

In my family, we have the privilege of choosing to drink non-fluoridated, reverse-osmosis filtered spring water, and I'm sure it goes without saying that we eschew industrial dentistry and any fluoride-containing dental products. I have been living a relatively fluoride-free lifestyle since the age of fifteen, when I made myself aware of the many risks of this industrial byproduct (to the consternation and ridicule of most of my friends and family, many of whom have, at long last, come around), and I have noticed significant and sometimes dramatic changes in the people I know and love who have more recently removed fluoride from their daily exposure (specifically my husband Lee, who was, when we first met, initially highly doubtful that fluoride could possibly be something to avoid, but who has since radically changed his mind—structurally, chemically, spiritually, and figuratively).

That said, in keeping with my general philosophy on nourishment, I am unruffled by the certainty that it is impossible for me to entirely eliminate all forms of fluoride exposure, and I know that my general habits, along with the resilience, fortitude, and flexibility of mind and body are more than adequate for the restoration of my pineal gland's vibrancy, and yours as well.

The notion of "structured water" has become increasingly popular, especially among biohackers and their ilk. As a proud biophile,[46] I see this current of appreciating the invisible, resonant structure of all things as an important one. Broadly, water molecules are said to have a naturally

---

[46] I am not interested in "hacking" anything, and I refuse to view humanness or the silly things that we humans do to ourselves and the planet as a technical problem to overcome.

hexagonal "shape," in their wildest form, when coursing through geological formations, springs, and glaciers according to the pulse and vibration of the earth's magnetic symmetry, forming a gel-like arrangement referred to as the "structure" of water or EZ-water. It is this crystalline coherent class of water which surrounds the hydrophilic surfaces within our body, and through which electrical currents flow.[47]

Processing, stagnation, and chemical additives, however, can have a "flattening" effect on the compositional shape of water, making it less dense, viscous, and highly charged, while reducing its bioavailability. The process of "restructuring" the water we drink is understood to increase our ability to absorb (and therefore benefit from) hydration. This is a fascinating theory to me, not least because it seems to reflect the idea of *tensegrity*[48]—the tensional integrity that allows the human body [of water] to maintain its optimal litheness and range of motion, thanks to the fascial web that is, in a way, simultaneously both an electrical grid and an irrigation system.

Fascia[49] is the gel-like network of electrically conductive matter that both supports and cushions every bone, organ, and cell in our bodies. Fascia is one of the most beautiful, mystical, psychedelic, fascinating, and sophisticated aspects of our bodies, and its complexity and mystery proves,

---

[47] To learn more about structured and EZ (Exclusion Zone) water, I highly recommend the work of Dr. Gerald Pollack on the fourth stage of water, as well as the written works of Masaru Emoto.

[48] *Tensegrity* is a term that was coined by architect, designer, and theorist Buckminster Fuller, which refers to "tensional integrity," a structural system in which each element of the structure is under both compression and tension, or compression via tension, so that every section is held up, and remains whole and distinct on account of every other part of that structure that is exerting a force of equal measure from within and in opposition to the whole.

[49] I had the immense privilege of briefly studying myofascial release with movement therapist, healer, and Pilates instructor Lee Miller, who trained directly with John Barnes, one of the world's foremost experts in myofascial release. Lee Miller's approach was incredibly intuitive and energetic, and she taught me that fascia can be manipulated and activated with featherlight touch.

to me, that the human body/mind is the most meta structure that exists. If the pineal gland is in some sense the "motherboard," fascia is the electric superhighway of the body—the fibrous circuitry—illuminating our corporeal being with the current of sentience, and providing a framework of support for the amplification of the heart's incredible electromagnetic toroidal field. (The immense power of fascia to hold memory and transmit energy proves that, within our organism, we, the human being, possess a far more elaborate and powerful technology than anything the nihilistic technofascists could possibly come up with.)

Every part of our bodies, including the mobility and pliancy of our fascia, is benefitted from consuming structured water. Ideally, we would be drinking directly from an artesian spring, but in the absence of this opportunity, water can be "structured" by the sun—this "activation" can be achieved at home by placing purified water in direct sunlight, through the magnetic motion of the spiral. There are also various products now available, such as glass carafes and bottles manufactured in such a way that they purportedly "structure" water through the crystalline formation of the glass itself, as well as via the exertion of an electrified magnetic vortex which inspires a self-structuring spiral motion.

Electric Feel

All along the Western front
People line up to receive
She got the power in her hand
To shock you like you won't believe
Saw her in the Amazon
With the voltage running through her skin
Standing there with nothing on
She gonna teach me how to swim…

All along the Eastern shore
Put your circuits in the sea

This is what the world is for
Making electricity
You can feel it in your mind
You can do it all the time
Plug it in, change the world
You are my electric girl.[50]

This epic, now-classic song from the aughts by psychedelic indie rock band MGMT gorgeously describes the body's magnificence as a generator and receiver, which also brings to mind Walt Whitman's iconic poem, "I Sing the Body Electric," in which the poet declares,

> *I sing the body electric,*
> *The armies of those I love engirth me and I engirth them,*
> *They will not let me off till I go with them, respond to them,*
> *And discorrupt them, and charge them full with the charge of the soul.*

From the shudder of love, to the arc of a melody or resonance of a note, to the sonorous stanza of a poem, everything that happens to us is carried forth by our cellular structure, through our atomic memory, and is crystallized within the fascial grid of our bodies. The way that we perceive and tell our stories is not only a cognitive exercise. Narrative accounts, and The Word itself, are transmitted into and through the body, across space and time, conveyed through fascia—the connective tissue that weaves together every muscle, piece of bone, ounce of flesh, and nerve.

Not only is enlivened fascia responsible for transporting electricity throughout the body, but, additionally, it gives our bodies form and balance, and acts as the conduit for emotions that are experienced in the present moment, as well as carrying longer-chain wavelengths of energy

---

[50] From the 2007 song "Electric Feel," by MGMT.

that are formed from the past through our ancestral line which we plug into, draw from, and pull into the future. One might argue that our bodies become ensouled as a bridge between planes of existence, and that the fascial system is evidence of the body's function primarily as the channel for recollection, materialized.

This is why movement, bodywork, somatic therapy, platonic healing touch, and lovemaking offer so much more than simply comfort or calm. Touch is crucial. During pregnancy especially, palpation, massage, caressing, and connected, nurturing, loving sexual expression are a form of direct healing of the past and future via the fascia and the lymphatic system.

In addition to the constant cuddling I am so lucky to have available to me as a mother of many children, and the immensely precious physical relationship I have with my adoring husband, I aim to schedule at least one monthly session with a bodyworker (more frequently, if possible, when I'm pregnant). Touch, and conscious myofascial manipulation, are also a part of my own daily grooming and care rituals—I wake up and stretch the "fuzz" (as integral anatomist Gil Hedley[51] describes the fascia), my oral health routine involves water irrigation and regular manual gum massage, I dry-brush my skin and use a gua sha stone for optimal circulation (and pleasure), and I move my body in a variety of complex ways as much as possible throughout the day.

Most significantly, I know the power of communicating with my baby through palpation. I know it is my role, responsibility, and privilege as a mother to connect with my baby's body, presence, and soul, and I know that I can do this at any time, by simply placing my hands on my abdomen

---

[51] Hedley, Gil. 2009. "Fascia and Stretching: The Fuzz Speech."
https://www.youtube.com/watch?v=_FtSP-tkSug. Hedley's "The Fuzz Speech" has rightfully become a classic call-to-movement, is much beloved by movement therapists and bodyworkers of all stripes, and should be required watching for anyone interested in the amazing human body.

and transposing my consciousness into their field of energy. And you can do the same. The ability to anchor to the essence of the child in our womb is a power and a sensitivity possessed by every mother.

ENERGY IN MOTION

Movement—pure, simple, joyful movement—is an essential devotional practice. I have advanced through each of my pregnancies in various states of physical fitness, with varying daily rhythms and routines, and as a result the experience of occupying my body as a pregnant mother has been vastly different each time.

But the cultural messaging around the physical experience of pregnancy is just as strangely negative and distorted as it vis a vis the process of birth. Just as we automatically preempt the supposed pain of birth, so are we primed to anticipate some degree of physical infirmity leading up to birth as well. We are told that aches and pains, and even gradations of debilitation (including round ligament pain, back pain, and pubic symphysis "disorder") are normal during pregnancy, and that these afflictions are even to be expected. This presupposition that our bodies will eventually fail us during pregnancy (or, for that matter, that degeneration is a normal part of aging) is as embedded in our culture as is the anticipation that birth will hurt.

None of this is true and yet the belief is so thoroughly ingrained via the social engineering of perception that it becomes installed in our subconscious minds, and, as a result, our behaviours and our very cells will rearrange to bring that perception-informed expectation to fruition.

The involuntary calling forth of dilapidation through belief is far more powerful than most people realise, especially given the truth that our bodies are always oriented towards healing and vitality. Just as in birth, the key directive is to simply stop inhibiting our own flourishing, which, unfortunately, we are entrained and encouraged to do from multiple directions.

The naturalization of pain, discomfort, and even enfeeblement during pregnancy is yet another artefact—an implanted relic, and a convention that need not be our reality. The body does not—and cannot ever—fail or betray us. Our bodies will only ever reflect to us the precise truth about the choices we are making and the commitments we are upholding in every action we take (or decline to take).

To be sure, joint, muscle, and nerve pain during pregnancy can certainly be disruptive, and disconcerting. But the discomfort brought by sensation is both purposeful and optional. When we do feel soreness, tenderness, or irritation, this is not a sign of dysfunction at all, but a message: an indication that certain muscles or areas in the body may be requesting attention, rest, or opportunities for more, or better, forms of movement.

Most women are aware at this point that cultural prohibitions against pregnant mothers lifting heavy things are absolute nonsense. That myth has, for the most part, been duly deflated. In fact, lifting heavy objects— whether they be older children, laundry baskets, or weights—is not only unavoidable for most women, but is highly beneficial and vitalizing as we approach birth. Vestiges remain, however, of the message that pregnancy is a form of disability and a source of depletion. Both notions are incorrect.

Human beings thrive on and require constant movement, muscle activation, and challenge, including walking, running, squatting, lifting, stretching, wiggling, and trembling. We flourish when we are engaged in activities that generate core power, and the maintenance of muscle strength around our joints and organs is essential in order to support and protect the internal workings of the body. Movement is pivotal (literally), and there is no age or stage of life at which inertia or stasis are natural, or beneficial. While growing our babies, movement diversity becomes more crucial than ever.

Furthermore, pregnancy is a time of *peak* vitality and physical potency. While it's certainly true that we need adequate and ample rest while nurturing a developing human being, movement itself is energizing. When we commit to spending a significant portion of our day moving in complex, vigorous, and joyful ways, the characteristic exhaustion that so many of us experience—especially during the first and last seasons of pregnancy which can be decidedly challenging—will be far more manageable.

All that said, there is nothing wrong, unvirtuous, or dangerous about choosing *not* to move during pregnancy. Birth works phenomenally well (when it's not being sabotaged) and I resoundingly disagree with the fateful proclamations of many birth and exercise gurus who suggest that being "unfit" during pregnancy has any direct result on poor birth-outcomes, or difficulties during birth, or that sedentariness is a direct contributor to "malpositioned" babies. This is merely more fear-based propaganda. But it must also be acknowledged that declining to move during pregnancy will, almost inevitably, result in discomfort. Whenever we thwart the body's need for movement, it will respond with a powerful message, requesting a correction.

In my work with thousands of women over the years, I have not observed any distinct correlation between physical fitness and the ease or difficulty (and painfulness, or not) of birth. I do suspect, however, that there *is* a direct (if perhaps difficult to deconstruct) correlation between the mental fortitude and discipline required to harness our intention during birth, and the ability to push the limits of the body in the context of fitness. (A similar kind of discipline is required when we respond to our bodies' indications that a change of habit is necessary for optimal performance.)

It is also undeniably true that mental fortitude and discipline can be harnessed and employed in many different ways. Birth is not really a marathon—it is certainly not a competition. Birth *is* absolutely movement: the continuous movement of the body, the movement of energy, and the movement of Spirit in service to transformation. Birth is everything.

I have spent a couple of my own pregnancies primarily sitting. And I've spent several of my pregnancies moving, walking, dancing, carrying heavy things, and spending a significant amount of time deliberately training at the gym. Sure enough, during my predominantly sedentary pregnancies, I experienced pelvic pain, stiffness, round ligament issues, constipation, haemorrhoids, pelvic lattice problems, and other indications that my body was bereft of care and attention, and crying out for movement and the infusion of energy. I made my choices, and I experienced the consequences of those choices: pain and unpleasantness. Nothing about my situation was surprising, and when I noticed feelings of outrage and betrayal arise, I reminded myself that I was receiving a perfect response to the input I had chosen to provide.

We are all aware that physical fitness influences our overall health, and the health of our bodies is connected to the health of our babies and connected to the totality of our experience of birth. But as with every other form of feedback during pregnancy, from nutrition to spiritual contemplation to emotional equilibrium, the effects and impacts of our habits and behaviour on birth itself are not as clear and predictable as many assume.

Thankfully (but unsurprisingly) all of my births, including those following pregnancies during which I did *not* honour and nurture my body as fully as is required for optimal thriving, have been well within the (vast) spectrum of perfectly normal and straightforward—fitness is not a requirement for birth to function normally. The birth process is its own terrain, a distinctive place, entirely outside of the quotidian.

After the births of each of my babies, however, my experience of recovery and restructuring postpartum has been in perfect alignment with the degree of care, attention, strength, tuning, and toning I have offered my body during pregnancy. And in some cases, this was a potent reckoning.

Yes, being physically fit, lithe, limber, flexible, vital, and energised will ensure a (dramatically) smoother, swifter postpartum renewal. In the end though, the most significant reason to move during pregnancy (I think) is because it feels good. Frequent movement will result in a multitude of peripheral benefits, to be sure, but in general, allowing the justification for any choice to be joy, will garner the greatest rewards.

There is no one correct way to maintain strength, mobility, agility, and suppleness. It's wonderful that there are such a variety of approaches to fitness that continue to be developed, popularized, revisited, or revived, and all modalities have their benefits. My own life has been enriched by many of them. However you most enjoy moving your body is correct, and I want to emphasise above all the importance of giving ourselves the gift of daily movement. Movement itself is really what matters most.

At this stage in my life, I have enough self-knowledge to feel confident in my own personal movement observances, which involve a combination of various rituals and routines including daily Pilates, weight-lifting a few times a week, bicycling for pleasure and transportation, and as much fun as possible playing pickle-ball and swimming whenever I can. The particulars of what one happens to do for exercise are not nearly as important as what I think of as the core principle of simply cultivating joy in kinesis. As I have mentioned, there are no precise, categorical movement protocols or programs that I would specifically endorse during pregnancy or at any other time (there are an infinitude of valid methodologies to choose from), but I do recommend the following two activities without reservation:

First, I encourage every pregnant mother (and every person at whatever life-stage) to take a walk outside every day. This is such a simple pleasure, and endlessly sustaining and life-affirming in every way. I try to walk each morning, with the only goal being to situate myself on earth, while observing and absorbing the vibratory frequency of the trees and animals and people around me, sometimes watching my dogs and my older children discharge their boundless energy if they have joined me too and dwelling in my body as I move.

The second mostly-non-negotiable devotional practice that I enjoy with a sense of ease, and which I also highly recommend, is dance. I usually begin my daily dance sessions on the floor, lying on my back or on my side, using the floor as a cradle, while in a sense moving through the stages of development an infant undergoes over the course of their first year, in the space of an hour or so. In this way I offer myself a kind of daily rebirth through energy in motion.

With arms and legs exploring the space above me, I eventually roll over onto my hands and knees, circling my pelvis, negotiating the space that my body takes up in a totally intuitive way. At times, the primeval, animal potency of this kind of action brings up intense feeling, especially movements that open the pelvis, and I notice too that when I allow myself to engage in this kind of exploration in an environment of total privacy and sanctity, I instinctively tremor in a way that initiates a trauma-release formation, and this too is very powerful.

Often, I include my kids in a daily dance party if they're around, but it's also precious to do this alone. Neither is premeditated, and I allow the context to unfold as the day presents.

INSPIRATION

I have to confess that, until recently, I had always found the concept of "breathwork" somewhat contrived…or rather, perhaps intimidating and mysterious (and anything that I'm initially intimidated by, my challenger-persona likes to condescendingly diminish). I don't feel this way anymore, mostly because when I was in the throes of excruciating pain during the second trimester of my pregnancy with Helio, breathing deeply (diaphragmatic or belly breathing) and breathing in a methodical, structured way, which involved holding my breath after both an inhale and exhale (a technique which I later learned has been termed "box-breathing") automatically and intuitively became my mainstay, and a matter of survival when I felt like I was drowning.[52]

I learned instinctively and by necessity, to breathe correctly, and I immediately felt a throughline and sense of connection in this experience (obvious, maybe for those more enlightened than I) between pain, surrender, love, and the first act of inspiration that our children make which brings them into embodiment at the moment of birth.

It may seem surprising—I suppose it is to me—that it's taken me so long to "get" the significance of the breath in this way, especially because I had done so much work in yoga and meditation. But that was certainly part of my revelation: I saw that throughout my life I had been *avoiding* the breath, holding my breath, shuddering to think, hyperventilating, catching my breath. Given my own traumatic entry into the world (during which I was taken from my mother's womb, umbilical cord cut before I had even fully emerged into a room wracked with conflict, anxiety, and tension, prior to being carried by a stranger to an incubator in another ward of the hospital) it makes perfect sense that full inspiration would feel deeply unsettling.

While in a sea of pain for so many weeks as my body healed from the kidney issues I experienced that second trimester, I did feel like I was dying, or that I wanted to die. Learning how to breathe as an access point to transposing my awareness to a different interval was the only way I could rescue myself and survive the intensity of sensation that was truly a foreign landscape. This, too, was a rebirth, and I emerged with a new way of

---

[52] To access and download my audio meditation "The Breath," please visit my website, www.yolandenorris-clark.com.

experiencing the breath, which was suddenly available to me as a luminous coherent lifeline during subsequent moments of crisis, and I have since used conscious breathing with a completely different sense of confidence, appreciation, and understanding.

I have also increasingly engaged in breathwork as a swift passageway to realming, and I now turn to the breath very deliberately as a way of falling asleep if my thoughts are scattered, and of achieving that state "akin to sleep" which Neville Goddard identifies as the humus—the fertile soil—of manifestation. Similarly, I use intentional forms of breathing consciously throughout the day as a direct and immediate entry-point to calm, if I'm feeling activated at any point.

Through the baptism of birth itself, I learned that channelling my energy through the breath is the simplest, most accessible, and most direct livewire to God, to my baby, to my Guide-Self, and to discharging pain and welcoming pleasure. The breath is both anchor and touchstone—the first and last measure of life.

EARTHING

Early morning.

The earth is still, and everywhere
    around me
    the living world thrums
    with persistent vitality.

Birdsong.

Wind rustling through the branches
    of the Madrona tree.

A brilliant blue Urraca alights

on a limb above
cocking its head
in acknowledgement.

The sun moves closer, spilling
a lustrous beam across my body,
and I receive.

This is a way of knowing.

A being of the earth,
like the plants, like
the animals, I belong
here.

As with the intimacy and nearness of our own breath, nature is our innate medicine and teacher. Nature is never absent. Bathing ourselves in the living world is the most potent form of prenatal care available. Every element of the natural world is replicated in our bodies' chemical structure and biological operations, and the rhythm of our anatomy is modulated and calibrated by the motions and magnetism of the unfettered wild.

Just as the labyrinthine mechanism of our physiology remains indecipherable, so too persists the unfathomable mystery of how nature achieves its perfect symmetry and balance. The impetus of individual cells to produce bark, pistil and stamen, iridescent feather, jewel-like insect, will always be beyond our grasp. With lofty confidence we name the world—xylem, phloem, nucleus and organelle—and we even name the patterns in the sky, in hopes of divining the answer to the question of the shape of the earth, but no one knows anything, except through the acute clairsentience of embodiment.

Despite our charmingly remedial "scientific" attempts to eviscerate and anatomize the mechanisms of nature—from dissections of the smallest life-forms to the loftiest quantum calculations made in hopes of demystifying the numinousness of "space"—we know precious little of our home, except via the truth-telling interface of the body. In many ways, it is symptomatic of our alienation from the earth that contemporary humans have felt the need to formalize the concept of "earthing" or "grounding"—a "technique" that involves standing or walking barefoot on the earth, or lying directly on the ground—in order to allow our bodies (electric, water-based conductors of energy that we are) to gather up electrons that neutralize the free radicals that lead to lowered inflammation, a reduction of many forms of discomfort and pain, and a balancing of the body's energy systems among other benefits.

But no matter the goofiness of the special names we come up with to describe what has always, until recently, been entirely normal human behaviour, it is a blessing that more mothers, especially, are seeing the value of slowing down, putting our feet in the sand, the sea, and the dirt, and simply allowing ourselves to exist as an intrinsic part of the entirety of nature.

Throughout my pregnancy, I accessed nature as medicine directly and mostly unconsciously, and I brought its cleansing balm into my birth in a multitude of ways. I remember feeling drawn to being outside as often as possible, and I was particularly enthralled by the ocean, the trees, and the sun. This is, I now know, partly why I ended up moving my family to Nicaragua. I felt a compulsion to follow the sun and be in a place where I could feel the sun on my skin as much as possible.

Several times a week as Helio grew inside my womb, I would go to the beach, lie partly in the water with my skin on the sand, just at the margin where the waves meet the shore, and move through a short, entirely spontaneous meditative experience of being held by the earth, gathering in the force of the elements, softening, and melting into the archaic cadence of sheer vibration; a conduit of the cardinal motions of the cosmos.

Solar Activation

We are being deliberately convinced to deprive ourselves of the sun, through weather manipulation and propaganda. Everyone alive right now has been bombarded with programming telling us that the sun is dangerous, that it's unhealthy, that there are holes in the ozone layer, that the sun causes melanoma, etc. The widespread heliophobia inspired by cancer and climate-change evangelism is, in my view, literal insanity.

State campaigns that convince people to smear toxic creams all over our skin verge on criminality, and yet we consent, denying the lived, embodied, material reality of our senses, and our extra-sensory perception. Human beings need the sun not only to be in a state of optimal health, wholeness, and happiness, but also simply to survive.

I have never cowered from the sun, and yet I came to a deeper realisation, during my pregnancy with Helio, of the sun's necessity for our spiritual and physical purification. Pregnant mothers, above all, need the sun on our bellies and on as much surface area of the skin at all stages of gestation.

I now actively seek out the sun, at all times. I want as much exposure as I can have, and I always ask for more. I don't particularly enjoy the sensation of my skin burning, and while this still happens occasionally if I'm outside under the blazing sun all day, I know that my skin will recover easily, and that temporary discomfort is the greatest risk. In general, the more I have deliberately and carefully sought out the sun's rays, the less prone to burns my very fair skin seems to be, overall. I think this is also due, in part at least, to cultivating a sense of spiritual devotion to the sun, which I know to be a conveyance and expression of God's beneficence.

In order that nothing should come between the sun and myself, I have never used sunscreen, I don't wear sunglasses, and I intend to retain my twenty-twenty vision for the rest of my life. I also avoid artificial light, especially light-emitting diodes or LEDs, which have become increasingly prevalent, and which (unlike the sun) are disruptive to our hormonal and circadian rhythms.[53]

We are first and foremost solar beings. Our skin is a solar panel, and we are specifically and directly activated by the sun. Stimulating the solar plexus, the pineal gland, and every organ through the medicinal qualities of direct sunlight is essential. Allowing the sun to shine on our gut, as well as our eyes, third eye, and crown, offers particular animation and enlightenment to all the ways in which we see, intuit, and know.

As much as any plant, humans wither without sunlight. We all know this fundamentally, and this is also why devices like infrared saunas, light therapy bulbs, etc. have become so popular though these will forever remain inferior to the unrivalled resplendency of the sun's therapeutic power. We require nutritive light to thrive, and yet there is no substitute for sunlight that comes remotely close to being as life-giving as the sun itself. The sun is so much more than vitamin D or positive energy. The sun is direct inspiration—as important to life as water and the breath.

Over the course of my own life, I have repeatedly encountered the idea that the moon is a symbol of femininity, and that women align with the moon, moonlight, or moon energy. But as I have allowed myself to tune into my body, and to revel more and more in the sun, I have found myself increasingly disinterested in exposing myself to the lambent glow of the moon, or even in staying awake after the sunset.[54] Night is for rest, renewal, and dreamtime realming.

---

[53] My home is lit only using old-fashioned incandescent tungsten-filament light bulbs and beeswax candles, but I also don't get too worked up about encountering artificial light from time to time.

[54] Grey, Alicen. 2021. "The Moon Is Not What We've Been Told." *Substack*, March 26, 2021. https://alicengrey.substack.com/p/fake-moon. I have been interested to note that my own newfound sensitivity to the moon has been reflected in others' perceptions as

In several mythological traditions, the light of the moon is seen as an aggravating factor for mental issues—hence the term *lunatic*, which comes from the Latin *lunaticos* which means "moonsick," but also relates to the French *lunatique* which literally means "insane." In Old English, the less romantic term was *moensoc*—which means, again, "moonsick." I don't share this to deter you if you love the moon. If you feel energized by moonlight, that's wonderful. But I increasingly recognize our human beingness as heliocentric in the most profoundly real and relevant way.

I also acknowledge that the sun shines less brightly and less frequently than it has in the past, and I do think there are nefarious forces at play, attempting to dilute our capacity to receive our due from the sun's rays.[55] This is, of course, in no way a "conspiracy theory," but a very well documented conspiracy fact. We strengthen our bodies and minds via the sun's energy, and this is precisely why geomanipulation is so prevalent and often so effective.

I am immensely grateful for those who focus their activism on bringing awareness to geoengineering, but this is not my wheelhouse, and I cannot and will not expend my energy on that particular battle. I also know that by enrobing myself in a forcefield of energetic protection, embracing the sun fully when it does beam freely and completely, and reminding myself

---

well. Various lunar theories abound, from Eric Dubay's belief that the moon is a plasma-based entity that emits a damp, septic, and even putrefying or necrotic light, to the description my friend Alicen Grey—writer and musician extraordinaire—has offered, with characteristic insouciant profundity, that the moon is a "fake ass bitch." Grey writes extensively on spirituality, art, feminism, realming, psychic phenomenon, the occult, and the fake moon.

[55] Elana Freeland's work in this area is especially enlightening, but there have also been articles published by the establishment media in recent years which have very clearly delineated plans to "dim" the sun under the pretext of whatever environmental crisis or catastrophe is being invoked. This is all part of the law of disclosure, which states that these kinds of expressions of evil must be consented to, at the very least by omission, and so they must first be confessed.

that nature will always prevail no matter the would-be controllers' hostile intentions, I and my children will always be as safe as we can possibly be.

While pregnant with Helio I took as many opportunities as I could to luxuriate in the sun, and I found myself following an instinctive procedure that involved, ideally, reclining and relaxing in the sun, but also taking moments to receive the sun's energy while standing as well, if necessary. Regardless of where I happened to be when the sun would start to beam, I would become inspired to simply stand there, or lie down (sometimes, if necessary, on the tarmac of parking lots, to my older children's profound embarrassment), and allow the sun's rays to touch my skin—especially my pregnant belly.

Even now, I do this daily, whenever possible: As I lie, or stand there, focusing on the feeling of penetrating warmth, I turn my head up to the glow, and (with my eyes closed) I consciously take in the sun's reparative energy, letting it radiate into my head and into my eyes through my closed eyelids. This has an almost immediate effect of both grounding me into my body while also transporting me elsewhere, in a sense, and this simple process feels like a revelation: so effortless, so totally accessible to all of us, and so profound. Even just a few minutes in this state was something that allows me to collect myself, to retrieve myself, to heal myself, and to just *be,* a process which I now know prepared me so well for a pleasurable and easy birth.

When we surrender to the energy of the sun, we are actually practising what it is to be in the state of the wish fulfilled.[56] We are practising what it is to actively fuel ourselves, to be the engine of our own power and desire, and on the most primal, elemental level, we are choosing abundance.

---

[56] Neville Goddard's all-encompassing key to manifestation.

Yolande Norris-Clark

BENEDICTION

Everything that is real to us and in us—all materiality and experience—is animated through consciousness and imagination, via language. We can never really be human beyond language or without language, and yet it is precisely those regions outside of language that hold the energy of our most authentic being—our soul-being—through birth, sleep, orgasm, and death. And yet, The Word consolidates, disseminates, and diffuses, functioning as an extra-material imaginal representation of the energy field. Speech is both solve and coagula. Articulation is alchemy.

Incantation, benediction, affirmation, and prayer are all immeasurably important instruments to which I repeatedly turn to infuse my awareness with the consciousness of being that I wish to cultivate. The invocation of power through the word is a way of remembering my Guide-Self, of reifying my agency, and of surrendering to that which I am: a mother who knows her child, a woman who knows her body, and a person who is in alignment with the divine perfection of the process of life.

The sign and signification of the word is as much a facet of its rhythm and musicality as its etymological or definitive meaning. Breath, music, and language exist on the same continuum. I learned to speak and read at the same time that I learned to play the piano (according to my mother, I was improvising at the keyboard as soon as I was able to toddle over to it, and I had a brief early career as a classical pianist[57]), and I write with as much a focus on the mellifluousness of the phrase as I do its definition (hopefully not to my detriment). Both writing and speaking words are forms of breath-work and song, and every piece of writing I have ever created—including

---

[57] My career as a musician was not particularly long or illustrious, but, as a child, I won several regional piano composition competitions, and placed second in a number of classical performance festivals, before quitting after having somewhat miraculously achieved my grade 9 Toronto Royal Conservatory of Music designation, despite never having learned to read music. I love the piano, but I'm still somewhat traumatized by that period of my life.

this book—has been edited and shaped through the performance of it as spoken word.

We narrate ourselves and our dream of life into existence, and this is true for the vision we have of our births as well. My daily writing practice includes journalling, creative artistic expression, political documentation, speaking my invocations aloud, and reciting prayers in order to reconsolidate my self and reinforce the vision I have of whatever it is that I am bringing into fruition in my life. These are all non-negotiable components of my daily ritual.

I have a little notebook in which I have collected various affirmations, poems, and sayings, and each morning I read through these aloud (and add to them when the impulse arises), with an attitude of reverence.[58] What I have noticed occurring over the years is that the repetition of these contemplative phrases often begin to develop into "earworms" that echo in my head throughout the day.

While I was pregnant with Helio, especially as I approached the veil, I remember intoning in my head—while walking, while swimming, and sometimes when I felt annoyance or irritation rise, *How can this be so perfect?* It's a funny one—both a question and an answer, and also a kind of placation, but somehow the quirkiness of the phrase worked for me, and was a comfort. I also often find myself turning to the mantras *This is moving through me,* and the simple, and always perfectly appropriate, *Thank you, God.*

There is nothing special or complicated about this. Yet I cannot overstate the power of the word channelled through the body, spoken aloud, and therefore made flesh.

---

[58] The audio recording of my Benediction meditation is available on my website.

INTEGRATION QUESTIONS

1. When you imagine yourself in a state of grace, peace, and ease, in connection with nature, what do you know to be true about your essential Self?

2. What are the messages you receive from your baby when you're in this state?

3. What commitment (of time, energy, intention) can you make to yourself, starting now and through the duration of your pregnancy or pre-conception, to enter into this realm of connectedness?

CHAPTER TEN

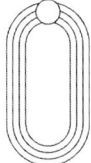

TRANSFIGURATION

SIMPLY BIRTH

Birth is simple. Birth is sacred. Birth is the wild unknown.

Mundane and extraordinary, giving birth to a child is as safe as any other plunge into the void of liminal space…and there is nothing else like it.

Liberated birth is the rewilding of the body, heart, and soul. It is the clearest mirror of our internal condition, and the most exquisite biofeedback system.

Birth is the holographic imprint of our essential being.

To reclaim your power to simply give birth is to remember your primeval origins, and to reacquaint yourself with your true, instinctive, divinely-appointed potency.

Spontaneous, undisturbed birth is the easiest thing on earth. It is utterly commonplace, and elementary. It's like falling off a log.

And there is no odyssey more sacred.

PORTAL

Freebirth is the path into and through the wilderness—an adventure that I, and increasing numbers of women, choose willingly, and eagerly. For me, electing to give birth outside of institutional influence, as far away as possible from medical technology, health professionals, midwives, obstetricians, and false authorities of every category, offers the greatest guarantee of sanctity, sanity, and safety. (Also, there are no guarantees at all. The very idea of "safety" is subjective and illusory.)

It just so happens that embodied, ecstatic transcendence and orgasmic bliss are facilitated by the very same contextual features that optimize both mother and baby's instinctive orientation towards survival and thriving. Darkness, silence, the familiarity of home, the absence of scrutiny, all provide the quintessential conditions for ease, euphoria, and security.

HOW BIRTH WORKS

In the absence of sabotage, interruption, destruction, observation, surveillance, humiliation, mutilation, violation, and rape, birth usually works without a hitch.

At the perfect time (generally between thirty-five and forty-five weeks' gestation) mother and baby begin to radiate, saturating each other with the ideal measure of intoxicating spirits, and the birth-dance begins its crescendo. Sometimes, the bag of waters[59] opens with a trickle or a flash flood many days before she even feels a twinge, and in other cases the mother may feel sensations for weeks or months before her baby comes to earth, and her waters might break only as the baby makes their entrance, still en-caul.[60]

---

[59] The amniotic sac, which encases and protects the child and its amniotic water within the mother's womb, is made up of two laminated collagen-based membranes, the interior of which is closest to the baby—the amnion—and the chorion, which is the outer layer.

[60] An "en-caul" birth occurs when the baby is born still shrouded in the amniotic sac. According to lore (primarily European) being born en-caul is a sign of good luck, confers upon the child the power to ward off evil spirits, and offers them protection against

When no one is sticking their fingers in the mother's yoni, mocking or verbally assaulting her, asking her inane and irrelevant questions, shining artificial light into her eyes and orifices, manhandling her, or tethering her to beeping machines, she and her baby float and flow together through the ether.

The mother's uterus gathers into itself, knitting its fibrous tissues into a wall of muscle, condensing and retracting—*accelerando, ritardando*—as the baby shifts and twists, pressing onward. Over the space of hours, or days, according to the rhythmic thrum of heartbeat, breath, autonomic pulsation, and in alignment with divine timing, the child, propelled by the formidable, insistent power of the womb, begins to spiral to the surface.

Emergence itself can be long and languid, or swift and propulsive. Occasionally, newly born babies will take a breath immediately, and exclaim their arrival with a cry, but more often than not they hover between worlds, not-yet-breathing but alive, poised, and ready to claim inspiration as they are beheld by their one and only mother in that exquisite first moment of witnessing.

Occasionally, as devastating as it is, for reasons that can never be known, a baby will be born still, or with organs that have developed in a way that precludes their compatibility with life on earth. Not every child is destined for this world, and no amount of technology, interventions, or preemptive measures can predict or prevent this heartbreak.

But for the most part, when we give birth in a space of sanctuary, away from the butchers and the saboteurs, the meddlers and the peddlers, and the cult priests of the church of obstetrics and their handmaidens, birth is

---

drowning at sea. My third child was born in the caul, and my intention was to keep the shrivelled membrane as a relic, in keeping with tradition, but unfortunately, I turned my back at the wrong moment, and our faithful dog at the time gobbled it up, with relish. I was quite upset.

remarkably straightforward and dependable, and generally unfolds in splendour.

Life wants to be lived. Babies want to be born. And we are made to flourish by the transformation.

LIMITATIONS OF THE HORMONAL BLUEPRINT

Over the past twenty years, the idea of the "hormonal blueprint"[61] has worked its way into the zeitgeist. Many birthworkers use the schema of hormonal changes and activations to explain the nature of the birth experience, and to attempt to illustrate the often-shocking alteration of reality that birth is designed to produce.

For some women, a description of the hormonal blueprint can be an important bridge between theory and perception, especially for those who are new to the idea of spontaneous birth, and who are coming into their awareness from an existing medical perspective. But an overemphasis on the hormonal "matrix" can also reinforce medical abstraction and obscurantism.

Despite advancements in technology, birth remains a total mystery, especially to researchers who approach the topic from a clinical standpoint. Most of us have a baseline understanding that what underlies the physiology of birth is the excretion of one hormone that then triggers another and so on. But what most people do not recognize or have the capacity to synthesize, is that the potency, quality, modulation, and appropriateness of the elixir that is concocted by the brain and body, which then floods the system, occurs in coherence with our thoughts and emotions, which transpire largely in response to nervous system stimulants that are given by our external and internal environment.

---

[61] Popularized and described in great detail by Dr. Sarah Buckley in various articles and in her book *Gentle Birth, Gentle Mothering.*

This, in turn, is what builds the organic, continuous alchemical feedback loop that allows birth to proceed in its dependable—yet always variable—cadence. Throughout birth, the crucial factor—the fulcrum—is the power of our minds, and (as always) we have far more agency in that regard than most of us recognize, although the catalytic olio of chemical compounds that we and our babies are bathed in as birth proceeds is undeniably important.

Oxytocin, known as the hormone of love and attachment, is identified as being primarily responsible for the rhythmic, pulsing expansions of the uterus. Prolactin (the hormone of nurturing) is tied to milk production. Estrogen, cortisol, and (of course) chemicals like DMT all play important roles in supporting the incredibly intricate sequential patterning of birth. The catecholamine hormones (foremost of which are adrenaline and epinephrine) provoke the fight or flight response, and these are designed to spike before a mother's baby emerges, giving her a burst of energy.

Furthermore, if a birthing woman is subjected to undue fear or pressure in the earlier stages of her birth process, the overflow of catecholamines will purposefully slow or stop her birth altogether, giving her an opportunity to find safety (which is why so many hospital births "fail to progress"). When a mother is being harassed and agitated, and if her nervous system is being constantly enervated in any way, she will be far more likely to experience birth as intense, painful, and highly stressful.

There is no "failure to progress." There is only ever a failure on the part of well-meaning but ignorant birth professionals and bystanders to honour birthing women and support the birth process appropriately. I emphasise the following in every teaching I've ever done on birth, and it bears repeating here: when the birth process seemingly lulls, this is *not* your body in a state of dysfunction. It is quite the opposite. This is your body's profound intelligence letting you know that you and your baby are in danger. This is, in fact, birth working perfectly. Birth *works*, and our bodies are always telling us the truth about the choices we have made and our present environment, whether our external environment or our internal environment (and there is an endless interplay, communication, and mirroring between the two).

Above all, birth is an alchemical and spiritual transformation. Within the scientific community, however, birth is described as an experience of psychophysiological stress, and it is from this fundamental presupposition (that birth is an intrinsically stressful experience) that the clinical and institutional study of birth, as well as the relationship between the birth process and what is now widely understood as "the hormonal blueprint," is undertaken. To define birth primarily as a form of "stress" is a terrible reduction. More than anything, birth is an experience of infinite paradox: expansion, interiority, immanent transcendence.

The word *stress* is a shortening of the term *distress,* and derives from the Old French, *estrece* which means "narrowness" and "oppression." When we can contextualize the assumption that birth is inherently "stressful" and oppressive as having come into being within an environment of normalized surveillance, violation, and abuse (which defines the institutional obstetric model), and when we compare this with the kind of birth that is possible *outside* of that industrial setting, the negative premise that birth is naturally or primarily "stressful" falls apart.

It is impossible to even remotely approximate an accurate measure or calculation of which specific hormones are doing what (and at what point) during birth. Moreover, fixing our lens on hormones too narrowly can distract us from the totality of it all, and pull our focus away from the spiritual fullness of the experience. The human being cannot *ever* function in isolation from the infinitely variable inputs of our environment, or the emotional landscape of what is occurring. If a woman is being tested, observed, scrutinized, or studied during birth, that alone will dramatically alter her physiological and biochemical responses.

In truth, no one really understands why birth works the way that it does, and the attempt to distill and analyze isolated chemical compounds in a birthing woman's body represents the least enlightening, significant, or rational method of acquiring wisdom or insight on the topic. Necessarily, if a woman's blood hormone levels are being measured or monitored, her birth experience is being modified in ways that will automatically preclude the quantum sum and magnitude of the process. Undisturbed birth, ipso facto, cannot be studied.

This is only one of the many reasons why I feel so ambivalent about the increasing research being done within the realm of "science" to deconstruct and analyze the brain's chemical composition. I am not convinced by any means that the wisest or most useful avenue for better understanding ourselves or our place in the world (or health and healing) lies within the fractionalization of constituent parts of the body.

What the hormonal blueprint and its attendant theories *do* tell us is that everything about sex, birth, life, and mothering is driven by instinct. This instinct derives not only from the interplay of hormones, but from the divine matrix of all life, and above all, from our relationship with our babies, ourselves, our environment, our spiritual condition, and from the vibratory frequency of the people around us. Our hormones are not the chief animating force. Instead, our hormones are inseparable and indissoluble from the entire psycho-spiritual ecosystem that we create from within our consciousness in response to the internal and external terrain.

Even if science were somehow unerringly correct, unprejudiced, or honest (which, in the vast majority of cases, it is not), the ephemeral and ineffable is so much truer and more compelling, in my view. It's not that I am proposing that we should discard the hormonal blueprint concept altogether, or at all. It can be a useful frame. But to overly focus on the isolation of various chemical components is, to me, a reductive approach to an experience that is far more dependent on the relational nuances between a mother and baby's subtle bodies, and a mother's internal communication with her baby and God, than anything else.

DISSOCIATION, EMBODIMENT, AND TRANSCENDENCE

Birth is engineered, hormonally and spiritually, to create an altered state of consciousness from within, through the delicate mechanism of our body/mind/psyche. The biological and psycho-spiritual blueprint of the birth process is calibrated to facilitate a form of realming—a voyaging through the multiverse of consciousness—that is pure transcendent immanence.[62] Based on my own experiences in birth, and observations from years of witnessing homebirths with a very low level of disturbance and sabotage, this immaculate transcendence is best described as ecstasy *through* embodiment.

This deeply internal (yet also profoundly integrated) incarnate state of alteration is the antithesis of dissociation. Rather than the numb escape that comes from splitting the self from the body, detaching, and untethering our consciousness from the extant situation—which we automatically do during instances of severe trauma when our sense of survival is being threatened—the transcendence of undisturbed birth is a unique, exquisite experience of deep and abiding attunement, clarity, and presence. This state can only be accessed when we are completely safe.

Again, some form of transcendence—of moving beyond or outside of what are perceived to be the usual limits of normal perception—is always a requirement of birth, and dissociation is certainly a category of transcendence. When a mother is interfered with, watched, penetrated, violated, or distracted during birth, however, she is effectively forbidden from organically moving into an altered state via instantiation and

---

[62] Derived from the Latin immanere, which means "to dwell in," or "to remain," immanence is a term traditionally used in contradistinction to transcendence, referring to the fact or condition of being entirely within something.

incorporation. It then becomes imperative for her psychic survival that she remove herself from the situation somehow. Given that physically getting up to leave is usually not a viable (or comfortable) alternative (although I have known a couple of women who have actually left the hospital or banished their midwives in the midst of birth) the mother is left with only two remaining options.

The first is to reflexively induce dissociation through an out-of-body experience. This is, as the term suggests, a phenomenon by which a person unintentionally abandons corporeality, projects their consciousness outside of their physical being, and finds themselves observing their body from afar—often from the other side of the room, or in my own case when I experienced this exact folding of the material domain while I gave birth to my third child, from the top of the ceiling.

The second option is to force dissociation using pharmacological drugs—either analgesics or direct dissociatives. This allows the woman to leave her body because, at the very least, when the epidural is inserted she will no longer experience the physical sensations of birth. This will offer some form of reprieve from the torture of this kind of captivity and will facilitate her psychic and emotional dissociation as well.

Dissociation using narcotics is, without a doubt, a very clear example of spiritual bypassing, which, under the extreme circumstances of obstetric abuse, makes perfect sense. I too, can imagine being more than eager to take whatever drugs might be on offer, were I to find myself attempting to give birth in confinement. (We also ought not forget that everything a mother ingests or receives into her body is felt and experienced in a similar way by her baby as well.)

Nitrous oxide gas (also known as "laughing gas") is another drug often used during birth. Nitrous oxide is a neurotoxin, and (along with its capacity to numb sensation) it scrambles the brain, offering a kind of relief from both the physical and mental conflict that inevitably occur when mothers give birth in a state of subjugation.

Pitocin,[63] the synthetic ersatz clone of oxytocin (the hormone of attachment and euphoric love), is one of the most widely used obstetric drugs, and the justification for its ubiquity is the so-called "induction" or "augmentation" of the birth process. The prevalence of pitocin is an object lesson in the weaponization of the scientific "understanding" of the hormones of birth.

Whenever a mother is seen to have "failed" to expel her baby within the appointed, mandated timeline (usually prior to forty-two weeks, though the arbitrary schedules differ across various jurisdictions), a mother will be offered (and then vigorously pressured into accepting) the introduction of Pitocin into her body via intravenous drip.

Pitocin magnifies the intensity of birth sensations to a degree that, for most women, is unbearable, and exponentially increases the likelihood that she will ask for, or accept, chemical desensitization. The use of Pitocin also brings with it an increased risk of fetal distress, uterine rupture, and the disruption of the mother's own internal elemental balance, which has profound implications for emotional regulation and mothering. Whatever the particular drug employed, the pharmaceutical path to transcendence via dissociation is actively encouraged by the system, in part because drugging women makes us less "difficult," and more compliant. But the use of drugs is also a core component of the occult ritual of obstetric traumatization.

My personal theory is that any exogenous chemical that reduces sensation, perception, or cognition, or which provokes any degree of paralysis in mind or body, can be a canalizing agent, allowing the infiltration and subsequent siphoning of dark energy. In a sense, this is exactly what is

---

[63] Pitocin is also known as Syntocinon, a portmanteau of "synthetic" and "oxytocin."

occurring when we elect to enter a state of dissociative transcendence using drugs as a form of self-protection. When pain, grief, and trauma are chemically suppressed, they do not disappear, or dissipate. That energy is simply converted, and reconstructed into a different kind of combustible—one that potentiates (even demands) a release at some point.

This release, like every other aspect of birth in bondage (and every kind of spiritual thievery), is engineered through the mining of our sentience. Just as babies are so often forcibly extracted from their mothers' vaginas, so too is trauma—in the form of stifled, unprocessed emotion—extracted from mother and baby in the form of pain and agony. This pain and agony is then consumed in an energetic feeding frenzy by the priests of the cult of obstetrics—institutional personnel—who gorge themselves on the suffering they have manufactured, while calling it policy, protocol, professional standards, or lifesaving.

Through two decades of birthwork, I have come to recognize that the collaborationism of those who repeatedly abuse birthing women and babies is an example of a vampiric, cannibalistic addiction to a kind of power that can only be fed by enacting the sexualized humiliation rites and rituals that the medicalization of birth has now perfected for this purpose. This is how doctors, nurses, and midwives can continue to return to their operating rooms to take up their syringes and their forceps, and to perpetrate obstetric rape, shielded by an endless chain of plausible deniability.

It's not just attachment to a paycheque that allows medical staff to shut down their capacity to feel compassion, and it's not only institutional brainwashing. It is also the result of a stimulated, driven compulsion to devour the reverberations of trauma, as the primary energy supply demanded by the same addiction to sadistic predatory power, that is on display and writ large in the corruption of governments and corporate organizations, as well as inflicted interpersonally by narcissistic abusers towards their prey.

Childbirth is the introduction to this dynamic for most of us, and it constitutes the intersection of institutional and interpersonal abuse, among so many other symbolic and literal convergences. This form of consumptive predation, especially the disingenuous collusion of the well-meaning drones who hide behind custom and credentialing, automatically re-enacting their own traumas, is emblematic of how true evil functions.

Disorientation during the immediate postpartum is a hallmark of disturbed birth (and often develops into postpartum anxiety and depression, which are primarily symptoms of the dysregulation that results from birth-related trauma). Crystalline, laser clarity of perception is what most women lay claim to, when they have carefully ensured that their births proceed without trespass, intrusion, or tampering. With the emergence of mother and baby together in full lucidity, their new state of being is both consolidated and defined, and they are reunited at last, interdependent still, even as they enact the beginning of their differentiation in the flesh.

The embodied transcendence of birth-in-presence is a closed system—a continuous helix of energy that is both boundaried and congruent with the field of body/mind/psyche. The baby, too, is an integral part of this circuitous, self-propelling feedback loop. When fully occupying her body at birth, the mother is using her own inner resources to fuel her power, and this magnetizes her to her baby in a state of electric connectivity. The infant being born to a fully-embodied woman in a state of spiritual and physical integrity exerts their own agency in concert with their mother, the consciousness of both intertwined but also powerfully distinct, leading each other to the apex of mutual ecstasy.

Yolande Norris-Clark

THERE IS NOTHING TO FIX

Birth is orgasm, yet most women do not feel safe enough to allow themselves to move through the portal to ecstasy.

What must we do to claim it, have it, *be* it? How do we get there?

First, we accept that there is nowhere to go and nothing to attain. There is no strategy. There is no "work." There is nothing to fix or to own. You simply get to choose. There is nothing *to do*.

In fact, the very notion of arriving at a destination or an achievement in birth is antithetical to the entire thrust and ethos of what I am attempting to impart.

If and when, as the waves begin, you find yourself experiencing anxiety, recurring disorganized fear, pain, or the feeling of panic, intensity, or suffering, this is the proof of your commitment to have that be your experience. And there is nothing wrong with that commitment.

But the excruciating truth of this life, and the gold of what I'm offering, is that the evidence of your choosing any given state of being—at any time, including birth—is the inhabiting or occupation of that state of being.

The evidence of your selection is the very fact itself of your experience. It's all you. There is no existence other than that of your choosing.

There is no other consciousness that can be perceived or experienced by you outside of that perception and experience, over which you have ultimate dominion, as granted by God.

The fractal choreography of birth will give you an opportunity like no other, to work with the fragmentation of your consciousness, to practice the intimacy and discipline of surrender, and to choose infinite presence, if you so desire.

PORTAL

We all have an enduringly accessible edition of ourselves—a part of ourselves that is always operating with all of her spiritual centres open and her consciousness in full alignment with the divine. You can lovingly summon her at any time. You can don the mantle of her aura in any moment, and be her. She is you, after all.

And she knows how to surrender.

THE DISCIPLINE OF SURRENDER

Surrender is one of the most essential components to the art of choosing. Surrender is not submission, or capitulation, or collapse, and yet it is also the antithesis of control. It's not floppy, or passive, or docile, or listless. Rather, surrender is an active, deliberate choice. Surrender must be undertaken with pure intent and unequivocal discipline, over and over and over again.

Surrender *is* a discipline, and may be the primary discipline required for the realization of any kind of achievement, or actualization. It is through the discipline of surrender, that we access and enact authentic power.

Cultivating the discipline of surrender arises from one's spiritual condition. This is not a judgement, nor a form of moralization, but rather an observation of reality. Learning to surrender—or rather, unlearning our resistance to it—is, in many ways, the foremost tool for making manifest any desire or dream. But surrender is also a kind of epiphany—a facet of enlightenment, even. It is a form of edification, and by surrendering fully to what we choose and what is true (which, though not ever really in conflict, may not always be perfectly parallel either—syncopated, in a way) we edify ourselves in faith.

To surrender is to release is to fragment—and the fragmentation is, I think, what we most fear. The fragmentation of self (ego), and the necessary abandonment of attachment to the conception of ourselves as identity, personality, and surface distinctions, is also what it is to be fully embodied.

Many of us are fundamentally adhered to the notion of embodiment-as-armouring, and we cling to an understanding of who we are as contained entities. Yet orgasm during sexual union, and the orgasmic eruption of emergence as we birth ourselves into being, both mother and child—and (perhaps surprisingly) also via the process of healing—are all similarly available to us most fully and integrally as experiences of simultaneous disintegration and apotheosis.

These forms of consolidation through dissolution initiate a shearing away of the self from the body, and an abstraction of our quintessence into The Everything. In the moment of undoing, we are briefly scattered—becoming breath, liquid, pure sound, light, essence—prior to the reconsolidation. In a sense, these are the ways in which we practice how to die, and yet here you are, still, for now. Immanent transcendence.

RIDING THE WAVE

As each wave rises upon the horizon, I stand, eager to meet it, to catch it at its crest.

Dancing and swaying, eyes closed, taking my consciousness to my third eye, and then connecting my whole self to God and my baby, I transpose my consciousness to my pelvis, tripping out in the pools and eddies of light and sensation, eruptions echoing throughout my being that are *so* gentle, and *so* beautiful, and *so* inevitable, and which I have so assiduously chosen over and over again.

Constant prayer, constant incantation.

Thank you thank you thank you.
Thank you God.
Thank you baby.

PORTAL

e you I love you I love you.
I love you baby.
I love you God.
Thank you.

With every cycle of sensation, I embrace the experience of bliss before the wave actually crashes, choosing powerfully, calmly, tenderly, with the laser focus of my attention on deep, sweet, surrender.

Here, I note that the sensation is…ample; extravagant. Now especially, I move towards the portal of love, surrender, trust, and gratitude, and I reorient my consciousness to the exact place where the sensation is the sharpest and most keen. I expand it, flood it with light, and it becomes a flowering, blossoming helix of resplendence, shattering into eternity.

During the expanse of timelessness between each sensation, I sleep—or rather, I lie back, and access placidness, drifting into the deep open sea.

ETERNAL REPOSE

After Helio's arrival, when I finally looked at the footage of his birth captured by the phone I had set up on a tripod at the end of the room,[64] it was interesting to me to note that I experienced almost no sensations closer together than twenty minutes throughout the entire process. This was a fact that (a) had not occurred to me at the time, let alone been remarkable or relevant and (b) would almost invariably have been pathologized by many birth professionals.

No matter the worldly time-signature of any birth, or whether it seems fast or slow to the mother during the experience, according to deep-reality and

---

[64] The video of Helio's birth is included as a component of my online course, also called "Portal," available at www.yolandenorris-clark.com.

deep-time there is only ever one sensation that we must navigate.[65] Just one, and that's *this* one: the one occurring in this moment that is now.

Know that there is always a break, a period of repose, relief, and respite, always. It might seem very brief—it might be only one second, according to an hourglass—and it might indeed feel like you're drowning and that the crash is relentless. This, like any other aspect of the experience outside of the now-moment, is a story that you are entitled to grasp onto or to dismiss.

You are free to use that precious instance to feel sorry for yourself, or instead, to take your rest and give thanks.

THE SHIMMERING NOW

A fear portal appears. Until this juncture, neither time nor fear has occurred to me, but they ride in together, and here is fear now: slow cold flames licking at the outer periphery of my attention, inviting me to play a different game.

The voice of my inner stealth saboteur whispers, *You've been here for a long time. You're getting tired.*

I immediately banish the delegate of darkness and despair and I choose again, relinquishing attachment, letting go of my urge to assess, diving back into the bliss of surrender. I also notice that my body is slowing down, and I respond with yielding, realizing a rallentando of my breath and my heartbeat.

As I move myself into a theta state, I breathe, saturating my baby with love and oxygen, again drawing my attention up to my third eye and to my

---

[65] I will never forget Gloria Lemay (my beloved midwife, teacher, and mentor) explaining this to me when I was nineteen years old and pregnant with my first baby, though it has taken me twenty-two years to really know this as a birthing mother.

crown to fuse with God, connecting specifically with the phosphenes in my field of vision as a compass; cosmographic landmarks. *You are here. You are still here.* And here is my baby too, swimming with me through the pool of the inner world, a place of knowing, trust, and rapture. We are safe. We have all the space in the time, we have all the time in the universe.

Everything is still. Here, the rest I am gifted is of the deepest tranquility I have ever known—not really sleep at all, but a preternaturally serene repose.

I am awake now.

To my immense surprise, my child is moving through my body.

What an unexpected thing—a birth! Who could have guessed?

I cry out for Lee as the gentle, shocking insistence of
emergence takes place, and the death
of the old
Me as I am
reborn.

Searing lightning
phoenix rising
pleasure beyond
orgasm
splendour
the sonorous quickening
please okay please okay
okay thank you
God

embers

Now   the glistening,
          luminous   body,
      shimmering   eternity

And You.

Your face.

Your infinite eyes.

The phosphorescence of
your perfect
aura.

Awe.

Birth Song

I have always justified the screaming and yelling I have done in all but one of my births (thus far) as full expression; as "letting go"—release—and as an indication of my unabashed embrace of my authentic self (the evidence of embodiment, even). As I mentioned in Chapter Two, I long held a kind of enthrallment for those women who were seemingly "able" to give birth in near-silence, and I wondered if quietude while giving birth might, at least tangentially, be related to modesty culture, or even certain forms of self-repression.

But I have also worked with countless women who have come to me for support in unravelling their trauma from obstetric violence, who have shared stories of having been told to "shut up" while giving birth, or of having nurses or doctors state that their utterances were "bothering" their fellow patients, or that on account of their vocalizing they must therefore be subdued by drugging.

Midwives, too, will often "shush" their clients in a degrading and infantilizing manner.

This particular kind of abuse—on top of the physical and sexualized assault that women routinely endure—is particularly cruel and demeaning. As always, giving birth in an environment in which one is being consistently objectified, humiliated, and treated with far less dignity than a calving heifer, will always lead to a very real and understandable (and literal) form of hysteria—induced by the industrial obstetric apparatus itself.

As my understanding of the psycho-spirituality of birth has evolved, however, my perspective on vocalization in birth has likewise shifted. I have also spent considerable time studying anthropological and historical accounts of birth, and it's fascinating to me that there are several indigenous birth traditions[66] that are known to have held a collective expectation that women give birth either entirely alone, or with few other people present, and that they do so with as minimal vocalization as possible.

The anthropological interpretation of these cultural distinctions in regards to birthing in quietude is always related to conceptualizations of decorum and bravery, but given my own relationship to birth, I think there is so much more to this than researchers who are evidently viewing these "phenomena" through an academic and industrial obstetric lens (clearly devoid of any experience in spontaneous, undisturbed, primal birth themselves), can possibly comprehend.

I now know, as a mother who spent her first eight births shrieking, screaming, yelling, and hollering, and—as I so proudly and publicly

---

[66] Two specific examples that I am presently researching include the women of the Piro Amazonian tribe of Peru, and the !Kung people of northwestern Botswana. Unassisted birth was, until very recently, the norm for both of these geographically disparate people, along with a similar cultural convention of birthing in relative silence.

announced years ago (which I'm delighted to see has become something of a popular slogan since then)—"roaring my babies into the world," none of that was necessary, or helpful, or any more "authentic" or "visceral" than the halcyon birth I had with Helio.

In fact, a subdued, tempered, channelling of energy through modulated vocal toning will almost always be more conducive to the deep, meditative surrender that facilitates orgasmic, euphoric ecstasy and rapture during birth, than howling and wailing, which are forms of resistance in action. The distinction here lies between discharging and expending energy, versus choosing to conduct and transmit one's energy as a means to cultivating ease, pleasure, and power. This is the melting openness of orgasm, which, in my experience, is rarely enabled by bellowing and thrashing about (despite the widespread portrayals of female orgasm as histrionic melodrama).

I must say too, that had anyone had the temerity to propose to me in my early years of mothering that I could have simply chosen to be quiet, and to deploy my energy differently during birth, I would have insisted, quite indignantly, that this suggestion was preposterous. I was convinced at the time that all my raving and berserking had been involuntary and in accordance with pure instinct. This simply isn't true—especially the rationalizing of my energetic and vocal incontinence as somehow reflexive.

But please understand that I say all of this from a deep well of tenderness and love for the woman I was, and for my commitment to the reality that I had chosen. There is absolutely nothing wrong with being loud and dramatically expressive during birth—every woman has the endless right to choose exactly the birth experience for her, and so did I. But as is the case with the craftiest versions of victim-consciousness, the idea that I was simply overwhelmed by the primordial force of birth was only made true by my devotion to it.

PORTAL

The tempestuous ranting and raving I did in each of my early births occurred, in every instance, as a form of resistance to full gratitude, presence, engagement, and feeling, and as the performance of spectacle (which was also partly in response to, and a result of, the self-sabotage of having invited various people into my birth-room, who had no purpose or utility in being there beyond my necessity for finding scapegoats for my theatricality).

During Helio's birth, in contrast, I discovered what it was to allow the sound and vibration of my voice and body to resonate as a source of healing, with what I realise now was truly an instinctive form of intention—no premeditation, no artifice, no force at all, but expressed in a state of receptivity to the coiling and uncoiling of energy throughout my body; consistently yielding, without contrivance or artifice; rhythmic, atonal, yet somehow also lyrical. My birth-song was beautiful (as is every single birthing woman's unique improvisation, always).

ATOMIC CHOICE

We do indeed reap what we sow, and yet there is no one-to-one ratio of cause and effect in the way many of us might assume there to be. That's not how manifestation, choice, "karma," prayer, or faith works. We never have access to the full picture—we are not God, nor gods. We, along with all of God's creation, are points of reflection of the dignity and ultimate perfection that *is* God.

And yet, cause and effect are always in play. You are constructing the "bridge of incidents" which will build your life in both large and small ways, and everything that happens in your external world is also occurring according to the laws of balance in your internal world, and vice versa. There will always be a correction. Like water, truth will always find its level.

As we have discussed, the macro choices that will establish the universe of your birth are crucial. These distinct, unambiguous choice-points will define your support system, where you give birth, and whether or not you birth within the vortex of industrial medicine or under the aegis of the God-given power of your body and intuitive self, but this is only the preliminary framework. This is simply the loam that will nourish your initial germination, from which the cornucopia of atomic choices you will then be offered (in accordance with the laws of the universe you have selected to inhabit) will arise.

During Helio's birth, I crafted a context that allowed me to choose surrender over and over and over again. Other choice-points included elements like my physical carriage, the way I held my face, my posture—arms outstretched, legs open, mouth relaxed, using my body as an instrument, a lightning rod—breathing with the intention of moving energy and *being* energy, which we all are, along with the word spells and incantations I spoke aloud in deliberate conjuration.

I have never felt less self-conscious, and this would not have been possible were I distracted by any bystanders, well-meaning helpers, or even my children and husband, whom I lovingly banished from the room a few times before they got the picture that this was not a party, but a pilgrimage.

I had entered this state of being, this space of full presence without any need for "help," or critique, or armouring, and that, too, was pure choice. As such, there was nothing to tolerate or to withstand. Once the birth began to gather momentum, I chose curiosity, and from that choice I could perceive with all my clairs[67] at once that the bliss portal was right there, in the field before me, and I knew that pain held no interest, no utility, no necessity, no place.

---

[67] Every person possesses God-given clairaudience, clairvoyance, clairsentience and claircognizance, though not every person is aware of these extra-sensory sensitivities, nor will every person choose to nurture or develop them.

PORTAL

Questions formed—or rather, an entity appeared that had the demeanour of a questioner, in the spirit of beneficence:

Can you feel it all?

Can you allow yourself to feel every distinction, isolation, and variation of what is being offered and of what you are?

What if? What if I don't resist?

What if I surrender fully?

Can I? Will I? Will I choose to experience magnification and magnificence? A full expansion? Will I allow myself to open every part of my body *and* my mind and spirit? Can I accept epiphany?

Can I—truly—open myself to knowing that the portals I have access to, in this moment, and in every moment, are infinite?

Can I open the portal of my mouth, my throat, my yoni, and my arms, and every portal to all my endless clefts and fissures, cracks and gaps, caves and chasms? Can I open the portal to all my lives and selves and to every iteration of existence I have ever known?

GIVING UP

You don't ever have to give up.

There is a powerful tendency that many of us have—that we all have, in various contexts and circumstances—to say to ourselves, *Meh. It's already done. I have already made this or that epically incoherent choice, so the plan is wrecked, and I may as well abandon the whole idea. There's no point trying anymore.*

Or, we tell ourselves, *I've tried it all. I made all the "right" choices, but it's probably not going to "work," because I'm always the woman who fails no matter what.*

Giving up is always an option, certainly. But it isn't necessary, and the opportunity to recalibrate, reconsolidate, and correct your course is always available, in every moment, at any point, even after what might feel like failure.

I am an epic self-saboteur, and yet I find myself constantly in the position of reaching an arm over the brink to grab myself by the scruff, and haul myself back up over the escarpment, bruised and tattered…but somehow ever-more determined to prevail, only by the grace of God. Maybe someday I'll stop that particular cycle, but for now, it remains an apparently irresistible pattern. The classic story of near failure to triumph is endlessly exciting, I suppose. And of course, we are always allowed to re-define failure, and to find the ways that our detour ends up being the right path after all.

I have spoken at length about the choice-points I encountered during Helio's birth, but one of the most fundamental of these was choosing to shift my attention from profound annoyance and even anger (my preferred way of initiating self-sabotage) to gratitude. You may remember, from the rendition of my birth-story from Chapter One, that I spent some time during the early days of the protracted multi-day birth after my waters had released, rage-cleaning the garage. This was definitely a form of both slopping about in the muck and channelling the frustration I felt about feeling trapped by my Self—by the familiar role that I had already noticed I was falling into—and of feeling hard-done-by and dissatisfied by my utter commitment to dissatisfaction (yes, it's always circular and self-perpetuating).

My sensations hadn't even really begun yet at that point—just a few undulations here and there—but when I finally decided to go to my room and allow myself to enter the ambiance of birth, I remember sitting on the edge of my bed, water dripping from my yoni, and finally, simply holding myself, loving myself, accepting myself, and gently embracing myself for exactly where I was, ultimately willing to offer myself forgiveness and mercy. I was about to set sail, I hadn't slept in weeks, and in that final plunge into the depths of acceptance, the shift occurred.

I peeled the layers back, and found who I really am, undefended. Gathering myself up, I chose and channelled joy and vibrancy (which we can always do, no matter our degree of exhaustion) and a spark ignited. This was the moment of full activation, and in that instance of potent, disciplined surrender, my sensations began, truly and fully. It was at that crossroads that I accepted and created the authentic world of my birth — a world constructed from the highest wisest version of who I am, and who I was in the midst of crystalizing, consolidating, and becoming.

You have the power to do exactly the same thing. You have the power to draw yourself back up from the verge, to enter whatever consciousness you choose to inhabit, and to summon your truest, bravest, most tender and compassionate self as you meet your baby.

HEAVEN ON EARTH

I feel the soul of my baby distinctly now. He and I are in full communication.

My whole being is suffused with intense adoration and the most resounding affirmation that this is the path of my soul's purpose
Good
True
Beautiful.[68]

---

[68] Plato, student of Socrates, formulated the view that the concept of the "good" was the source and state of being that made the perception of truth available, and that beauty was a way to orient towards the good and true through the inspiration

Yolande Norris-Clark

A soft, warm, leaking sensation arises, and it is so delicious
    so easy to allow.

Tears.

There are tears coming from my eyes
    and oceanic amniotic water coming from my yoni
        and more water from the interior of my body—pee, I
        recognize vaguely—
            and all is exquisite liquefaction.

I moan
and tone,
and speak aloud to my baby
and to God.

My eyes are closed.

I open them now to see
    the room
        warm glow   abstracted
            fractallate.

I love you baby
I love you baby
thank you God
I love you.

---

of desire. I agree, in a sense, though I think beauty, truth, and goodness are primarily accessed through embodiment (which includes the creation of art, the art of the intellect, and sensation).

PORTAL

Intervals splinter before me
        sundial,
                pinwheel,
                        maypole, and   more
                                I am opening   more and
                                      flowering again.

In each   decimal   moment   as the wave   comes
in
closer
        I meet it
        with no defence
                amphibious.

I am breathing underwater
        immersed
                in the love that is
                      openness
                      and gratitude.

Time folds into feeling
love folds into space
my body folds   into the spiral
            of all existence.

I am awash in love
and grace
and bliss
and holiness.

I am dancing the circle serpentine   sinuous   helical fluid.

This is the galactic   infinite.

The heavenly place
of choosing
       choosing
              choosing
                      constantly choosing
                              surrender.

INTEGRATION QUESTIONS

1. Have you ever had the experience of transposing your consciousness outside of your body, allowing access to what feels like a field of awareness that resonates as a sense of connection with all things?

2. If so, what was the context of this experience? What were the conditions?

3. If not, are you open to having such an experience via birth? How do you feel about the possibility of experiencing a full surrender of your Self and ego identification?

CHAPTER ELEVEN

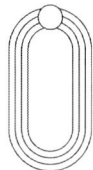

FEAR AND INTUITION

FEAR PROGRAMMING

Wild animals run from the dangers they actually see, and once they have escaped them worry no more. We however are tormented alike by what is past and what is to come. A number of our blessings do us harm, for memory brings back the agony of fear while foresight brings it on prematurely. No one confines his unhappiness to the present. —Seneca

Fear is one of the most significant issues we have to contend with as mothers. In many contexts, fear is normal, natural, and adaptive, but fear can also become warped and twisted into obsession, and this can be dangerous in and of itself.

The fostering of unbalanced, neurotic forms of fear is what has contributed to the creation of our culture of lack and dependency, and its cultivation and encouragement is largely what keeps mothers in the thrall of the perverse, inverted policies and procedures of the industrial obstetric complex. Fear is continuously projected, nurtured, and encouraged.

Fear is mandated, even. In many ways, fear is written into law. Fear is certainly inscribed on the mind and body.

Most of us are born into trauma which is masked as "safety," and throughout our lives that trauma is constantly reinforced as protection and survival. This is what the industrial obstetric paradigm both reiterates and fulfils. The perpetuation of institutional birth, and the allopathic program in general, requires that we be kept in a state of fear, particularly in regards to the purportedly inherent dysfunction of our own bodies.

One primary goals (and a frequent outcome) of the initiation ceremony of obstetric birth is to create a population of individuals who are deeply confused about fear, agency, and power, and for whom this confusion has been so internalized that we then struggle immensely to see the widespread dysregulation of fear as anything but normal. The obstetric mind-control program has succeeded to such an extent that the fear of birth, life, nature, sex, and death has become a cultural identity and a virtue. Courage, truth, and embodiment—the antidotes to fear—are actively disincentivized in this colonized, technocratic, globalist society.

We are discouraged from truly *feeling* fear, from excavating it, or from personalizing, examining, and interrogating it. We are cautioned against becoming intimate with fear, and from investigating which parts of it belong to us, and which parts were imposed on us by false authority or cultural tradition which we then blindly accept, contract into, and naturalize. Querying and exploring our fear is the only path to owning it, so that we can then repudiate and disavow the distortion, and subsequently move forward with courage and power.

All fear is, at its core, the fear of death in some form. This includes, of course, the fear of literal death—the death of our own bodies and the death of our babies. But fear is also a signifier of our aversion to other kinds of death: the death of aspects of ourselves that are no longer effective or suitable for the lives we are building into reality; the death of certain relationships with other people or institutions that no longer serve us; the death of certain beliefs and commitments; the death of our former social standing, of our reputations, of our sense of belonging to a particular culture or clan; and so on.

Fear is also often a disguise for the trepidation we feel when we are on the verge of losing our grasp on our stories of victimhood, or on the various concocted identities we cling to. The fear of discovering how powerful we truly are—and therefore how responsible we are for ourselves—is one of the most significant kinds of fear that we all carry.

At its core, every form of fear stems from our desire to survive, but also to expand, and that tension offers us a chance to know ourselves and to grow in faith. Birth, especially sovereign birth, gives us an incredibly rich opportunity to unravel and make sense of our fear programming.

FEAR, FAITH, AND DEATH

The elephant in the room when it comes to any conversation about birth, but especially the idea that we can choose the way our birth experience unfolds, is always death and loss. This can be a complex topic. The emotional geography of loss is always personal and informed by how we understand faith, choice, and power.

I am no stranger to loss. I was nineteen years old, and fourteen weeks into my first pregnancy when my baby died, and I miscarried. Miscarriage is not the same as stillbirth or the death of a child already born, and yet there is no hierarchy of loss. I had a profound soul-relationship with that being, and during and after the miscarriage I was in despair.

I arrived at faith, through the experience of finally choosing to trust that the outcome was correct, simply because it happened. And it was this devastating introduction to faith that was the permission I needed to surrender to the terrible yet infinitely precious *not-knowing* I was then thrust into, when, only two weeks after I miscarried, I discovered I was pregnant again, and en route to the birth of my first baby.

This episode marked a considerable shift in my relationship to fear, faith, trust, and surrender, but my tendency towards anxiety wasn't alleviated overnight. Rather, each of my subsequent pregnancies has offered new and different insights, and gradually, over twenty years of pregnancy, mothering, birth, and birth-work, I can honestly say that I am now at peace with the inherent uncertainty of life, and deeply anchored by a sense of trust in the outcome of birth, which is supported and informed by knowing that my actions are rooted in choices coherent with my values.

Ultimately, self-sabotage in the form of entertaining recurring, speculative fears or anxiety is always an expression of resistance and inconsistency—a lack of integrity. Any action taken from a state that precludes a sense of peace in, and acceptance of the consequence, will involve distortion, fabrication, and grasping for control.

Contrary to what many people believe, it is not faith that ensures a particular result. Our faith is not a factor in the final outcome. Faith is, instead, the state at which we arrive *through* the process of either triumph or loss. Faith is both the outcome of proving to ourselves that what we believed at one point was impossible was always within our grasp, *and* it is the balm that eases the pain of loss—succour and solace for the one who feels broken, and bereft.

Yes, faith can sometimes seem to come easily when it all works out in the end, but often, we are presented with the choice to be faithful, visited by faith, and sometimes inundated by it most strikingly, when things do *not* unfold according to our perceived wants. Faith is always possible, always on offer, always within our grasp.

We can have anything that we choose, and everything that occurs is a perfect mirror of our inner self. We create our state of being, which determines the outcome of our lives. But this does not mean that we control the content or the details of the outcome, or that we have the option to decide on the specifics of how our manifestations present themselves. We simply do not have access to all of the infinite, minute, fractionated elements of the workings of life, the universe, or God (and thank goodness for that—imagine what a mess things would be if we did).

The process of "successful" reality-creation necessitates that we get over the specificities of the result, while operating from the *feeling* of the desire fulfilled. The goal is to actually be *okay* with what plays out, beforehand, knowing that you have taken responsibility for being honest with yourself regarding the setup and the choice-points that led to the only elements that you actually have access to, and that is the feeling of *being* the woman for whom the energy and the state of the result is natural and assumed.

Assuming this state of being is also what will allow you to be at peace with the outcome as it materializes. I know that ultimately, I will survive (physically, for the duration of my lifeline, but also in a spiritual sense) if my baby dies, because I know that I owned every single choice along the way, and I know that those choices have built the structure of who I am in intrinsic integrity.

If, and when, during your pregnancy or birth, you find yourself experiencing chaotic anxiety, or recurring disorganized fear decoupled from reality, it is the feelings themselves that prove your commitment to experiencing your state of being in this way. Remember: surrender is the antithesis of control. We cannot control life or death, and we cannot choose life or death for anyone except ourselves.

I do, however, believe that we choose our own life and death on a continuous, contractual, primarily subconscious (but sometimes conscious), basis. It's still a mystery, fundamentally, but the passage of life and when and how we come and go is also something that I believe we volunteer for. I have never known of anyone who has died, and who has not on some level, by my observation, contracted into their own death.

My father, who died at the age of sixty-two in 2017, definitely chose his death. At the time, I was seriously annoyed with him for kicking the bucket and proving me wrong after all. But once I calmed down (which took me a couple of years) I could see quite clearly that he had been ready to exit the world in body, in mind, and on a spirit-soul level for quite some time. In the end, he was done, and he chose to check out. He simply couldn't do it anymore, or didn't want to, and the fact that he went out hacking and coughing and kicking and blustering was just his inimitable style.

Even a "freak" car accident, for example, while entirely outside the realm of blame or fault, always involves a series of choices and steps that each of the individuals involved in the calamity make, as the event is assembled into reality. It is the patchwork of choices made by everyone ensnared, even peripherally, in the incident, as random as it may seem, that results in certain people being on the same road, on the same day, at the same fateful moment in time, colliding.

Life is a co-creation. Our choices are always informed by, and being made in response to, the choices of everyone else around us, and yet our agency precludes control. This is an exquisitely heartbreaking dichotomy—this is *the* central paradox of life—that we have the infinite power of choice only insofar as, or to the extent to which, we are able to surrender to the truth that we have no real control at all. The one can only exist fully with the other. This is also both a paradox and, in a way, a promise. (As I see it, this understanding of how connected, and even dependent, these concepts are to one another—that is, the power of manifestation or reality-creation as inseparable from the concurrent power of the eternal unknown—is also the indestructible silk thread of truth that binds together all religions and belief systems.)

Again, I know that God grants us free will—a freedom of will that is nonetheless structured by the laws of this world. But we are not individual gods unto ourselves at all. The only executive power we have is over our own inner world, our responses, and the way that we take action and responsibility over our interior selves and our being. In this way, we do have the power to influence the physical, material context, and our environment, and to impact others, just as our thoughts have an energetic form, structure, and reverberation. But we don't have "control" in the way that most of us conceive control as a form of domination over others and our environment.

Tyranny is only ever a false sense of command. And when we do seek to exert force, and to dominate another—physically, emotionally, psychically, dogmatically, politically, financially, even—the scales of spiritual (if not worldly) justice will always be calibrated correctly.

Even mothers—as powerful as we are—do not have the authority to decide the destiny of another person's life-stream, including that of our children. I do know how devastating and heartbreaking this can be. None of us have the luxury to "manifest" our babies being born alive, or our babies being born with particular features, or the guarantee that our babies will be free from whatever condition or state their own souls have chosen with, or through God, to incarnate into. In the context of birth, motherhood, life, and death, this can be hard to grasp (and hard to swallow) but embracing this concept is one of the keys to freedom from fear.

I have worked with many women over the years who have experienced loss, whether in the form of miscarriage or stillbirth, or the loss of the idea they had of their child appearing with certain assumed abilities. Many of these women have shared with me in confidence that, in some capacity, they knew their baby was not destined for this world, or they knew their child would be different. This is not the case for all mothers, but for some it certainly is. We are all soul-beings that have multiple forms of agreements and contracts with God, and none of us are granted omniscience. That is the sole purview of the divine. But we (especially mothers) are often gifted prescience, visions, visitations, or other forms of God-given extra-sensory perception.

As I described earlier, during Ignatius' birth, I felt, as his body first emerged, his soul untethered, wavering in and out of this realm. I then sensed the clear choice he made to come into his body in those brief moments right after his birth. It was very evident to me that Iggy had to decide to enter his soma—and I know whatever action I might have taken to save him, or persuade him, would, if anything, have been discouraging to his tentative spirit. Had I taken action, however, and had that action changed the outcome, for better or worse, that too would have been correct, and a perfect example of the phenomenon of co-creation.

Initially, I don't think Ignatius was quite sure, at first, if he wanted to be here or not. This is entirely understandable—this world is a complex milieu, though Iggy has adjusted beautifully, and I think he has more than embraced and accepted his divinely ordained (and chosen) place here. Since his birth, Iggy has already lived through several tectonic planetary shifts, many of which inspired our family's move to a new country and culture, before he was even a full year old.

Ignatius is extremely sensitive, considerate, and careful, and even cautious, but also, resilient, brave, and open. Another of his many virtues is that he is extremely (perhaps inordinately) protective of his little brother Helio (who, at this stage, but also according to his character, charges forward into life with joyful abandon). Ignatius' energetic imprint, like that of each of our children, is a perfect measure and reflection of the timbre and frequency of his birth.

FEELING FEAR, BEING BRAVE

As a woman who has lived through many different iterations and degrees of identifying with fear, clutching at fear, and preoccupying myself with fear in the context of birth and motherhood, I can attest to the fact that there is a significant difference between *being* afraid of birth, versus experiencing the *feeling* of fear.

To allow ourselves to simply feel fear and then discharge it and move on, we usually have to first move through *being* afraid. In my case, I had to decide that I would not allow the feelings of fear I had about birth to overshadow my determination to not *be* afraid. *I can feel fear, but I am not afraid.*

This is, in essence, the difference between identifying with fear (I *am* scared of birth) versus noticing the feeling of fear come up, and reminding ourselves that *yes, I experience moments of the fear sensation, and I know exactly how to disavow those feelings.* This is an important distinction, and it refers back to the notion that we evolve into the energy of the belief system that our inner dialogue dictates. The more disciplined and specific we can be with our inner dialogue, the more powerfully we can choose in alignment with our true desires.

The key is to practice consciously disinheriting the ineffective state of being and shifting the focus of your attention. To *be* something is hardened and entrenched. To *feel* something is fluid and transitory.

I may feel fear, but I am not afraid. I am not afraid of birth. I am not afraid of death. Why? Because I know exactly who and what I am. I am right with God. How? Because I've given up on the negotiation. How do I know that to be true? Because before, it wasn't. Because I moved through it, and now this is what I am.

This does not mean that I am—or that I see myself as—impeccable or unerring, or that I'm always brave. Not at all. I screw up constantly, I say and do the wrong things, I let people down, I fail, I thrash and wail, I cower and tremble. But for the most part, I am willing and able to see my flaws and foibles, and I do have a sense of who I am beyond the gambits of my personality, and I trust in God's redemption. I feel fear, from time to time. But I know there is never any reason to *be* afraid.

PORTAL

THE TIGER

Fear is a survival mechanism, and it's a brilliant one. It primes us for action, flooding our body with the chemicals required to make a decisive move. It sharpens our senses, it makes us alert and aware, and it keeps us alive…in a way.

Humans are, however, designed to be fairly relaxed (but attentive), while also purpose-driven, in general. We are meant to be walking, gardening, napping, swimming, working with our hands, eating good food, making love, and connecting with our friends and family, for the most part, and continuously discharging any potential energy through movement.

Living in a state of relationship and reciprocity with each other and the natural world (as we did for aeons before the era of the machine) meant contending with potential danger, certainly, yet a life of action also gave rise to a very embodied, organic, fluid, and instinctive understanding of risk, based on moment-to-moment cause and effect in response to the messages of the body.

Once in a while, we would have to fight the tiger, yes, but not all the time, and in-between those bouts of fomentation we could rest, recuperate, and rally. Our fear-response served us, as opposed to living *in service to* fear.

Life has changed in recent years. I suspect the idea of "risk" in the way that we conceive of it (and obsess over it) in our contemporary world, wasn't often considered, let alone made a topic of discussion or consternation prior to industrialization. Now, however, we in the so-called "developed" world no longer progress through our days and years predominantly in motion, nor are we personally responsible for producing what we consume.

As we have steadily become more dependent on automation, the abstraction and outsourcing of our basic needs has increased exponentially to the point that for many of us, life is "lived" through the disembodied interface of the screen, which delivers lightening-fast simulated "experiences" of extreme violence, extreme sex, extreme social intrigue, and extreme forms of synthetic "work," all of which produce intense physiological and emotional responses in our brains, including arousal, jealousy, anger, and fear, all decoupled entirely from any groundedness in the material or natural world.

The more our existence has become controlled, regulated, governed, structured, corralled, and arguably, made physically "safe" by technological superintendence, the more fearful we have become. Because the amygdala—the most ancient, primal part of our brains—cannot distinguish between a virtual threat and a physical one, many people experience maladaptive fear on a near-constant basis.

For the most part, there is no tiger in the night which we must prepare ourselves to fight. Our fears are rooted primarily in fantasy scenarios that play out in our minds, yet our bodies are chronically flooded with cortisol, adrenaline and other stress hormones, priming us for reflexive action that we rarely have an opportunity to release. Our physical bodies—engineered for *embodiment*—haven't changed much at all since pre-industrial analog life, but the perception of danger, and thus our state of reactivity to it, has risen disproportionately while the degree and variety of actual threat has plummeted.

Even in this digitized existence, we do, of course, occasionally have experiences that come close to resembling those "fight the tiger" moments, which may or may not result in emergent physical (and emotional) exertion and trauma, and incidents in which our very survival is at stake can certainly intersect with the birth process. Birth is, without a doubt, a profoundly liminal space for mothers and our babies, and not every child will pass through the birth portal into life. But in my experience and by my observation, this is usually far more a spiritual issue than a medical one. The spiritual life-and-death nature of birth has become deeply confused with the idea that birth is inherently dangerous, or that the birth process is always an emergency, as opposed to simply an emergence, as Jeannine Parvati Baker said.

Due to the various forms and layers of programming, propaganda, and sabotage that we have discussed at length already, pregnancy and birth now tend to be experiences that amplify the confusion between truly protective versus unproductive fear, despite the fact that for the vast majority of women—especially women who have access to clean water, high-quality food, and who are lucky enough to live in places where war, famine, and strife are not the norm, being pregnant and giving birth could be among the most remarkably peaceful and straightforward of biological processes, if not for the detrimental influence of industrial obstetrics and midwifery.

Given our current upended hall-of-mirrors reality, however, humans today find ourselves in the unique position of either living in a state of sustained fight-or-flight, or of having to teach ourselves the following two critical yet largely under-developed skills: (a) how to distinguish between disordered, unproductive fear—fear that isn't ours—versus instinctive fear that is offering us accurate information about our environment requiring an immediate response that will keep us alive (a process that involves a combination of intellectual discernment, emotional intelligence, and the art of choosing), and (b) how to consciously and deliberately calm our autonomic nervous systems so that once we have determined that our fear is not serving us, we can set it aside then dispense with it somatically in order to feel safe in our bodies once again.

Fear dissolution—the resolution of (a) and (b)—is one of the most important aspects of the work I do prenatally with both my coaching clients, and the women I support one-on-one as a birth attendant, and this technique is an essential part of choosing pain-free birth.

Let us now break down the process of identifying the nature of our fear, determining whether or not it serves us to respond to or to simply feel, acknowledge, then release it, and how to do that in practical terms.

FEAR DISSOLUTION

Step One: Give Yourself Permission to Acknowledge Fear When It Appears.

There is no need to bypass fear, or to avoid it. Fear is not something to be ashamed of. Giving yourself permission to feel fear means being willing to identify it, and yet for many of us this simple step alone can be a challenge.

For example, my preferred emotion is anger. This is the emotion that I feel most comfortable with, and which was most commonly represented, allowed, and encouraged in my family of origin. Anger was seen as righteous, strong, acceptable, and was what I therefore entrained myself to "use" to mask many other emotions.

Even now, when I feel that initial flush of anger, what is often really erupting under the surface is fear. Even when I'm having a physical response that indicates that I feel afraid (which is usually identifiable as a sensation in the belly, including churning, fluttering, and tightening) the first-line intellectual interpretation that I apply to what I'm experiencing is rage.

During my first pregnancy, prior to exiting the industrial obstetric system entirely, I had hired a regulated, academically-trained midwife to support me, and it took me a few weeks to realise that her lens was just as medicalized as an obstetrician's. She didn't actually work for me at all, but for the allopathic system, and after each of the three appointments I had with her before I ended our relationship, I would come home feeling furious (and I would subsequently bang out a written diatribe about my disillusionment—which was, I admit, cathartic).

But what I soon recognized is that while much of the anger I felt was authentic (and galvanizing), I was also feeling scared. In part, this was a sign that the midwife was following the mandate of her training: to provoke the appropriate degree of fear in me, the pregnant mother, so that I would comply with the demands of her "scope of practice." But she overplayed her hand, and I was not, apparently, sufficiently malleable or pre-programmed. I did feel fear (along with anger), but my fear was as a result of seeing this contorted, manipulative dynamic for what it was, and it fueled my defiance. I knew that this was a dysfunctional, unbalanced alliance, completely lacking in integrity—on both our parts—and this recognition represented a fundamental choice-point for me.

Had I been unwilling to take the first step in simply identifying my fear, the entire trajectory of not only my first birth, but of my life, would have been drastically different from what it was, and is.

You may feel comfortable with fear and have no trouble noticing when you feel it. But you also might find yourself feeling sad, dejected, or confused, or even deflecting the deeper emotion with humour and silliness, when what those conditioned responses might be hiding is fear.

A quick reliable method for deciphering the emotion of fear, especially if you have some ingrained confusion around your feelings like many of us do, is to intentionally tune in to your body and pinpoint the location of the most prominent sensations. As I said, you will most likely feel fear in your belly, your gut, or your solar plexus—somewhere within the core area of your body. When you do, put a hand on that place, acknowledge the feeling, sit with it for a moment, and allow it to be there. *I feel scared.*

Step Two: Tune into the Quality and Texture of the Fear Sensation You're Experiencing.

Now it's time to tune into the more granular characteristics and specifics of the fear you're feeling, whether that be a generative fear, chaotic unproductive fear, or an immediate, protective animal-survival fear. Let's start with the latter.

First of all, we have to backpedal a little bit, because it's important to note that if you're actually dealing with a fear that signals an abrupt, precipitous requirement to fight the tiger, it is unlikely that you will be in a position to question what you're feeling at all. You'll be too busy running or battling for your life. The very fact that you are able to take even a moment to sit with your fear probably indicates that you're not going to die, for a minute or two at least. How wonderful!

But on some level, fear is always related to our survival—just not always literally. All fear is self-protective. The difference is that chaotic, unproductive fear is usually about protecting the ego, or our subconscious self-concept, from moving into a zone of unfamiliarity, because (as you'll remember) discomfort is a kind of death of the old self.

There can also be some in-between states—situations in which our life or wellbeing may indeed be at risk unless further action is taken, which means that we don't want to disavow our fear entirely, but should respond to it, and let it work for us. It's generally when we mistakenly confuse the ego-fabricated chaos-fear instances with those marginal situations (that nonetheless do involve real risk) that we unwittingly invite unnecessary drama into our lives, and enact sabotage. And this frequently occurs during pregnancy and birth.

What I am describing is, effectively, the difference between fear and intuition, or impotent fear versus intuitive fear. One will lead us away from what we truly desire, and the other is giving us a clear call-to-action, in service to keeping us in alignment. How can we tell them apart? The more we practise, the better we become at deciphering the following distinction: fear that is true in a physical, embodied sense, and which provides us with a signal that we must respond to in the world of the material in order to stay alive or to move forward, has a crystalline clarity to it that we can feel in our bodies—it has a kind of auric quality that slices through the moment, grabs us by the scruff of our shirts, smacks us across the face, and demands our attention. Unproductive, chaotic, impotent fear, on the other hand, has a foggy, sogginess to it—a density that many of us might recognize as anxiety.

Step Three: What Are You Afraid Of?

You also want to be noting the subject of your fear, if you can determine it. What is it that you feel afraid of?

This may be more complicated in practice than it sounds, but if you do have a sense of the concept, idea, or scenario from which your fear originates, seek to acknowledge it. Often, what we discover is that our fears are somewhat shapeless: *What if? What if my baby dies?* I have felt this particular fear many times. In fact, there is at least one point in each of my pregnancies during which the question, *What if this time, I am the mother initiated into that terrible sisterhood of bereavement?* and I experience a familiar woozy sense of dread, horror, grief, despair, and shifting anxiety.

Many women have expressed to me over the years that the fear they have of their babies dying represents the kind of grief they suspect they could never recover from. Yet I have also supported many mothers through loss, and what I have observed, overwhelmingly, is that women do endure, even the death of a child, and that they often grow in enormously beautiful—if painful—ways from the experience.

I have also come to know that for myself, and among many other women, underlying the initial (very accurate and significant) assessment of loss as the primary reason for fear is yet another layer of terror, rooted in the dread that if my baby were to die, I would, in addition to being grief-stricken, then be judged as a terrible mother, ostracised by my friends and family, criminalised, have my older children taken from me, fall into a catatonic depression, find myself living on the streets, lose all my teeth, and then, unloved and loathed even, I myself would die alone. This may sound extreme or hyperbolic, but this potential fear scenario, or some variation thereof, is not uncommon.

Don't forget that the most potent threat to our sense of survival—the thing we are hardwired to fear the most—is social isolation. This is, in essence, the worst kind of death—the obliteration we feel when we are ousted from the clan. What I have found, however, is that there is an incredible sense of freedom in facing this, and in allowing my mind to (briefly) travel to that worst-case scenario, whatever it might be. The strategy of allowing oneself to entertain the most catastrophic outcome—to stare into the void of our darkest fear—also happens to be at the core of stoic philosophy, which is as useful and relevant today as it was in ancient Rome.

According to Roman statesman, playwright, satirist, and stoic philosopher Seneca, indulging the most reprehensible of potential eventualities can actually be quite therapeutic and liberating, when done in a measured, limited way. This may seem contradictory to Neville Goddard's directive to eschew all but the most single-minded focus on inhabiting the imaginal state of the wish-fulfilled, but in my experience, one facilitates the other.

Seneca's recommendation to dwell, for a time, in the "premeditation of evils," gives us an opportunity to recognize that (usually) what we have ideated as the worst-case scenario isn't nearly as bad as we think it might be, or that our fantasy is perhaps somewhat overblown. (I don't *really* think I would lose all my friends or that everyone would hate me if my child were to tragically die. I think probably I would find myself deeply loved and supported by many). But in humouring the fantasy, we get to then return, relieved, to what is often the far more fortunate reality that we currently occupy.

There are fates worse than death, yet even those are, at long last, relieved by death, thank God. I genuinely console myself with the thought that if I do end up toothless, childless, and homeless, I'll at least have one heck of a story to tell before I go. Again, this is not at all to dismiss or diminish the incredible devastation that so many mothers and children endure in the very real, tangible realm of waking life, but to point out that no one is immune to loss. To be a mother is, inevitably, to know sorrow.

Step Four: What Evidence Do You Have to Prove That Your Feeling of Fear Represents a Clear and Present Danger?

Once you have identified the quality, texture, and clarity of the fear you're experiencing and its origin—whether this is the fear of a specific aspect of mothering, or the fear of bleeding, or the fear of death itself—the next step is to ask yourself whether or not this fear represents a clear and present danger in this worldly domain. What is the existing evidence which confirms that what you are feeling fear in relation to is immediate?

This is a slightly different question than whether or not there is evidence of risk, overall. Risk, like danger, is quantified according to parameters that are changeable and shifting, including our own values and priorities. But risk is far more abstract, notional, and speculative than danger. Ground yourself in the current, tangible moment of now, and ask yourself what is true? What is the real situation at hand? Are you in danger?

Bring yourself back into your body. Is your baby kicking and moving in your womb? Is your baby perhaps sleeping, yet vibrating with a palpable energy? Breathe. What is the state of your heart? How is your body actually feeling in this moment? Allow yourself to orient to a sense of comfort and safety—to seek it, even—within yourself. Surrender to the substantiation that your body will always provide.

Most of us are so accustomed to chronic anxiety stemming from our fear-and-chaos programming, that we feel uneasy and apprehensive about the possibility of being comforted by our bodies' grounded truth, which is often informing us demonstrably and assuredly that there is no true evidence of a problem in this moment, even if we might be feeling a physical sense of agitated fear. I have also practised this in reverse, in a sense, when I have initially noticed certain unexpected physical symptoms, and then sought clarity on the correct course of action by attending to the emotional quality of my response, and then noting if I can allow my body to calibrate accordingly.

As an example, during the end of my fourth pregnancy I felt quite light-headed and nauseous, my ankles became swollen, and I developed a headache. I was aware that these markers can sometimes be associated with forms of blood-pressure dysregulation that can be dangerous for pregnant women and their babies, yet I really didn't feel any fear at all, certainly not to a degree that was calling me to take action. As always, I asked myself, *What kind of risk are you willing to take?* And when I briefly assessed my options, taking each to its logical conclusion, the one that was most clearly resonant in my emotional body, was to simply drink some water, allow myself to fully relax, have a nap, and wait and see. I did all that, and within a few hours, the symptoms subsided, and I felt much better.

There is no risk-free option. It is only when the outcome of a choice is positive or satisfactory, that we can allow ourselves, in hindsight, to believe that we selected correctly. But as I have detailed in previous chapters, we always end up choosing in alignment with our true desires.

If we decide to go to the hospital in response to a fear or a symptom, and we realise after the fact that there was no real medical need for such an undertaking and that we ended up submitting to a bunch of procedures that were counterproductive, or the outcome was catastrophic, we can rest assured that our true desire was to either reinforce our allegiance to the obstetric realm, or to receive another opportunity to re-assess that allegiance, and grow in self-awareness.

If, however, we choose not to engage with medical authority and calamity ensues, most of us will assume that this therefore indicates that had we made the opposite choice—had we gone into the hospital, for example—a more positive outcome would have transpired. But this is not necessarily true either. There are infinite variables, and we are not omniscient beings. Everyone speculates, everyone projects. But really, all we can know of what is true is the truth of the now, or of the past as we have interpreted it through the lens of our existing biases, assumptions, and beliefs. And we are all, always, in the business of confirming their biases.

Given the circumstances of your current situation, in the context of your body, your emotions, and the character and quality of the fear you're feeling, what is the true evidence that right now, in this present moment, you are in danger? If you find that there is no real evidence, move on to the next step.

Step Five: Reorient to the Crystalline Path and Close the Fear Portal

Once you have identified the quality of your fear, centred yourself within the physical and emotional truth of what is occurring now, determined that you are not actually in immediate physical danger, then taken a grounding, clarifying breath, it's time to reorient yourself to the truth. How do we know what is true? By attuning to the resonance of authenticity.

To do so, I recommend objectifying the fear you're feeling, and looking at it as an entity or a portal. I often think of my feelings of fear as having created a tunnel, an opening, or a pool in the panorama of my mind. I have the option of either stepping into that dark tunnel, passing through the opening, or immersing myself in the pool and languishing in it. Or I can decline the invitation altogether, and allow these sombre pools and portals to vanish.

When you find yourself in a similar position, vaporise the fear first by *blessing* it and thanking it for bringing you the gift of inquiry, presence, truth, and the integration you are now claiming. Honouring our fear is a crucial step. Fear is precious. It shows us what and who we love (our babies, ourselves), and what we value (our health, our lives).

Although I use the expression "fear dissolution," you are in actuality simply reinforcing the boundary between the reality you are choosing to occupy and the fear that you know is not yours, and which is instead a reflection of a state of consciousness you have no obligation to enter, adopt, or reside in.

In the past, when I have tried to eradicate my fears, it would invariably backfire, and I would find myself looping in obsessive thought-patterns. Cherishing my fear, while also lovingly holding a boundary around it is *so* very helpful. I'm not in denial: the portal—the possibility of fear—is there, and can be summoned again. It may be appropriate for me to enter that fear portal at some point, but I'm choosing not to at this moment because I have recognized that, ultimately, it does not serve me or my child at this time.

Now, redirect your attention to your preferred, chosen, desired outcome—the birth of your healthy baby, the knowing that your child is well, vigorous, and alive, or the vitality of your own body. You will now transpose your consciousness into that particular reality, the reality of your desire. Here's how: take a moment to become keenly aware of how your body feels. What you will likely experience—if indeed you have arrived at the truth—is a profound sense of tranquillity, relief, and ease. It is this feeling of composure shimmering through your senses, your nervous system, and your cells, that is the foremost signal that you are on the correct path.

What I find particularly fascinating is that there is a strong similarity between the kind of fear that is *true*, and the peace of knowing that your feelings of fear are unnecessary and maladaptive. Authentic, actionable fear (strangely enough) is also a crystalline state, and the truth has several universal characteristics, common across emotional states. Whether it's the transparent immediacy of an adrenaline-fueled message to fight the tiger, or the lucidity of knowing that yes, this really is an instance in which calling 911 is the right choice, or, the recognition that your agitated anxiety can securely be replaced by calm, all of these responses share the thread of coherence and peace, even when the truth is that your fear *is* warranted and that intervention is the appropriate response.

This process is relatively similar both in terms of feeling fear during pregnancy, and when fear arises during birth itself. Yet it's also the case that the way we relate to our fears before birth has a major impact not only on how we handle fear during birth, but also the degree to which we experience fear during birth (or not). The more we can acknowledge, honour, and process our fears during pregnancy, the less intensively or significantly we will feel maladaptive fear as our babies are emerging, and, in general, the less pain we will experience as well.

WHAT IF

We all have widely varying beliefs, priorities, preconceptions, and preoccupations. For many mothers, danger, risk, and the fear of complications or emergencies are principal considerations, especially early on in their journeys. These concerns are generally the primary stumbling blocks that women face, initially, to contemplating birth outside the system. Because of this, the fear of the "what if" has a major impact, directly and indirectly, on our experience of birth.

Women often approach me wanting to know what I would do if I were faced with the hypothetical situation that exemplifies their worst fears. *What if your baby is born prematurely? What if your baby is prenatally diagnosed with some problem or other? What if your baby has a congenital distinction and you only discover it at birth? What would you do?*

These questions reveal, first and foremost, a certain degree of dissociation from the questioner's inner authority. This is not a problem, and in no way does it make anyone wrong—most of us have to move through a process of rediscovering our instinctive knowing, and often part of that process is observing another person who has already undertaken the passage of reclamation.

My answer to these questions is always, ultimately, *I don't know*, because I don't live in the realm of the theoretical when it comes to my births. In fact, I have actively trained myself to *decline* the invitation to dwell in the arena of the potential disaster scenario. I'll briefly check in there, as Seneca has suggested, and I know the universe of fear is always available and beckoning, of course. But I have consciously disciplined myself to turn down the proposal to spend much time there, if any.

There is, however, a more pragmatic reason for what might seem like my studied rejection of fear, and this is intimately connected with my repudiation of diagnostic testing, which I simply do not engage in during my pregnancy whatsoever. Foremost among my reasons for eschewing prenatal diagnostics is that there is *no* diagnostic technology in existence that is 100 percent accurate.

One of the questions that consistently comes up among pregnant women and their partners is, *How will I know that my baby is healthy or if they have a problem or a congenital distinction if I don't have an ultrasound?* (Or a blood test, or DNA screening). The answer is, of course, *You won't.* You won't know. You won't know one way or another. We cannot ever know.

Every diagnostic procedure available has a rate of false-positives and false-negatives, and there is no way to confirm a result unquestionably. Given that there is no way to be entirely sure of the conclusion a diagnostic or genetic testing procedure provides, I see no value in cultivating anxiety over tests and results that cannot be definitive.

Furthermore, the assumption that a problem *might* be present inevitably leads to further testing, greater scrutiny, and increased pressure to submit to surveillance and monitoring. This in turn can create more problems, or exacerbate existing ones.

In most situations in which a potential problem or congenital variation has been diagnosed (on the basis of a test that cannot actually be confirmed) there is nothing that can be done prior to birth to treat the condition. Prenatal surgery (the practice of opening up a woman's womb and performing a medical operation on her pre-born baby) is not *entirely* unheard of, and in a minutely rare number of situations it may be offered, but I would never even consider such an option, myself.

I would also never even contemplate aborting my child no matter their potential condition—certainly not on the basis of a diagnostic test that might be incorrect. I know many families who were told that their child had a serious or even fatal condition determined by the results of prenatal surveillance or genetic testing, who ended up choosing not to "terminate" their child's life, only to discover at birth, that there had never been anything "wrong" with their baby after all.

In other circumstances, what may be very real issues discovered through technology (and subsequently catastrophized) may resolve spontaneously. I have known several mothers whose babies were diagnosed with heart conditions which healed naturally without surgery (but not without first the immense stress and strain of a pregnancy that was suddenly labeled "high risk," resulting in constant subsequent testing, and a very difficult technocratic birth).

Furthermore, most diagnostic procedures (like amniocentesis, ultrasound, and even the drawing of blood) pose risk, or increase certain risks in and of themselves. Ultrasound has never been proven safe, is known to damage cells and mammalian tissue, and is correlated in numerous animal studies with a multitude of adverse outcomes, including an increased potential harm to organs, cavitation, miscarriage, and behavioural ill-effects.

Amniocentesis, which is most often used when attempting to determine whether or not a preborn child carries the markers for Down syndrome (also known as trisomy 21) can also significantly elevate the chances of miscarriage. Of course, the underlying assumption that fuels the widespread testing for conditions like Down syndrome is that people with an additional chromosome are faulty and unwanted in their perceived imperfection, and most people "test" for Down syndrome, with the intention of at least considering abortion if their baby is believed to have it.

As my dear friend, colleague, and editor Sophia Zaferes has observed, Down syndrome testing is nothing more than sanitized eugenics. This is especially tragic given the fact that people with Down syndrome have a very unique set of aptitudes, sensitivities, and gifts to offer this world.

Because I do not value or believe in what the medical system offers, I choose to experience pregnancy and birth outside of the realm of industrial medicine and obstetric interventions altogether, and far from the domain of cyborgicity. I simply don't have any interest in participating in technocratic pregnancy or birth.

It's not only the questionable effectiveness and ethics of obstetric testing methodologies that disinterests me, but the entire apparatus. It's the coercion, manipulation, and indignities that mothers are subjected to; the layers of alienation involved in allowing parts of our bodies to be segregated from other parts, blood drawn, tissue removed, and the bifurcation of the body with machines and screens. The entire rigamarole often causes immense stress to mothers and babies, even prior to the potential anxieties (and sometimes devastation) of a diagnosis. All of these forms of submission have costs beyond the physical and psychological risks, and the ritual itself takes a heavy spiritual toll.

Ultimately, there is no compelling statistical evidence showing that any prenatal procedures, diagnostics, or protocols actually improve outcomes. This is true for ultrasound and amniocentesis, and it's certainly true for all the goofy pseudo-scientific silliness that comprises the nuts and bolts of "routine" prenatal care.

There is no real information of note to be derived from draping a plastic measuring tape over a woman's abdomen in an attempt to "measure her fundus." Charting a mother's weight gain is an antiquated exercise in shaming women for their very existence. The obsessive focus on a baby's position in utero, which has become so fashionable, is primarily a way to instill a completely fabricated, unnecessary fear in a mother in response to a totally normal situation—a baby that is simply moving around in the womb, or who has assumed a particular position instinctively—that is in no way, shape, or form pathological. There is certainly very little authentic "care" involved in what women are put through at the doctor's office or midwifery clinic.

I have chosen to be at peace with the unknown, and this approach is an option for every woman. I will always do my very best, given the material, physical, spiritual, and internal resources I have available, to nurture and care for the child growing inside me to the best of my ability, but I am, for the most part, untroubled by the ever-present possibility of death. I have the right, as does every living being, to choose to embrace the mysteries of life and death.

I do not in any way see myself as untouchable, or immortal, or special at all, but I have come to not only accept, but *value* the space of not-knowing. I also know that no one can ever know inarguably whether or not their baby is developing "properly," not even with the purported benefits of technology, which we are increasingly taught to perceive as omniscient, despite this nonetheless being an illusion. I have also come to the conclusion that *especially* if there were something wrong with, or distinct about the way my child was developing, I would not want to know prior to birth, even if unequivocal knowing were possible (which it isn't). My choice remains to experience the sacred enigma of pregnancy, and then to give birth at home, to receive my child into my hands, and behold them as they are, with love and acceptance. If, at that point, I were to perceive with all my senses a reason to seek medical attention, I would take whatever action might seem correct or appropriate in the moment.

Once a mother has enrolled in the medical technocratic program during pregnancy, and offered up her body to be scrutinized, assessed, measured, documented, and surveilled to any extent, it is very difficult to disengage from that framework. The structure of the medical establishment creates a complex set of explicit and implicit expectations and motivations on the part of medical practitioners who, as a result of that structure, are incentivized primarily by their existing allegiance to their profession, and the threat of liability.

Women are assured that their right to "informed consent" will be maintained, but the only true form of decision-making power we have is whether or not we consent to enter the system in the first place. Once that initial consent is given to allow ourselves to be contracted into the industrial sphere as a patient, our choices from then on will be engineered and manipulated, and our capitulation is all but guaranteed.

You may not share my perspective on medical intervention at all, nor do you have any obligation to. But if your goal is to manifest—through choosing—a pain-free, blissful birth, and you recognize any degree of connection between the set and setting of your birth and the outcome, I encourage you to interrogate the nature of the cognitive frame you are electing to adopt through your level of engagement with the medical apparatus, and how (and in what ways) you hope to benefit from such involvement.

PORTAL

EMERGENCY

This is not, as I'm sure you have gleaned by now, a book about the specifics of the birth process or its physiology, but I do want to briefly touch on emergencies.[69] What if there *is* an emergency? How would you know?

What I know from my years of experience as a birth-witness is that the parameters (according to cultural consensus) as to what defines a normal birth have been artificially constrained, owing largely to the pervasiveness of medical fear-programming. Our collective assumptions, and the conditioned beliefs of most medical professionals do not, in my opinion, reflect the vast range of what birth can often reasonably and safely encompass.

I have only been involved in a handful of planned homebirths that have led to hospital transfer, and almost all of those transfers occurred as a result of the mother's fear and exhaustion—not pathology or tragedy at all. On the other hand, I have seen many instances during homebirths that I am confident would have been described as emergencies (and treated as such) had the mother given birth in an industrialised setting (which are often created in women's homes).

These extenuating circumstances have included the presence of meconium, births that stretched out over several days, babies that took many hours to emerge (including over ten hours of pushing), excessive bleeding immediately postpartum, broken umbilical cords, and babies who were born initially unresponsive, and more, all of which were handled calmly and efficiently at home with positive outcomes, and no medical involvement.

---

[69] If you wish to explore this topic in much greater detail, an excellent place to start is my online course, *The Complete Guide to Freebirth*, in addition to my other written work and my upcoming books.

How we define an "emergency" has everything to do with our fundamental understanding of how birth works. Many otherwise normal variations in birth are erroneously assumed to be dangerous, then treated as emergencies, which can lead to iatrogenic harm[70] — the unintentional manufacturing of a true emergency as a result of medical mismanagement.[71]

Thankfully, emergent, time-sensitive, life-threatening situations in birth are rare, especially among women who are fundamentally healthy and well-nourished. But they do sometimes occur, whether having arisen organically or fabricated through the ineptitude of so-called experts. In the unlikely event of a true emergency, of course, medical interventions can be lifesaving, and it's a blessing to have that option available to those who want or need it.

Many of us are subconsciously fearful that if we allow birth to be easy and blissful, we might then miss out on what we have all been conditioned to believe is the more impressive account of almost dying, or of needing to be airlifted to an obstetric hospital, or of our midwife having to perform

---

[70] A term coined by Ivan Illich in his excellent — and still highly relevant — 1974 book "Medical Nemesis."

[71] In 2016, researchers at Johns Hopkins Medicine (an institution for which I have no respect at all, but which incidentally comprises six academic and community hospitals, four suburban health care and surgery centres, over 40 patient care locations, a home care group and an international division, and which apparently commands considerable international respect among the scientific community), calculated that more than two hundred and fifty thousand deaths per year are due to medical error in the U.S. alone. This figure, published in *The BMJ*, surpasses the U.S. Centers for Disease Control and Prevention's (CDC) third leading cause of death — respiratory disease — which purportedly kills close to 150,000 people per year. Unsurprisingly, in 2021, McGill University's Office for Science and Society (a department bearing the byline "Separating Sense from Nonsense") argued, in an article inconspicuously titled "Medical Error is Not the Third Leading Cause of Death," that the 2016 Johns Hopkins assertion is "an alarming [and] highly problematic bit of data extrapolation" that "has been used to paint all of medicine as untrustworthy." Given what transpired in 2020, and the vested interests of the medical community in preserving what little faith remains among the population in medical science, one can almost sympathize with McGill's editorial note of desperation.

some medieval maneuver that saved the day. But most of those stories are examples of unnecessary, fabricated drama. I want to encourage you to explore the possibility that saving yourself, getting out of your own way, and allowing bliss can be the most exciting and romantic narrative of all.

Generally speaking, conditions that will almost always genuinely justify medical assistance include:

- uterine rupture (which involves the uterus actually breaking open, which can pose a serious risk to the lives of both mother and baby)
- placental abruption (which occurs when the placenta prematurely separates from the wall of the uterus before the baby is born, which can lead to a baby's death and dangerous levels of bleeding for the mother), and
- cord prolapse (when the baby's umbilical cord drops out of the mothers vagina before the baby begins to emerge, which can cause cord compression and hypoxia, a lack of oxygen to the baby).

Postpartum haemorrhage is also serious and potentially fatal, although there is widespread misunderstanding throughout the birth world about what constitutes postpartum haemorrhage (as opposed to normal blood loss postpartum), how to identify it, what to do about it, and, crucially, how to prevent it.

In my experience, the number one method I have successfully employed to prevent postpartum haemorrhage is to stay as far away as possible from anyone who might sabotage my birth, which is, in my view, the number one cause of pathological blood loss during and after birth. Among the many reasons I choose freebirth, primarily among them is my desire to keep myself and my babies safe, and alive.

In the case of uterine rupture (the risk of which is slightly elevated in women who have had prior surgical births) symptoms include bleeding, and often heavy bleeding before the baby is born, along with sudden, severe, and sharp abdominal pain that does not generally follow the usual pattern of the birth process. In this case, the rhythms of the mother's sensations may be irregular, and the birth process may start or stop in a manner that seems incongruous to the normal progression of birth. Symptoms can be somewhat similar in an instance of placental abruption.

Typically, heavy bleeding or sensations that depart from the expected pattern are not normal during birth and are signs that should be attended to closely. (Some blood, however, especially as the baby moves closer to the point of emergence, is often quite normal, especially spotting, or the spattering of blood as the baby begins to crown, or just prior to crowning.) Cord prolapse will also usually be evident, because the cord will likely be visible at, or close to, the mother's vaginal opening.

Ultimately, to the understandable consternation of so many mothers and fathers, there is no simple formula for knowing exactly when it's appropriate to seek medical help. As always, there are infinite variables. But you, the birthing woman, have been granted an incredibly sensitive inbuilt biofeedback mechanism: your physical body, your emotional body, and your instinctive knowing. The most important factors above all, in determining whether a situation is a true emergency or not, are your perception, your intuition, and the information you are receiving through all of your senses—including your attunement to any feelings of fear you might be experiencing.

I must reiterate here that there is never an incorrect decision. Or rather, that if there can possibly be an incorrect decision it can only be the one that you cannot live with. You are the sole authority over your birth experience. No one is more invested in your baby's well-being than you are. You get to decide exactly how your birth plays out. You have no obligation to justify to anyone why you might want to go to the hospital or stay home.

I know mothers whose babies have died at home, who are totally at peace with every choice that led to that experience. I know other mothers whose babies have died in the hospital, and who, a decade or more later, are still *not* at peace with the choice they made to leave the sanctuary of their homes to enter the hospital. And I know mothers who believe with every fibre of their being that they made the wrong decision in choosing homebirth or freebirth.

This is why it is *so* important for you (and every mother) to take the time to discover who you are and what you value (if possible *before* becoming pregnant) and to find peace in that discovery. Because the idea that it is even possible to outsource responsibility for your choices during birth—to a doctor, or a midwife, or a doula—is a fantasy and a delusion. No other person or institution (a) shares your unique subjective value system, and (b) has to live with the outcome of your choices.

In all likelihood, however, if you do find yourself in the midst of a true emergency, the fear you experience will have a clarity to it that is absent from the opening up of maladaptive and unhelpful fear portals as you traverse the landscape of an otherwise healthy birth. When your fear has the force and cogency that would be present if you were facing a tiger—the incisive, penetrating, razor-sharp sense of knowing that something is wrong—you are being called to respond.

As we have discussed throughout this chapter, doing the work of clearing away all that might distract you from honing in on your intuition, or which might occlude your clear vision of the truth, is the best way to reinforce your connection to your instincts and your clairs. This, in turn, will make available to you (in any situation, including if you find yourself faced with a true emergency) the most valuable "diagnostic" tool of all: your unimpeded self.

THE RELATIONSHIP BETWEEN FEAR AND PAIN

Birth is a universe unto itself. Birth has its own timeline and lifestream. Birth is always an initiation, and every interval propels us on to the next stage. The feeling of fear as it passes through one's consciousness like lightning while in the throes of birth isn't anything to be afraid of.

And yet, you should know that fear and pain are always intertwined. The physiological effect of fear is ultimately constriction, resistance, and the priming of all our body systems for conflict or impact, which evokes pain preemptively. As you'll recall, fear also produces adrenaline and cortisol, and excess stress hormones flowing through the body can inhibit the appropriate distribution of oxytocin (the hormone of love, connection, orgasm, and uterine expansion), the body's natural opiates (which not only suppress pain but support the essential drift into an altered state of consciousness), and will, I believe, prohibit DMT, which facilitates our direct communication with God.

Because of this dynamic, it will serve you well to have practised the fear dissolution process (consciously redirecting your attention and energy *away* from unnecessary fear portals) prior to birth. And fundamentally, of course, this method is the same in every context throughout our lives. When you know that the fear you're feeling lacks the clarity of purpose that distinguishes it from protective fear, you will focus your attention instead on intentionally entering into the portal of love, coherence, and trust.

This refocusing is central to summoning bliss as your baby makes his or her way through your body. Actively disavowing fear, and embodying calm, love, gratitude, trust, and connection facilitates surrender. It is surrender, in the end, that will:

- automatically move you away from a state of fear,
- give you the opportunity to release pain with ease,

- facilitate the physiological process of birth, and
- optimize your safety and wellbeing and that of your baby.

During pregnancy, we are often projecting our minds into the future, and our concerns are usually related to whether or not our babies will be healthy once they are born, or how we will handle birth when it comes. The way fear appears during birth itself, however, almost invariably has some unique features and characteristics, and I want to attempt to prepare you for what fear—specifically during the birth-dance—can feel like, because it's often distinct from the fear ideations of pregnancy, in ways that can be common among many mothers.

The physicality and imminence of actually occupying birth is a singular dynamic, and one of the most frequent expressions of fear that I encounter among birthing women is that it feels like their babies are "stuck." In fact, this thought/feeling formation—that there is some kind of obstruction or immobility—is one that almost every woman experiences at some point during her birth process, and for some mothers, this fear can be persistent or recurring.

But babies don't really get "stuck." It just doesn't really happen. There is no "stuck" (in birth or in life, in spite of how convincing the sense of being trapped can often feel). We cannot ever be in stasis. We are always in motion, and there is only ever change. I have personally witnessed mothers push for ten hours before their beautifully healthy babies emerged, and I have witnessed a baby crowning (the child's head sitting visible at the mother's perineum) for eight hours before she spilled out of her mother's yoni, immediately pink and vigorous. I have also personally known babies who have floated between two worlds—head protruding, body not yet born—for over ten minutes before restitution occurred and their shoulders and then bodies spiralled forth (with no interference or touching from anyone at all).

True shoulder dystocia, while very serious, is vanishingly rare. Many mothers are told that they and their babies "had" shoulder dystocia, when what they were in fact suffering from was the ignorance and impatience of their doctor or midwife who, in all likelihood, truly believed that his or her well-meaning sabotage saved the day, and then felt compelled to attach to the event an alarming and dramatic term, imbued with formidable cultural significance ("shoulder dystocia") to justify their actions and illustrate their valour.

Birth is highly variable. In my experience, it is nearly always true that when a mother thinks that nothing is happening—*everything has stalled, and I think my baby is stuck*—this is actually an indication that *everything* is happening, and that she is right on the cusp of a major shift in energy.

During your own birth, you can facilitate this shift, and support yourself and your baby, by choosing—always choosing—to summon your courage, and to orient to the power of surrender. *The moment of emergence is approaching.*

This is where your inner dialogue is especially important. Here is an example of a variation of what might go on in your mind as you *midwife yourself* through fear during birth. It may not unfold in your head in as organised and sequential a way as what follows, but this might serve as a general template:

What is the subject and nature of your agitation?

I think my baby is stuck.

Where is the physical sensation, and what feeling is associated with it?

Heaviness in my belly. Tension. Fear.

What is the quality of this fear?

Nervous, panicky, sweaty, shaky, disoriented.

PORTAL

What do you absolutely know to be true about your situation at this moment?

I am giving birth.

Is there any evidence to suggest that there might be a problem with your birth, or any clear evidence that points to your baby actually being stuck?

No. Because I also know that the feeling of stuckness or blockage is very common, and even universal among birthing women. Every mother that has birthed in consciousness has been here.

When you come into presence, and tune into your body, and your baby, what is it that you know to be true beyond a shadow of a doubt?

I am strong, I am healthy, I am connected, and I'm in the birth process. This means that everything is happening, and there is constant movement, and I am free to move, more or differently. I know on the deepest level that I am alive, and I love my child.

Now, as you merge with your Guide-Self, you will allow the fear portal— *it's right there*—to pass by, and you will actively choose the portal of serenity—*here it is*—and move in that direction.

Follow the breath. Let joy, gratitude, and love be your compass, and know that you are safe (if that's true).

SUFFERING IS OPTIONAL

Suffering is optional. Fear, and even pain, are volitional experiences. Most of us, however, do not have the skill to renounce all pain and fear entirely—I certainly don't (not yet anyway).

I succumb to both pain and fear quite regularly. But I also know that it's entirely unnecessary to live there long-term, and I now have the tools and the framework to work through those states, or to allow them to move through me—body, mind, and psyche—far more readily and skillfully than I ever did before.

We don't want to exile fear and pain entirely; they remain important messengers—emissaries; and prophets, even. We can feel them, acknowledge them, thank them, and then move into a different state of being. The possibilities offered by the process of consciously disavowing and discharging pain and fear, and of lovingly reorienting our bodies and minds towards healing, are infinite.

You will choose whether or not your birth is blissful. You will choose whether or not your birth is painful. And your ability to choose is determined by your spiritual condition, your self-responsibility, and your willingness to feel and witness, all of which arise from your fundamental *being*. No questioning or analysis necessary, simply the practice of life.

Birth is the template for living, and life is the template for birth. Brook and creek, rivulet and stream: all tributaries flow to the sea.

INTEGRATION QUESTIONS

1. What fears, if any, do you have around your upcoming birth? What do you notice registering in your mind and in your body when you imagine your birth?

2. What would the logical conclusion be, in regards to your upcoming birth, if you were to follow feelings of ungrounded fear, and respond to its triggers?

3. Moving forward, when fear comes up, how do you commit to responding to it?

CHAPTER TWELVE

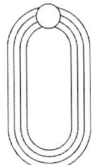

TRANSMUTATION

FRACTURE

Each of my babies has made their presence (or impending incarnation) known within my energetic field and my body in different ways. Helio's conception was announced by what felt like a vision from God. Yet in direct contrast to that brief moment of beatification, his gestation was one of the most challenging of the nine I have experienced thus far.

That entire year—2021—was a terrible, wonderful, shocking test of faith for me, Lee, and our children. We had left Canada for Central America the year before, yet it was only in 2021 that we fully realized that the world we had assumed was ours had never been real, and that we could never go back. Not to Canada, not to our old lives. The very idea of home itself had been shattered, and in the wake of the demolition I saw how battered and cracked the casement had already become over so many years prior.

I hated Costa Rica. The shocking beauty of the landscape, which I found initially entrancing, soon struck me as despotic and oppressive. It was gorgeous, dense, brutal, and unrelenting. I decided the climate was *drastically* inappropriate for my constitution, and to prove it, I cultivated a constant rotation of open festering sores all over my body from the bug-bites that I would ragefully tear open with my claws, and which would then inevitably become inflamed and pustulating.

The eternal dampness and intensity of the jungle corroded *everything*—my books, my clothes, my documents, my flesh, and, I was convinced, my soul. I hated it all.

More than anything, I missed the sense of having a comprehensible future. I missed the idea of stability, the idea of normalcy. I know, of course, that both are a fantasy, and that life is transitory in all ways, but I mourned the accessibility and plausibility of the delusion, and my former innocence. The reconstruction—the re-*membering*—would be extensive. And pregnancy would become the site of my healing.

My divination that our baby was on the wind was the strangest experience of feeling utterly elated and aligned with what was meant to be, while also being at something of a loss, given that the space between knowing he would come, and actually becoming pregnant, was one of the most potent proofs of manifestation I had experienced up to that point in my life.

I saw the object of my desire and felt the presence of my desired one; I experienced his energy, and I knew we were meant for each other. I was his mother already. *I am his mother now and always.* It was so relaxed, and so inevitable, even before his body came into mine, that, paradoxically, I also felt very little attachment. I almost had a sense that had it not happened at all, that would have been fine too. Another life, perhaps. But when I discovered I was indeed pregnant just a few days after our child appeared in spirit, I felt disoriented. The only explanation is that it was ordained (as is everything that happens under the sun).

Yet within the context of my entire lifeline, it also made perfect sense. I have chosen—and been chosen *for*—the act and art of mothering and the fathoming of its depths. I was also in a state of fracture.

I was, in a way, homeless—out of place, off-kilter, lost. I expressed this sense of precariousness in ways that were physical, emotional, and psychological (not to mention spiritual) but the physical elucidation was the most intense and unfamiliar.

I am an expert in self-sabotage, as I've mentioned, and I have always known intellectually that physical breakdown is an indication of inner conflict, but I was not expecting that my body would break down quite the way it did.

HEALING PAIN

Pain is the most potent sign and signifier of healing.

Pain is the blade and the chalice;[72] the wound and the weapon; the container and that which we endeavour to contain. Pain can so quickly become everything, eclipsing the self, the other, the love, and the world outside.

But pain can also be harnessed, tended to, made to heel, and nurtured into oblivion. Pain is never *just,* or *simply.*

Pain is eclectic and scattered, wild and shifting.

---

[72] Riane Eisler's 1987 book *The Chalice and the Blade* is premised on the work of controversial archaeologist Marija Gimbutas, who suggests that feminine neolithic statues and figures represented mother-goddess worship. The book puts forth the idea that, prior to the establishment of Indo-European civilizations and the dawn of agriculture, human societies were matrifocal (if not matriarchal), and that the central theme of history has been "the struggle between so-called feminine and masculine values." Eisler positions women and women's culture in conflict with the aggression and domination of masculinity and "the patriarchy," and suggests that it is a return to the fundamentally peaceful virtues of femininity that will restore balance to human culture. I disagree with Eisler's conclusions almost entirely, but I appreciate her book in many ways, and it remains an interesting lens, as well as an important documentation of second-wave feminist thought.

The pain-body—Eckhart Tolle's description of the viral, roving, protean entity of despair and negativity that can morph just as easily from irritation to anger to physical agony—is what creates the cycling spectacle of tension, and the chronic seeking of release through drama, and self-obliteration.

Pain is also political. When we are effectively disciplined to only know pain as the companion to dysfunction and the precursor to decay and death, our collective loathing and abhorrence of it—our fear of pain—makes perfect sense to tend to, propagate, and financialize.[73]

Pain is so much more than what this culture of avoidance has taught us that it is.

Pain is a message from the body. Pain is a form of primitive wisdom; one of our most profound teachers. Pain is an invitation into various pathways of self-exploration and self-knowing. Pain is an access-point to God. Pain is a teacher and a gift.

Pain is real, and pain is also, in so many ways, merely a remnant—a relic.

THE SCIENCE OF SUFFERING

Despite fairly extensive scientific research on the nature, substance, and treatment of pain, a deeper understanding of what it is, how it works, and why it comes and goes, remains elusive. This reality only underscores the enormous limitations of theory and the fact that our bodies incorporate so much more complexity than what science can account for.

---

[73] Increasingly, the pharmaceutical mitigation of pain is viewed as an entitlement—a human right, even—and at the same time, birth has always been instrumentalized to sell the fear of pain. During the 1960s and 1970s and beyond, the second-wave feminist movement in particular was hijacked by the industrial obstetric complex to propagandize and promote the epidural on the basis that women "deserve" to be relieved of the pain and indignities of childbirth.

The scientific community has attempted—absurdly—to organize pain into three main categories: nociceptive pain, neuropathic pain, and…all the rest.

Nociceptive pain[74] refers to the signals the body receives when the sensory nervous system (the central nervous system and peripheral nervous system working in conjunction) detects a threatening or noxious input. For example, the heat from a fire will send a pain-signal to the brain indicating potential damage to nerves and tissue.

But "nociception" itself—the triggering mechanism—is not the same as the *feeling* of pain. Pain is often (but not always) the result of a nociceptive response. In fact, we move through our daily lives continuously responding to numerous nociceptive inputs that won't necessarily become pain, because we make adjustments to preempt that outcome. Low-level discomfort (like the impetus to stretch or reposition our bodies) is a nociceptive response.

Neuropathic pain denotes the sensation that results from physical damage to the nervous system directly, which includes injury to nerves but also more abstract and seemingly impenetrable issues like autoimmune disorders, headaches, and so-called "dis-eases" like fibromyalgia that are seen by some as primarily a pain-system dysfunction.

These distinctions seem utterly specious and farcical to me, especially given my extensive personal expertise in pain, including (among a lifetime of other examples) the purportedly nociceptive pain of kidney stones, and what we have come to understand as the semi-official special category of "pain in childbirth"—neither of which are experiences that I could ever classify within the pitifully limited, reductive scientific frame.

---

[74] Ingraham, Paul. 2023. "The 3 Basic Types of Pain." *Www.PainScience.Com*, January. https://www.painscience.com/articles/pain-types.php#:~:text=Somatic%20pain%20is%20experienced%20in,classification%20systems%20have%20full%20overlap.

All pain is, in a sense, psychosomatic, or imaginary, in that it occurs in our brains, whether in response to a material input, or perception, or both. Yet even science recognizes that belief and anticipation have an enormous impact on our degree of sensitization or desensitization to pain, even in the context of what might be considered the simpler or more straightforward nociceptive pain category.

One recent study on pain[75] involved exposing participants to "thermal stimulation of varied temperatures" and then assessing both the autonomic (involuntary) responses (pupil dilation and skin conductance) in addition to the participants' subjective assessment of the pain, and how both their responses and assessments differed based on expectation.

What researchers observed is that while the heat stimulation accurately predicted skin conductance and pupil dilation, "the individual pain experience statistically mediated effects of noxious heat." Furthermore, "moderated mediation revealed that evidence for this process was stronger when stimulation was *perceived* as painful compared with when stimulation was perceived as non-painful " (emphasis added). This indicates that our perception—even when it comes to pain that most of us would assume to be totally involuntary and dependent only on outside stimulation—actually informs the physical and autonomic response and the extent of injury itself.

This is wildly exciting to me, and I think it proves, at the very least, that we underestimate our power to consciously generate our own experience through belief, and also that sensation and healing (which we describe as pain, symptomology, injury, or dysfunction) are always intertwined, cannot ever really be compartmentalized, and exist on a continuum.

---

[75] Mischkowski, Dominik, Esther E. Palacios-Barrios, Lauren A. Banker, Troy C. Dildine, and Lauren Y. Atlas. 2018. "Pain or Nociception? Subjective Experience Mediates the Effects of Acute Noxious Heat on Autonomic Responses." *Pain* 159 (4): 699–711. https://doi.org/10.1097/j.pain.0000000000001132.

Birth, unlike pathology, is a transformation. Birth is also, in so many ways, a form of regeneration and re-membering in so many ways, but it is not a pathology. Pregnancy and birth do incorporate various forms of ancillary healing, but procreation itself is not corrective in the way that the healing response to an adaptation or compensation following an overt biological conflict[76] will be.

Birth is not an injury, nor, I would argue, primarily a corrective process of repair. Yet we have all, to some degree, been conditioned to believe that it is. Nonetheless, every experience we have of healing can give us profound insight into aspects of birth that intersect with restoration, including pain of various kinds and modes.

Every experience, especially pain or discomfort during pregnancy, is in service to your learning about pain, working with pain, and increasing the power and capacity you have to hold pain with reverence and appreciation, and then to disavow or renounce it, and to dissolve it entirely, which I now know can be done in any context, under any circumstance.

As lived experience (and science) suggests, our bodies will always reflect to us the underlying composition of our beliefs. The fact that birth is so widely understood (and promoted) as a problem to be solved through surgery, chemistry, or professional maneuvering, has choreographed our perception of it.

I came across a riveting example of the power and influence of this kind of framing of the scientific explanations for pain in birth in the following abstract of an article from a journal of obstetrics and gynaecology:[77]

---

[76] According to the Germanic Healing Framework developed by Dr. Ryke Geert Hamer.
[77] Rowlands, Shelley, and Michael Permezel. 1998. "1 Physiology of Pain in Labour." *Baillière's Clinical Obstetrics and Gynaecology* 12 (3): 347–62. https://doi.org/10.1016/s0950-3552(98)80071-0.

PORTAL

Labour pain is the result of many complex interactions. Although not fully determined, the pain arises from distension of the lower uterine segment and cervical dilatation. The neural mechanism of labour has some features similar to other forms of acute pain; nociceptive information is relayed in small A delta and C afferent fibres to the dorsal horn of the spinal cord, mediated by neurotransmitters; from there it may be involved in the initiation of segmental spinal reflexes or pass through the spinothalamic tract to the brain. Many factors are activated during labour which may modify the nociceptive impulse at different stages of its passage. Some of these factors act synergistically to promote anti-nociception that peaks at delivery.

What strikes me most pointedly about this summary is its simultaneous layering of both obfuscation and, in a way, honesty. Revealed so clearly in the arrogant, convoluted, alienating medical terminology of this synopsis is the fact that doctors and scientists have absolutely no idea why some women experience birth as pain, not to mention why some other women experience not only an absence of pain in birth, but ecstatic, exhilarating pleasure.

DESCENT

At around nine weeks into my pregnancy, I began to notice that my belly was protruding to an extent that was irregular and incongruous with what I knew to be my stage of gestation. I looked, quite truly, like a woman far closer to thirty weeks pregnant than someone still in the earliest season. It was quite bizarre and alarming.

A few days after this unseemly swelling and inflammation began—with my abdomen still shockingly distended—I experienced my first attack. This episode constituted repeated waves of the most ferociously extreme, excruciating, acute pain I have ever experienced in my life—which continued for about four to five hours, unrelentingly.

I had had gallbladder problems as a teenager, and the sensation was somewhat similar, though this seemed worse, by my recollection. Of course, every physical issue we experience throughout our lives is connected to each one that came before, on every level, and I was very aware of the parallels and similarities between the gallstones of my childhood, and what was occurring now. Clearly too, this particular geographic region of my body, where filtration, processing, modulation, digestion, and integration take place, was carrying the effects of both ongoing healing, and the recurring cycle of unresolved and unprocessed conflict.

I can only describe the sensation that erupted and then continued for hours on end as being what (I imagine) it would feel like to be stabbed repeatedly in the gut with a sharp knife, over and over again. The pain was so intense that I would frequently heave, and sometimes vomit. My body temperature would vacillate wildly between freezing and shaking, then moments later I would be burning up, drenched in sweat, and weeping from the anguish of it all. It was an appalling and terrifying experience.

During this first occurrence of outrageous pain, not only did I feel desperation and despair, but it registered to me that the pain was so monstrous that I actually wanted to die. In addition to the pain though, the wretchedness and misery were also shocking, and this compounded the horrific physicality of it all. I remember recognizing, with real alarm, that I was screaming like an animal. And I screamed for hours, flinging myself around, writhing, and repetitively banging various parts of my body against things—there was a big cupboard in our room, and I smashed my head and my fists on the door of that cupboard hundreds of times during that first episode alone, and all the episodes that followed. There were many moments when I left my body, only to observe my own debasement and the loss of everything I thought was dignity, with disgust.

I begged—frenziedly, incoherently—for God to deliver me, or to let me die. I begged Lee to take me to the hospital. I was desperate and feral. I had to make this stop. I had to fix it, and make it stop. I also felt a sickening mix of frantically needing and desiring to protect my baby, but also, to my shame, feeling deeply resentful of him or her. If it weren't for this creature inside me that I already loved, I could just go to the hospital, and they would tap a vein, and give me a hit of morphine and I would slip away into euphoric nothingness.

This abject insanity continued for an afternoon and into the evening — hysterical screaming, flailing and wailing, begging and bargaining — and then it stopped. And suddenly I was fine. I was exhausted and traumatized, but physically I was fine. It was as though a switch had been flipped. Spent, I went to sleep.

The next day, I woke up, and carried on with my life. But later that afternoon, it all began again. At first, the pain was mild, but within a few minutes, the stabbing had reached a fever pitch, and I was thrown into terror and torment once more. This time, the attack was closer to six or seven hours' duration, and once again, I moved through the cycle of frantically trying to figure this out — thinking and thinking, wracking my mind for some explanation, and then having to abandon my attempts at analysis, and devolving in a babbling psychotic mess, emitting an effluvial torrent of stream-of-consciousness and invective.

THE FUNCTION OF DIS-EASE

I recalled, in my pain-addled fervour, conversations with my mother when I was a child, during which she explained to me that having kidney stones was widely acknowledged to be far more painful than childbirth (an assertion I have a very different perspective on now, given the rearrangement of how I understand "normal" birth *and* kidney stones, but which, at the same time, is not wrong).

Even from that first attack, the most plausible explanation to me was that I was, undeniably, experiencing what is described as kidney stones. The possibility of an ectopic pregnancy or a ruptured ovarian cyst crossed my mind, although I eliminated those fairly quickly, given the specificity of the symptoms and the cyclical, episodic nature of the attacks. (Lee himself had endured kidney stones a few years before, and he also recognized the patterns.)

I had been a long-time student of self-healing, vibrational and energy medicine, and, in particular, the Germanic Healing Framework,[78] for several years already at this point, and I turned once more to the principles of GHK for insight into the brutal healing or resolution process I was clearly undergoing.

I have always held the perspective that an individual's susceptibility to disease or healing is entirely dependent on their beliefs, in the same way that our propensity to claim power or victimhood, or love or hate (or pleasure or pain during birth) is a reflection of our philosophical orientation. For someone who believes in viral contagion, for example, viruses are inescapably real, and the world is a precarious minefield of potential infection. For the person who believes that we can never "catch" a disease (and that what scientists have decided to call a "virus" is but the evidence of a cell undergoing the natural process of excretion, cleansing, and reparation), the world—and the body—is a sanctuary.

Similarly, an experience which involves acute pain will mean something quite distinct for a person who believes, according to the principles of GHK developed by Dr. Ryke Geert Hamer, that dis-ease, far from being a form of dysfunction, is instead a brilliant survival mechanism: the evidence of the healing itself having already taken place, and a sign indicating the aftereffects of what Hamer called a *biological shock*. A biological shock is an instance of unexpected distress that threatens a

---

[78] Also known as German New Medicine (GNM) or Germanic Healing Knowledge (GHK).

person's sense of physical, spiritual, or relational survival, also understood as a *conflict shock*.

These conflict shocks result in a three-fold response on the level of the psyche, the brain, and a corresponding organ in the body, prompting the organ to either grow more cells, or to diminish cell growth, as part of the brilliant, instinctive, adaptive healing mechanism that all mammals possess—the special (or splendid) biological program. The "new medicine," as the Germanic Healing framework is often named, is known throughout the Spanish-speaking world as "the sacred medicine" (*la medicina sagrada*)—and Hamer's discoveries, in my experience, do truly constitute sacred and universal knowledge that has offered me and so many others immense freedom.

Kidney stones, according to the Germanic Healing perspective, are indicative of a biological conflict rooted in a person's inability to maintain boundaries, to truly stand for their convictions with power and sovereignty, or to commit fully to their life path. This conflict can also be intertwined with a state of internal antagonism driven by isolation and abandonment—which impacts the kidney collecting tubules and amplifies the individual's issues with boundaries and choice-points. This was a perfect characterization of the existential crisis I faced in those intensely challenging years, full of displacement and alienation, prior to becoming pregnant with Helio.

But understanding dis-ease from an abstract or theoretical standpoint is very different from actually shifting the subconscious beliefs we have about ourselves and our place in the world that give rise to painful and challenging physiological expressions of healing. It is only by modifying our frequency signature from the inside out that our physiology can then accord with a new resonant range and oscillation of being, and therefore expression.

This recalibration often involves a reconfiguration of our very understanding of the meaning, cause, significance, and story of dis-ease, not to mention our relationship to the symptoms that we're experiencing, along with our beliefs about how those symptoms might be relieved or resolved. Most people unwittingly perpetuate dis-ease and extend the healing process through their commitment to resistance, victimhood, drama, and wilful-yet-unconscious self-subjugation, exactly as I was doing.

In spite of the fact that I recognized myself immediately in the description of the conflicts that give rise to kidney stones and "kidney colic," the resolution eluded me at first, and from the initial onslaught of pain when I was nine weeks pregnant, I had an attack every single day for the subsequent two and a half months. Each bout lasted for a minimum of three hours, but at times extended up to eight hours. These episodes usually began in the afternoon or evening and persisted into the night.

The inflammation in my kidneys was so severe that I was unable to lie down at all while the pain was raging, so I devised several coping strategies, including a clever way of assembling my pillows into a tube so that I could at least attempt to rest, even while the pain persisted. It was often two or three o'clock in the morning before I was finally able to sleep for a few hours, only to wake up and move through the circuit once again.

HEAVEN ON EARTH

Pain became the organising principle of my existence—the master to which I conceded everything. I was quickly conditioned to anticipate the attacks, and I scheduled my work and time with my children in the mornings so that I could maintain a semblance of normalcy, while living what felt like—and was—a double-life. Half of my time was spent in a zombified stupor, carrying out as many basic tasks as I could, and my afternoons and evenings were dedicated to pitiful supplication: begging for mercy, begging for drugs, screaming for deliverance (literally), and fully ensnared within a state of profound victimization. It's remarkable what we can become accustomed to and survive. It was a kind of hell on earth.

This time of perdition was also one of the most enlightening, educational, and important experiences of my life, and it offered me a completely new perspective on, and understanding of pain, and of the *immense* power that we have over our experience and perception of it—a far greater power than most of us recognize. The protracted nature of the experience, especially, was an absolute gift. Horrific, without a doubt, but there was something deeply interesting to me about this invitation to not only put into practice my theories and notions, but also to test my own fundamental beliefs about the mechanisms of healing, the body, and the mind, and to discover myself anew.

As I became more familiar with the sequence I was moving through—as I started to "expect" that the pain was going to begin every day at a certain time, and that this was what I was being "dealt"—I got mad. I became *enraged*, and railed against the pain, and against God. I *hated* God. I swore at God. I swore at myself. I told God this, that, and the other, and worked myself into a lather while He only responded by giving me more. When my husband Lee then tried to help me, I lashed out at him, and I lashed out at him when he left me alone. I was grotesque. Strangely enough, spewing hatred and behaving badly didn't do much to help.

Nonetheless, for a couple of weeks, anger was the only octave I was capable of expressing, and while the quality of the pain itself didn't deviate, there was a flicker of child-like power in my rage. It was not authentic power at all—I was still fully in a state of victimization, at this point more than ever, perhaps—but the anger also felt akin to desire; to a will to survive, a determination to continue to exist; an assertion of myself.

As the spiral continued, however, I began to grow weary. I hadn't slept or eaten properly in over a month, and I was breaking mentally and physically. Each day, when afternoon rolled around and I could sense the portentous indicators with which I had become so familiar, that foretold that an attack was near, I began to revisit the idea of death, but this time in a more listless, lethargic, and resigned version of despair, increasingly tinged with grief and fear.

I felt delirious in a new key. I was sad and scared, and more afraid of the depths of my sadness and my increasing passivity than anything. Between rounds of screaming and moaning, I wept and cried and mourned—I had been damaged too much already, and I suspected I was breaking down. I would never be the same. Surely my child was already damaged beyond repair.

Many people have asked me why I didn't go to the hospital at some point during this extended ordeal. I certainly wanted to, or rather I *thought* that I wanted to many times. I considered it frequently, and on occasion, ardently, and even obsessively. There were many moments when I said to Lee, in all seriousness, *That's it, let's go. I can't do this anymore.* And he would get up and say, *Alright. I'm ready. I'll help you out to the car…* genuinely hoping, in many ways, I know, that I would succumb, for his sake as well as mine.

But in the end, I couldn't do it (and Lee knew that too). Partly, I am indeed too stubborn, proud, and vain. I couldn't handle the idea of finding salvation *there*. While this confession is, I'm quite aware, deeply unflattering, it's also just as valid, I suspect, as the inverse motivation. But I also knew that the logical conclusion of the choice to submit to the medical establishment would not, ultimately, have offered me or my unborn child any real benefit.

Yes, the pain I felt would have been relieved immediately by prescription drugs. But it is an indisputable fact that morphine and other pharmaceutical analgesics are harmful to developing babies, whereas it was not entirely clear or even likely that the pain I was experiencing was actually injurious to my baby. Had I gone into a medical facility, I know it would have been nearly impossible to have avoided the insistence that my child be subjected to various forms of surveillance and testing, including ultrasound and doppler exposure, among other procedures—a risk I was not willing to take. Furthermore, even within the allopathic sphere, there is no real "cure" for kidney stones or kidney infection apart from antibiotics, pain meds, and (at the far end of the spectrum) surgery, all of which were out of the question.

Ultimately, the longer I stayed alive and endured the pain (a capacity on my part which seemed miraculous to me at this point), the more aware I became of the fact that it wasn't killing me. It wasn't killing my baby, either, though at times I felt exceedingly guilty over what I was putting him through.

I am well aware that pre-born children feel everything their mothers do, but I also know that there are infinite variables, and that babies, even before birth, are expressing, experiencing, and integrating life through their unique lens of perception. All I could do was choose, guided by love, what I believed to be the most protective, nurturing option, and to trust that my baby was resilient and thriving.

As the attacks of kidney pain continued and I fell into an awful routine of anticipation, endurance, and survival, I started to lose it: my mind, my tether on what I thought was reality, any grasp of time.

But as a result of this descent into near-madness, something else started to happen: began to communicate more directly with my baby, with myself, and with God…and that's when everything changed.

BECOMING ALIVE

The successive weeks of agony had taken a colossal toll. Mentally, physically, emotionally, and spiritually, I felt like I had been assaulted and tortured, and yet in part, it was the intensity of this new level of delirium that catalyzed a shift.

As my sense of internal unravelling accelerated, I felt a heightening passion—a critical mass of emotion—while, at the very same time, an almost demented sense of neutrality, humour, and even indifference to the drama, descended.

I found myself thanking God, and almost exultantly asking for more. *Is that all you've got? Is this it, you bastard?* Then, unbidden, a series of further questions appeared on the skyline of my consciousness.

What am I getting out of this?

What do I love about this?

Why have I chosen this?

Why have I selected such a commitment, such an investment?

What is it that I think I'm atoning for, by nurturing so much pain?

What am I waiting for?

This seemingly spontaneous line of inquiry was sobering, yet also enlivening and enlightening. I found a burgeoning levity, and curiosity. Belief is the crux of all healing, after all. Belief is everything.

So I started to play. Instead of resisting the sensation, which had been my modus operandi up to this point, I saturated the space of perception with every atom of my awareness, and I allowed myself—tentatively at first, but soon all-consumingly—to feel it all; to feel beyond feeling.

I chose, in that moment, to discern the sensation of what I had been calling "pain" so fully and so devotedly that the feeling itself became abstract, compelling, and precious. What then blossomed was the most profoundly beautiful realisation: *I am alive.* This is what it is to be alive.

This cannot be wrong. And this sensation is a treasure, because the pain itself *is* the sign that nothing can really hurt me.

I tilted towards the pain, and it washed over me. I noticed that when I, conversely, micronized my consciousness, and made my awareness nanoscopic, I could move between the interstices of the intensity's topography to find entire expanses—open plains—of space, and relief. In the three-dimensional world, these openings occurred within an infinitesimal decimal point of a second, but they were undeniably there, and available to me once I was willing to encounter them on another plane, through a distinctive experience of time.

Again and again, when the wave of sensation came, I transposed every particle of my attention into the centre of the typhoon, and God, my baby, my Guide-Self, and peace were there, waiting. I conveyed my awareness to the round world of my womb, and to the energy of my child, and I flooded him with love (and some strands of contrition) and I felt his love in return, encompass and suffuse my whole being. I felt grateful, and the pain became something else. I had graduated.

The next day, another level of training was presented to me, and this time, in response, I immediately chose to softly, nonchalantly focus my attention and claim surrender with ease... and the conversion was immediate. The idea itself of "pain" began to instantly lose its charge.

The meditative, disciplined, yet exquisitely simple form of concentration required to surrender in this way meant that I had no residual energy left for yelling and screaming or forcefully launching my energy into the desolate dark, but I also had no interest in doing so either. The seduction was gone.

It took sustained focus to maintain my devotion to surrendering to the fullness of this newfound embodiment. The connection I felt with my baby and with God was electric, and I was dazzled by the relief of releasing my hold on hardness and disaffection.

Finally, I took a breath, inspiring deeply, exhaling fully, noticing, as though for the first time, the beauty of my body, and its perfect wisdom. I was flooded with an all-consuming, astronomical feeling of gratitude, and as this thankfulness engulfed me, the residual miasmic traces of pain dissolved.

Thank you.
Thank you God.
I love you baby.
Thank you God.
This is fine.
This is fine.
This is fine.
This is passing through me.
All is passing through me.
This is fine.

Everything was fine. I was at home in the world, at home in my body, and my child was at home within me. God is always present, and He has vested in me (and in every person), the power to choose love.

Over the next two days, the episodes of pain declined sharply, and then stopped—completely. The remainder of my pregnancy was blessedly uneventful (and I have had no issues with my kidneys since then).

Why did the pain diminish and then cease at that point in time? Was it simply that my perception of the pain, and therefore my relationship to it, shifted? Or was it perhaps simply a coincidence that I experienced such a radical reconfiguration of how I situated myself in association with the pain at the very moment that my kidney issues just happened to abate, at random? I don't think so. I don't think we can ever isolate the body from the mind from the psyche from the landscape of the spirit or the map of emotion, or from the power of our awareness or from the art of choosing.

I don't believe that there are any coincidences. But if my belief in my own power to alchemize pain and to heal is but a delusion, it is a delusion I am delighted to embrace and maintain.

THE GIFT OF PAIN

Of the many lessons and epiphanies I received and integrated from my experience of spontaneously healing my kidneys, one of the most potent and formidable among them was the realisation that a crucial aspect of the body's impeccable design is that there is no amount of pain that you (or I) cannot handle.

I beseeched God to allow me to lose consciousness while in the throes of my two-month-long ordeal, on the basis of my assertion that I simply couldn't bear it. But God, in His infinite (and often exasperating) wisdom, refused to grant me my request (He's not much of a genie), thereby demonstrating just how wrong I was. It turns out, I *could* bear it after all — for weeks on end, no less.

The fact that you feel pain means, categorically, that you can handle it. If you can proclaim your inability to abide the pain, you are proving yourself wrong, then and there.

The only evidence we are ever offered to indicate that pain is unbearable, is loss of consciousness. If you are conscious, you can, by definition, tolerate the pain and that, in and of itself, is a fact that you can choose to derive comfort from. Any form of pain you are experiencing is pain you can withstand.[79]

Throughout my journey into and out of pain, I was struck by the power of assuming studied indifference in the face of it; not complacency, exactly,

---

[79] People do occasionally pass out from pain alone, but this is quite rare. For the most part, fainting happens on account of blood-loss, fear, or a vaso-vagal response, which can certainly be related to pain, but isn't always.

but, as we examined in the context of fear, an acknowledgement of the relative insignificance of this especially deciduous sensation. The clichés, as always, are true—*this too shall pass.* More than grief, which can really hang around, and more than sadness, which can seep as silent as mildew into the soft parts of everything, pain may throb and persist, and saw and gnaw, but it's always, in some sense, passing through. Even chronic pain has its ebb and flow.

Our relationship to pain evolves in stages. I wonder if it's necessary to move through them all, at least fleetingly—denial, desperation, anger, fear, sadness, curiosity, presence, expansion, gratitude—to then access detachment and acceptance, which, in my experience, tend to be inextricable from pain's eventual leaving. Pain, like every symptom, is healing in motion.

It is true, axiomatically, that we have infinite options as to how we choose to experience, interpret, and define pain, and what it is that the presence of pain reveals to us about ourselves and our decisions. But we also have far more agency over, and influence on, the visceral experience of pain—how it actually feels in the body—than we have been conditioned to expect or believe.

Pain is bewitchingly subjective, and our commonly held cultural beliefs and assumptions about what it is and how it works are often highly incongruent with the incredibly diverse and sometimes seemingly extreme experiences that people have with pain—including the vastly differing perceptions that exist of how the sensations of birth are embossed upon the body and the psyche.

Just as fear and struggle during pregnancy are powerful hooks, rooted in the commitment to reinforce our sense of identity and significance, so too is the story of birth-as-pain.

The legend of suffering through childbirth is an antiquity that we do not actually require for survival or substantiation. The narrative of struggle and extreme endurance that our culture suggests is endemic to birth is a vortex of belief whose resonance we can step outside of, and disavow, through the act of becoming.

In the simplest terms, the process of pain dissolution[80] is as follows:

- Come into presence: Bring yourself to your body. Here you are, having an experience, being called to a place of intimacy on account of a sensation.
- Notice: Where in your body are you feeling this sensation?
- Assess: How can you describe the quality of the sensation? Is it pressure, knotting, pounding, clenching, pinching, sharpness, twisting, vibrating, throbbing, or churning? What is the most factual, substantive way you can describe the physical feeling, without emotion or story?
- Acknowledge: Remind yourself, briefly, that you know what it is to experience ease, and that the ease is forthcoming, sometime, because everything changes. Everything you're experiencing right now is temporary.
- Discern: What emotions are you experiencing, overlaid with the sensation?
- Accept the emotion: Separate the emotion from the physical sensation and acknowledge it. You feel angry and scared.
- Feel: Feel your fear and your anger. Sit for a moment and allow those feelings to be fully present. Honour yourself for your courage in seeing and feeling it all.
- Touch: Take your hands to the location in your body where the sharpest sensation resides, and send the energy from your palm beaming through skin, fascia, muscle, tendon, organ, bone.

---

[80] A pain dissolution meditation is available on my website, www.yolandenorris-clark.com.

- Realm: Transpose your consciousness to the place where the pain resides.
- Attune: Notice the subtle pulsation of the sensation. Pain is almost never fixed. It always changes. Between every peak of throbbing, stabbing, or piercing, there is a space. Find it.
- Micronize: Make your attention as small as an atom, and fit your awareness between those moments of peak sensation. Be in the space and grace of the rest that is always available.
- Move: Wherever the sensation resides most prominently, allow yourself to move that body part. Even if the movement is granular or microscopic, there is always a way of moving that will change the way the pain feels in a way that is, at the very least, curious and interesting.
- Breathe: Breathe. Breathe into the place where the sensation exists.
- Sing: As you breathe into the pain, allow yourself to vocalise freely, without performance, strategy, or effort.
- Radiate: During the apex of sensation—at its highest, most seemingly offensive peak—stay with it, and expand it, making it bigger, and allow yourself to see and feel that you are still alive. Flood that place with the warmth and light that you are able to harness with your mind.
- Dissolve: Let the light fill the area, and then as it filters away, notice how the pain also subsides.
- Allow: Affirm that there is no problem, nothing to fix, nothing to change.
- Bless: Offer thanks—to God, to Spirit, to whatever force you know and love, and to the pain itself for this exquisite experience that proves your aliveness.

- Be grateful: Allow yourself to feel the transformational glow of gratitude fully.

Now, do it all again.

INTEGRATION QUESTIONS

1. When you move with discipline and devotion through the steps of pain dissolution, how does your self-concept change?

2. How do your symptoms and the quality and sensation of pain shift or change?

3. Write about your birthing experience from the point of view of your healed self, who has completely transformed her view of pain from inevitable and necessary to optional.

CHAPTER THIRTEEN

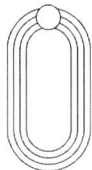

INTEGRATION

HELIO

Heart.
Breath.

Moving shadows.

The sound of light
        pulsing
                gloaming.

The dance is on.

I turn inward
        silent
              charged   connected.

The rise comes softly   electric
        and I am opening once more.

PORTAL

Song of devotion.

Orison.

I reach my arms to the ceiling
the sky
the heavens
willing.

I am willing.

I am soft
        and willing
                and surrendering
                      over   and   over   again
                      returning
                          to surrender.

Laser.
Beacon.

Focus
        coaxes me back
            home to the all-encompassing
            immanence of God
                the presence of my baby's soul
                    the innate comprehension of
                    myself
                      as love.

The joy of it is so intense I start to weep.

There is no pain at all, only   rippling   fractals

      sheer   diaphanous   rhapsodic
    multitudinous
      melodic   pleasure
        beaming.

Thank you God.
Thank you God.
Thank you baby.
I love you baby.
I love you so much baby.
Thank you.

I move in circles now
    spiraling back to the median
        coiling and uncoiling   my hips   my ribs
      my arms uplifted
        surrendering again
        and again
          loose   open   choosing
  riveted
  yet completely at ease.

Another surge builds.

This time
    I see the wave in the distance
    moving towards me.

I open myself to it   fully
    and there is only the swell.

I see it all   now
    the fear portal here,

PORTAL

      the pain portal there
          the ecstasy portal   resplendent   in the
      distance.

I consider
wavering
but then
I turn
into the riptide
too curious to know
the crush
of bliss
to accept
the temptation
to doubt it.

Again and again I lean into the gyre
      yielding to the rhythm   falling   through
    layers and
    strata of
    whorls and
    eddies of
    being and
    consciousness,
    into and
out of the larger looping cycle of sensation,
      feeding into ever-finer spirals,
          helixes
              holograms.

Eyes closed
      panorama
keen

    knowing

I dive into the pools of light as they appear.

Elysian.

I embrace the all
        more and higher
        higher   more.

Water.

Vapour.

Primaeval swimmers in the ocean of   deep   time.

My baby is moving through my body.

Thank you God.
Thank you God.
I love you baby.
Thank you God.
Thank you baby.
I love you.

Suddenly, I need to go outside
        to be
            with the trees and feel
            the sun again.

I stagger into the courtyard.

Lee is outside.

PORTAL

    He sees me emerge and
    gets up to follow at a distance.

Walking is strange and unfamiliar, but tentatively, I make it out into the walled garden, where the late-afternoon shafts shine luminous through the mango and moringa trees, between the tines of the gate, flooding the flagstones.

I place my hands on the coarse, cratered bark of the massive guanacaste[81]
    hovering   receiving.

My body is a solar panel.

The flaxen glow melts into my skin
    and I radiate.

I turn my face up to the light and feel pure pleasure.

Another sensation rocks me, its shockwaves fluttering through my body.

A consecration.

I have received my illumination.

Suffused, and incandescent, I drift back to my den.

---

[81] Van Velzer, Ryan. 2023. "National Tree." *Costarica.Com.* February 24, 2023. https://www.costarica.com/culture/national-tree. "The Guanacaste tree is said to represent universal equilibrium and sacred creation, the renewal of faith, the power of Mother Nature, and the transient condition of human life. It is a symbol of stability and growth, and its strong and firm roots represent the attachment to life. Its hard trunk expresses human will and its branches are the protectors of creative peace. The tree's canopy is associated with spiritual consciousness."

Yolande Norris-Clark

In the sacred dark there are no distractions.

I am alone, in the presence of God
        my baby
        my heart
        the music
            soft song of my body.

With every successive sensation
I accept the summoning
sidestep the snares
soliciting
        the lure to question time
        to consider exhaustion
        to doubt my energy my stamina.

In each instance
in every moment
at every interval
I choose
to choose
to walk through
the portal of euphoria
again
and again.

        A thought arises
this is my first time
the first instance of ever having allowed
this quality or texture of pleasure
into my nebula
        let alone my flesh.

PORTAL

It's a miracle
    to have this
    to know this
    to be human
        and alive.

I lovingly refuse
    the seduction of attempting to quantify or question time.

I don't want or need this to end or
    to be anything other than what it is.

When each swell subsides
I rest
    In the perfect moment.

There is nothing to change and yet
the flow is constant
    fluctuation
    evolution
    Morphing   shifting circling   transforming.

I am in the vortex
    of the vortex
        of the vortex
            of the ever-spiraling
            vortex.

I am being offered everything.
I receive it all.

Aurora.

Helio.

Darkness descends. Without feeling the need to assign a value or story to this, I can feel the energy of my physical body dwindling, and I allow that too, partly curious to know what will happen, but also dispassionate, and ultimately at ease.

Someone—Lee or maybe Treva—hands me a glass of water. I drink, then I lie down. Shapes and light-forms flicker across my vision. I sense someone's presence in the room, then I slip away, out into the fathomless shadow realm.

How long do I sleep? Minutes, hours, days, lifetimes, maybe.

Abruptly, I am in my body again. I call out. *Something is happening. Where am I?*

There is a power and force in my pelvis that I haven't sensed before. It shocks me, and then I remember the offer of ecstasy, and I dive back into the current of trust, closing my eyes, plunging into the hallowed darkness.

Endless time passes and we move through all the universes of the heart and skin, flesh and muscle—holy prayer.

I make myself a ray of light, and I know this is it. I call for my husband and—

Hello baby I love you.
Hello baby I love you.
Thank you God.
Okay baby, come now.

You are mine and I am yours.

PORTAL

I love you. Thank you God. Thank you God. Thank you God. Thank you baby. I love you.

You are mine and I am yours and this is life, becoming.

We are a single stream of consciousness;
    a column of fire
        as deep as water
           as steady as earth
              as fluid as wind.

From the conflagration of all
the elements
my yoni
    blooms
and my baby's head
    blossoms
        from my body
           in an exquisite emanation.

I hear my breath
    ragged and serene.

I touch my baby's
    soft
        damp
           downy skull
           round
    at the core of me
    the meat of me
    the heart of me
    part of me.

Yolande Norris-Clark

I see Lee on the periphery.
He is nervous.
This is fine.

Everything is fine.

I am the world and the world is moving through me.

I am reclined
        still stretched out on my back.

Now that my baby's head is   there
        between my thighs
        I feel the urge to
            rise.

I rotate
draw myself to my knees,
arch my back,
        and with jubilant   intoxicating   orgasmic
            relief
            my baby is born.

I immediately pick his slippery body up in my hands and reflexively
uncoil his lifeline—the umbilical cord—from around his neck
and we reach for each other.

He cries out   briefly
        nuzzles into my breasts for a moment
then he turns to me
his gorgeous face frosted with vernix.

PORTAL

He lifts his arm up, and I grasp his tiny hand.

He opens his eyes
    looking into mine
        and I gaze into the sapphire deepness of existence.

We call our new sun Helio.

CONTINUUM

Motherhood is a continuum—an elliptical orbit through time and space, and across ancestral flight paths. We traverse the labyrinth into and out of the spiral with every child, and every micro-stage of each macro-stage has its own crescendo, apex, denouement, resolution, and seeming completion…and then we embark again on the next mission, whether toddlerhood, the teenage years, grandbabies, cronedom, or ascension to the beyond.

Your newborn baby will need you every moment of every day and night, and will be nursing almost all the time. Knowing this, expecting it, and ensuring that those around you know and expect it too, will make an enormous difference in your capacity to choose to melt into the dreamlike tapestry of newborn life: days upon nights upon days of languid succulent softness. Mornings and afternoons folding into each other, as you simply allow yourself to float and be, seeing the world through and in the eyes of your child, taking in every ounce of the tenderness of their unfurling.

In the hours and days that proceed from the birth of your baby, you will weep and sleep and radiate and absorb love and elation, and you will bleed. You may feel strong warm gushes of blood periodically over the first few days, especially if you're lying down or reclining in bed. This is normal. You may also feel cramping accompanied by the passing of larger blood clots, which is also normal, and then your bleeding will subside to the extent that it will feel like a heavy period, for some time—days or weeks, and it may come and go, ebb and flow, letting you know when more rest is in order.

If your yoni has torn at all, you may feel burning when you urinate during the first week of postpartum as your tissues reassemble (which they will, especially if you allow yourself to rest and to relax).[82] Your entire body may ache, especially in the tenderest of places, and you will likely feel exhausted in general. Rest and sleep.

Every physical, mental, emotional, and spiritual challenge or dilemma following birth will be soothed by rest and sleep. Keep your baby with you, and ideally *on* you, at all times. The longer you can stay in bed, naked, with your baby nursing, nestled in the curve of your body, or laying on your pillowy belly, kneading your newfound softness with their tiny toes, the swifter and better all your aching parts will heal.

Watch and listen to your baby. Talk to him. Be curious; be open. Every phase is fleeting, but the timing of the stream of life is always perfect, as long as we are willing to pay the price: to pay attention. Children do not "grow up too fast," it only feels that way when we miss out on being present, which can seem burdensome in this era of constant diversions which pull us away from full engagement with our aliveness. Not only do we chronically absent ourselves from the now through our absorption in technology, but we distract ourselves with unnecessary fear, anxiety, and worry, which can rob us blind.

---

[82] Norris-Clark, Yolande. "Make Your Own Honey." *Substack*, June 18, 2022. https://yolandenorrisclark.substack.com/p/make-your-own-honey. I have written extensively on perineal tearing and healing elsewhere. However, in general terms, our yonis and the mucosal folds of the vagina are designed to sometimes tear, and to heal beautifully, especially when no one has poked you with a needle and thread. Even severe, so-called "third degree" tears heal best without suturing, in my experience. Resting is the most effective path to quick and efficient healing—for all of our body parts postpartum, but especially when it comes to perineal tears. See my *Substack* article for more information.

PORTAL

Motherhood is rich and fascinating if we choose to see it that way, and children are whole people—entirely themselves—from the very beginning. Caring for our babies is designed to be as easy, pleasurable, spontaneous, and magical as birth. Invariably, the one experience will perfectly reflect the other. As always, choose discerningly, and carefully, and know that in every gesture and inflection we select our orientation to one universe or another.

AFTERMATH

The time and space after birth can be a vortex of intensity and tenderness. In the aftermath of emergence, you will move through yet another stage in the transubstantiation of motherhood: the realignment of your body, along with a breakdown of your identity and sense of self, and a shifting of all the elements that you once thought made you who you were.

For many of us, especially those for whom birth constitutes an evolution into an entirely new range and palette of awareness and power—not to mention ecstasy, grace, or bliss—the early postpartum period can be disorienting in its expansion to the point of near-alienation. The distinctiveness of the kind of radical shift into what for most women is the singular and remarkably unfamiliar experience of sovereignty and self-responsibility that liberated birth offers can be so uncomfortable that many mothers feel an almost irresistible temptation to unconsciously sabotage their otherwise-perfect birth experiences by imagining various problems or conditions, and even making up justifications for transferring to the hospital.

In my practice, I repeatedly encounter versions of the story of the mother who has had a wonderful birth at home, but who then decides to go to the hospital to get "assessed" because she feels faint, or because she is bleeding, or because her baby is gurgly, or any other version of pathologizing what in most cases are the completely normal consequences of birth. Only rarely are these kinds of transfers medically necessary. Instead, they primarily serve the purpose of reinforcing the woman's underlying allegiance to the medical industrial complex and recapitulating her victim-consciousness.

Whether the new mother who has sought clinical help leaves the hospital convinced that in the end, she really *did* need medical assistance after all and the professionals heroically saved her, or if the hospital staff end up villainizing her and embroiling her in a child protective services investigation as a form of social sanction and punishment for having given birth outside the system (which is disturbingly common), she has, in some way, reconfirmed her familiar identity as a victim — either a victim of her ultimate dependency on the system, or a victim of the system itself.

Often women transfer to the hospital postpartum to be "checked" by medical staff simply because they have a subconscious (and very legitimate) need for attention, validation, or witnessing — a common dynamic among mothers who lack appropriate support systems and self-awareness (and one of the potential pitfalls of choosing freebirth). When she is then told that her placenta needed to be manually extracted, or that the clots were alarming and abnormal, or that she was dehydrated and needed an injection of IV fluids for a few minutes, this justifies both her story of needing to be saved, and the power of medicine to do the saving.

In no way is it a sign of weakness or failure to engage with the medical system because we want to be seen, loved, or acknowledged — those needs are real. But ensnaring ourselves in an unnecessary medical drama almost always ends up being a poor substitute for the tenderness, devotion, and deep adoration many women are really looking for, following their initiation into new motherhood. We can avoid drama (if we so choose) by learning to know ourselves, identify our emotions, and ask for (then instantiate) what we truly desire.

Drama, however, is the dynamic that many of us seek out and cultivate. We tend to be highly attached to the drama of victimhood — it is certainly enticing for most of us, especially when individuation, independence, and self-responsibility are so deeply threatening to the status quo, in this culture of acquiescence. Most of us are extremely uncomfortable with power, peace, and healing.

On the surface, maintaining a commitment to the medical complex can seem like the safest way to preserve our habitual place within the culture and family system to which we belonged prior to motherhood, and in a way, this is true. Withdrawing our allegiance to the medico-pharmaceutical establishment is a risk. But the deeper truth is that we mothers who have liberated our instinct and potential through birth represent a threat to the masquerade.

I am in no way suggesting that it is *never* appropriate to seek medical attention postpartum—as always, there are endless exceptions. You know if your story of hospital transfer is among those exceptions, because you will be reading this without any sense of defensiveness or sensitivity at all.

For the most part though, birth works, and the variations of what can be "normal" are far broader than most of us believe. The body adapts. This fourth "stage" of the birth process as you encounter your baby and your body finds its balance is intense. In many ways, the time immediately following birth is inherently destabilising, at first. Most mothers will shake, ache, quake, flutter, fluctuate, bleed (sometimes quite heavily), cramp, weep, and tremble in the hours after birth, and most babies will snort, snuffle, cough, sleep, and cry.

The birth of the placenta can occur according to varying timelines (usually placentas are ready to emerge from between thirty minutes to an hour postpartum and while there is very little reason *not* to facilitate the release of our placentas during that time, I know of mothers who have waited much longer before safely and easily birthing their placentas at home without any medical interference). Patience is an essential part of allowing our bodies and our psyches to calibrate.

Barring an unforeseen major underlying condition or dis-ease, most women who have experienced a relatively undisturbed birth can expect that just as their bodies successfully grew and sustained their babies for ten months and allowed those babies to be born, so too will they recuperate postpartum. There is always some grief and loss interwoven with the ecstasy.

Sovereign birth rearranges everything. Have courage.

DENOUEMENT

In the moments that followed Helio's emergence, Lee called from the courtyard into the jungle where our older children had been playing, and they streamed into the bedroom, jostling for position, eager to see their new baby.

I loved the chaos and the sweetness of all the big brothers and sisters clambering over each other, elated to finally meet their new sibling, touching him, kissing him, helping to ensure his optimal thriving by perfectly complicating his microbiome with all the grime from climbing trees and playing in the dirt all day.

Eventually I settled myself in bed, surrounded by my family, and Helio latched on to my nipple for the first time and began to nurse peacefully. Around forty-five minutes after he was born, I started to feel uncomfortable. Suddenly shaky, sweaty, and cold, I knew these signs of shock indicated that I needed to eat and drink, and that it was time to release my baby's placenta.

Lee brought me tea and fruit, and an empty bowl, and I knelt over it, bearing down while offering some gentle traction on the umbilical cord, and the bloody organ slipped out of my body easily, followed by a torrent of blood. Relieved and woozy, I sat back once more, situated Helio in my arms again, and we all cuddled in.

I then began to notice the feeling of after-birth sensations (also known as *after-pains* which tend to be stronger with the birth of each subsequent baby, and which, after past births, I have experienced as terribly painful, far "worse" than the birth process, in some cases). Lee offered me a hot water bottle, and I held it against my womb, which felt soothing. I then closed my eyes and quietly moved through the pain dissolution process, and within a few moments, the tightenings were no longer perceptible (and never returned).

Some hours later, with the cord laying limp and cold across our baby's body, we decided at last to separate our son from his placenta. Lee brought my beeswax candles and the cord-burning box, and the kids gathered around again, and we all watched in awe as Helio's once-vibrant, vital, pulsating, lifeline crackled and blackened between the two points of flame until eventually, it was but a brittle filament.

The kids cheered and I cried when the last strand broke, marking our child as fully born, and consecrated, in a way, through this ceremony of completion. Then, still naked and bloody, I lay down with my baby, breathing in his intoxicating scent, his little face at my bare breasts, and we slept as we would sleep for all the days and nights of his life over the following year and more.

I stayed in bed (for the most part) for a few days, nursing and napping and envisioning the fibres, tissues, and muscles of my pelvic lattice knitting back together, and I learned to pee and poop again like a baby myself. I got annoyed with my husband, I sobbed in despair and loneliness, and I witnessed my baby, hour after delicious, sensual hour, as he dreamed and fed and practiced the art of embodiment with dazzling mastery. Together, we learned to breastfeed, we found our positions, and we nourished each other.

On day four, I woke up before sunrise feeling irritated with everyone. I also noticed that the yellowish hue of Helio's skin had intensified,[83] so I wrapped him up and took him out to the truck, and we drove slowly down the dirt road as day began to break.

We turned on to the shortcut through the cow fields and across the river, through Las Delicias, and down to Remanso. There, at the edge of the ocean—on the margins of the world—-I was alone with my baby, save for a few intrepid fishermen wading into the half-tide waves on the south-end of the bay. As the sun stretched its long warm caress up over the hill behind us, I watched the frigate birds diving for their breakfast while Helio slept in my lap, and we both basked in the dayspring's opulent first light.

Life outside had beckoned. Later that day the kids had a performance, then a class, then a beach party, and with that, Helio was inaugurated. From then on, he was routinely slung into the sweaty stretchy wrap in the slick tropical heat, carried out into the world where all the old ladies everywhere we went snatched him from us lovingly to kiss him a million times, and our friends at the mercadito put him on their produce scale to see how big he was, and the street dogs jumped up to sniff at him, and he was passed around constantly—as happy as could be—by all his siblings

---

[83] It is very common for babies' skin to turn a yellowish tinge during days 2-4 postpartum as a result of a build-up of bilirubin. Bilirubin—a normal substance produced during the breakdown of red blood cells—is processed slowly by their tiny bodies in the early stages of adjustment to the outside world. Jaundice is an adaptive, physiological response, and the best way to facilitate the clearing of bilirubin (thus resolving the yellowish discoloration of a baby's skin) is to breastfeed the baby continuously, and expose them to the rays of the sun to support the maturation of the baby's liver and internal systems. All of my babies have "had jaundice" to greater or lesser degrees, and this has never been even a remote concern to me. The risks of jaundice tend to be greatly exaggerated by medical professionals, and often mothers are pressured into allowing their newborns to be separated from them and put under artificial lights, despite the fact that sunlight (while in their mother's arms) is a far superior "treatment." In rare cases, severe jaundice, or significant jaundice at birth can indicate a problem, but this is unusual.

and their grubby friends, the rocked to sleep on my breast or in his daddy's arms to the lullaby din of the barrio.

POSTPARTUM

Postpartum is its own vast landscape; valleys, vistas, cliffs and crags; deep forests, and wild moors. We can get lost and lonely there, but it's also a place of liberation.

Matrescence epitomizes the most radical change a person will undergo outside of our initial arrival and our eventual departure. It can feel stunningly disorienting, at first, to mutate with such seeming suddenness, from the lush, round, taut blossoming of pregnancy, to being The Mother, in her full-fledged luxuriant garden of a body, ripe and fleshy, brimming with nectar.

Nothing can be contained postpartum: breasts, flesh, milk, tears, sweat, blood. Everything seeps and flows, bursting at the seams. Every emotion is abundant—the exquisite, earth-shattering adoration you have for your baby, the rightful pride, the beautiful slowness, and the crashing overwhelm, sometimes punctuated by pain, sometimes shame or regret, and occasionally faltering confidence, fear, exhaustion, or the terrible ache of absence and lack—a gap where we're told attachment should be, but is not, or isn't yet.

I have felt all of this, often all at once, and I know I'm not alone.

I have never done postpartum quite "right" (not according to the books or the experts), but I also wonder if there ever really can be (or has been) a correct ideal. Every family is a mess, all cultures that we know of are dysfunctional, every relationship is fraught, and no one has it all figured out. On one hand, there remains an enormous burden of pressure from our post-industrial consumer society for mothers to "bounce back" after birth. This is nonsense, of course, but in recent years, the backlash towards that expectation has been fierce, almost to the point of fashioning a different kind of unattainable fantasy.

Postpartum doulas, handbooks, and courses on postpartum caretaking and "re-villaging" abound, and there is now a glut of information and messaging on the importance of "self-care" postpartum: setting up systems, determining what specific kinds of support are best, along with various strictures on what foods new mothers should be eating (or not), and for how many days we should stay home in relative self-isolation with our babies. Most of that sounds grim, rigid, and awful to me.

Moreover, my observation is that for most women who experience any degree of deficit after birth, the issue isn't so much a lack of planning, foresight, or consideration at all, but rather a lack of resources, family cohesion, and authentic community. There is an interesting dichotomy between the idea of curating a postpartum experience, versus recognizing that our babies are born into the life we have created—a life that is real, and messy, and reflective of all that we are.

Yes, postpartum is a time when mothers are, ideally, nurtured, loved, revered, and doted on. But I am no longer entirely convinced that it is always to our benefit to contrive elaborate processes in the early days of motherhood that deviate too greatly from our day-to-day lives, or to treat postpartum as an "event."

Ascribing to the first forty days an undue degree of significance or expectation, over and above more or less allowing the experience to unravel organically in keeping with our existing way of life can sometimes result in feeling deflated or let down, especially if your postpartum support plan involves people spending a lot of time in your home that you aren't accustomed to accommodating (even if those people are acting in selfless service).

Occasionally, the entourage we find ourselves assembling can create friction, especially when one is not particularly adept at making one's wishes and desires known. If you find yourself suddenly thrust into an unwanted managerial role after giving birth, this can be just as draining (if not more so) as doing the work yourself (in my experience). Furthermore, at some point (presumably) all those people will leave, and you will once again be in the midst of your real life, now with your new baby.

This is not to say that it isn't important to put thought and intention into postpartum preparation. It is. But what is perhaps more important than calling in a temporary support team is doing what we can during pregnancy to set up our lives so that we can, as much as possible, transition fluently from one act to the next.

SEX AFTER BIRTH

People assume that becoming a mother automatically reduces a woman's sex drive, kills intimacy, dampens our sexuality, makes us asexual, or that motherhood (especially new motherhood and postpartum) is somehow a neutralizing, sexually deadening experience. None of this is true.

What does kill intimacy, affect the erotic impulse, damage the physical connection between women and their partners, and negatively affect the spark in a marriage or partnership, is being violently raped while giving birth by an obstetrician or a midwife while your husband watches, then being gaslit by everyone involved and the entire society around you, who tell you that this is just what it is to give birth, and to become a mother, and that the trauma, dissociation, and psychic dismemberment that so many women feel after giving birth is normal. Women are told that this is just how birth is, and what it does—what motherhood does—when in reality it's primarily obstetric violence that is neutering.

Most mothers have survived extraordinary abuse. The normalization of this abuse doesn't make it acceptable; in fact, it makes it so much more challenging to integrate. Because the programming is so persistent, and so ingrained, and the cognitive dissonance is so entrenched, many women are not even aware that what they have lived through is violation, sexualized abuse, and torture.

Not every woman needs to feel sexually activated after birth, and many women don't. Yet birth and mothering are integral to the sexual continuum, and there are mothers among us (especially those who have had ecstatic, wild births) who absolutely do feel erotically enlivened after birth—many of whom I have supported over the years. The mythological schism between birth and sex has contributed to the pernicious fabricated conflict between the archetypes of the mother vs. the seductress, a narrative that is not only unfortunate and unnecessary, but profoundly anti-human. In some cases, women who feel highly sexual postpartum wonder if there might be something wrong with them, when they feel desire even during the early days of new motherhood. Just as there is no "right" way to do birth, the same is true of sex and the sexual impulse.

There are various ways that the senseless cultural prohibition against postpartum sex (and motherhood as a time of sexual aliveness) is enforced, including the ridiculous and infantilizing idea that women must wait a predetermined number of weeks before re-establishing sexual congress with their partners, or that they have to receive "permission" from their medical practitioner to do so. This is part of the same necrotic, demeaning tradition that produces birth rape. There is no "dinner-plate-sized wound" inside the uterus postpartum, and any woman who feels ready for sex at any stage postpartum is free to listen to the messages from her body.

Lee and I made gentle love the day after our eldest daughter's easy, fast, arrival, and it was heavenly. I had experienced no tearing at all, my body felt utterly vibrant and whole, and there was no reason not to—just as women are free and safe to have sex while menstruating. Following the births of most of our babies, I have waited a couple of days before resuming intimacy, and I know that this has *contributed* to my always-efficient and integral recovery (as well as supporting the self-healing of prolapse, which

I have experienced on a couple of occasions, and repaired fully without any medical involvement or intervention).[84]

The Glowing Orb

Almighty God, unto whom all hearts be open, all desires known, and from whom no secrets are hid: cleanse the thoughts of our hearts by the inspiration of thy Holy Spirit, that we may perfectly love thee, and worthily magnify thy holy name.

The "Collect for Purity," a prayer of preparation, is recited at the beginning of the Anglican Eucharist. It was first published in the tenth century, but has been included in every Anglican and Episocpalian prayer book since the sixteenth century onward.[85] This was one of my favourite parts of the Anglican liturgy, which I grew up intoning every Sunday morning while sitting next to my mother in the oak pew at St. Philip's— third row from the front.

As a child, I found this prayer immensely comforting, and now even more so. It also seems perfectly emblematic of the transparency of choice in the context of our relationship to God, and illustrates so beautifully the deep truth of the art of choosing.

---

[84] My Salon on the Pelvic Lattice is available on my website www.yolandenorris-clark.com, and my program, "Lattice," on healing the pelvic lattice is forthcoming.

[85] Wikipedia. 2023. "The Cloud of Unknowing." *Wikipedia*, April. https://en.wikipedia.org/wiki/The_Cloud_of_Unknowing. I was thrilled to recently discover that The Collect for Purity was also published in The Cloud of Unknowing, which, according to Wikipedia, is "a spiritual guide on contemplative prayer in the Late Middle Ages...the underlying message [of which] suggests that the way to know God is to abandon consideration of God's particular activities and attributes, and be courageous enough to surrender one's mind and ego to the realm of "unknowing," at which point one may begin to glimpse the nature of God," which sounds very much in keeping with the message I am attempting to impart in this book.

Every aspect of who we are and what we love is open to God, from whom no secrets are hidden. We are always worthy, despite every desire—coherent or discordant—being fully known. What a relief.

You will remain in relationship with your child and with your birth experience (and each birth distinctly) for the rest of your life. Like any union or soul-contract, the tenor and tone of your affinity with birth may change drastically as you grow and mature, and the perception you have of your role, responsibility, and the part you played in the junctures, peaks, and hollows of the story of your child's arrival may change as well.

In the early, heady, milk-drunk days of your baby's life, you will likely ponder what transpired, perhaps even with a degree of ardour, or fixation. Was it everything you dreamed of, or hoped for? Was it orgasmic and blissful after all? Or was it blisteringly hard?

Maybe you adore every single part of it, unreservedly. Or you may feel a degree of ambivalence. You might already recognize that you made choices which were out of integrity, allowing for certain situations to occur that you now lament.

You may feel annoyed or bitter at having spent thirty bucks on a rambling book about portals and choices leading up to what was nonetheless the most painful experience of your life.

It could be that in spite of feeling fear and pain, you loved your birth so much that you can't wait to share your triumph and fulfillment with everyone in your circle.

But you might also feel confused, angry, or betrayed—by God, nature, your mother, your midwife, your partner, or yourself. You may feel reverberating elation.

You might possibly feel a strange sorrow that the thrill of birth has now passed into the archives of memory and lore.

As I have reinforced throughout this book, there is no way to fail at birth. There is no "wrong" way to give birth. There is no "bad" or truly inauthentic way to give birth.

There is no "easy out" in birth, either (except for choosing ease, which can feel insurmountably demanding until you do it, which can only happen at the appointed time, in the absence of force). There are only choices that take us here, or there.

However the experience of birth unfolded for you and your baby as you both made the journey, your chronicle is the correct one, because it happened the way it did. In the happening, and in your reflections on it, your responses to it, your feelings about it, and your willingness (or not) to hold it and examine it—like the glowing orb of insight that it is—you get to see what's true, if you want to.

Whether the feelings you have about your birth are conflicting or crystal clear, one of the most important, precious, and valuable assets in fully integrating birth and new motherhood postpartum, is the opportunity to tell your story. Ideally, this would occur in the context of true community.

I truly hope you are surrounded by sisters, aunts, cousins, and neighbours, who will, as Sister MorningStar says, "come running" to you, not only to cook and tidy up, and do your laundry, and serve you while you rest, and fall deeper in love with your baby, but also to sit at the foot of your bed, eager to listen to every detail of the tale of how your precious one came into the world, without judgement or opinion, only rapt attention and love.

If this kind of witnessing is woven into the warp of your life, you are very lucky. But if not, you can choose to view this dearth as a summoning: an invitation for you to create something new, and to draw out those women close to you who are similarly yearning for circles of support and beholding.

We are everywhere.

CODA

Birth has taught me that we all belong here, that God is real, that we are part of God, and that we are always in God's mercy, being held mercifully by Him.

You belong here, too, and you are always free to choose: your commitments, your beliefs, and your true desires.

Healing is an act of faith.

Birth is an act of love.

Life is an exquisite gift.

No matter your particular belief system or denomination, birth is the most lavish feast of love and tenderness available.

Birth is for melting into. Birth is *the* peak experience, not of striving, but of exquisite sensation.

It is sheer gorgeousness, and it is made for our thriving.

It is my conviction that the purpose of birth is to connect us to heaven.

Birth is the most psychedelic experience on earth.

It is the ultimate enigma—a map of the holy matrix.

And birth is yours to claim.

PORTAL

INTEGRATION QUESTIONS

1. Instead of anticipating depression after birth, how would it be if you anticipated bliss? What would change for you?

2. What do you suspect might be the costs—the challenges or even the downsides—to getting exactly the birth that you want?

3. What are some practices, activities, or ways of shifting the energy of fear that you can bring into postpartum as a way of integrating the expansion of your birth?

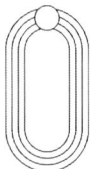

ACKNOWLEDGEMENTS

Had it not been for the support, challenge, existence, criticism, love, prodding, nurturing, and midwifing of the following individuals over the years, this book—and the version of myself that wrote it—would never have come to be. It is true that I couldn't—but most significantly, wouldn't—have done it without you. First, and always, I'm grateful to my family of origin, and all my ancestors, especially my mum and dad. Mum, you have never wavered for a moment in your conviction that I have a gift and a purpose, and everything I am is thanks to you. Funnily enough, the same is true about you, Dad. You would have been so proud of me (unbearably so). Thank you Gramps. You, in some ways more than anyone I've known, lived by the fundamental principles in *Portal* (and you would have had absolutely no interest in reading it, which would have been very funny and totally fine). Grandma, Granny, and Grandad, thank you for your fortitude, and your flaws, and for the stories of my lifeline. Unending thanks to my children for making me a mother, and for inspiring me in every way, at every moment. I love you all so much. Thank you Gloria, for your love, your wisdom, and your shining example. Thanks to all of my beloved birth-witnesses over the years: Wendy, Mandy, Cécile, Emily, Tegan, Katie, Eli, Danielle, Chantal, and Karen, Telka, and Joanna for your friendship way back when. Thank you to my many teachers: Sister MorningStar, Mrs. Drover, Brenda, Sharon, Ms. MacRae. Thank you to all the women who have invited me into their homes and their hearts, entrusting me with the honour and privilege of witnessing you as you courageously birthed your babies. You are all magnificent. Thank you to the people who have kept me and my family going as I pursued the hermitage necessary to complete this book: Karla, Brendaliz, Francys, Eliezer, Marie-Pier, and especially, Fernanda. Andrea, thank you for your coaching, your feedback, your conversation, and your friendship. Jenna Faye, your early support for the initial iterations of *Portal* were instrumental—thank you. To the women in the Bauhauswife Birth Circle community, thanks to all of you, for your boundless encouragement, your curiosity, your stories, and your sisterhood, especially Amanda, Emily, Lauren, Jessica, Cam, Isabel, Julie, Johanna, Krystal, Keirsten, everyone I'm missing, and all those of you who have stuck with me for so long. Thank you to all my midwifery students in the Radical Birth Keeper School. You give me so much hope in the future of humanity. Thank you to Christopher for your second-hand guidance on theological matters, and your indirect (but I know significant) peripheral support. Emilee: your relentless belief in me, your loving harassment, your ferocious friendship, your partnership, and your masterful leadership has changed my life. Thank you for dragging me into the fire, kicking and screaming. To my three Graces, Olivia, Sophia, Alicen—a dream-team. Let's do this again, but maybe with less drama (I promise). Alicen: You are magic. I am so grateful for your gentle midwifery, and your literary contribution to this project—and for the art you bestow upon the world. Olivia: Where to begin? Before you appeared in my life, I had no context for what it could feel like to be seen, anchored, managed, encouraged, beheld, and nurtured as an artist and a visionary in the way that you so lovingly, efficiently, and skillfully do. Your vision, guidance, patience, and encouragement are inimitable. You are such a gift to me, and every day I am grateful to have you at my right hand. Let's keep doing this. Sophia: You are brilliant. You are wonderful. You are an absolute gem. The time, energy, and sacrifice I know you have made to enable the birth of this book has been monumental—far above and beyond—all undertaken with immense kindness, forbearance, and good humour (not to mention inimitable precision). I don't take any of it lightly. Thank you. Finally, Lee: Thank you for telling me that it was worth it to keep going, and for being there for our beautiful children while I disappeared for months on end to bring this book to fruition. Thank you for tolerating me. Thank you for sitting there for hours in the dark after the babies were asleep, listening to every painstaking line. Thank you for our family. I love you.

And thank you to my many patrons over the years, especially to those of you who purchased the very first print edition of this book and to those who generously supported the first official publication run. I am deeply grateful. Along with the individuals who chose to remain anonymous, many thanks to: Ashley MG Anderson; Breanna Lohnes; Emily; Jessica Sherry Hoffmann; Taylor Storment; Ivy Royer; Annie; Dagmar Kleemiss; Fi Brown; Alicia Wilbur; Janine Heincker, Lightkeeper; Leila Forrest; Kristin; Chloé Pelletier Legros; Kath B; @elly.birthmagic; Tierza Hammond; Lindsay Robinson Crawshaw; Grace Vani; Sarah Epp; Jess DeMaster; Valerie Jakobsen; Erin Blank; Meghan Belgum; Iliana Elizabeth-Kay of Blossoming Wombs; Autumn Bailey; Katrina Holder; Lila Nicole Paillon; Frida Blackwell; Nina Nordin; Ana Aleksic; Saskia van Nieuwenhuyse; Britt; Lauren Aletheia; Etna; Kate Ekaitis; Yvonne Bucholtz; Nicole Schlögel; Monica; Megan Vincelett; Amanda; Jessica Epting - Sovrin Birth NYC; Evelyn Andersen; Erin Holmberg; Neleah Youngs; Ellah Ray; Bec Wild; Bobbie Sue; Tahnee Taylor; Aglaée Jacob; Gaby Machado Amaro; Clara; Carly Merz; Megan Tucholski; Sophia; Veronika Opela; Lea Dorothee Margarete; Kartmann; Dandilion Davenport; Teresa Haverkamp; Brittany Noelle Burke; Irene Armona Yoldi; Roxane de Sauvage; Victoria Trøster; Aubree Copling Barborka; Zara Domingues; Melissa; Dayman-Langen; Amy Abbott Pappageorge; Irina H. Fein; Sophia from Switzerland; Lori Dale Jaffe; Heather, fellow Mighty Mama; Ange Koutsofrigas; Lisa Kaiser; Jan M. Yanello; Caitlin Cole; Meagan Hamilton; Erika H Vernon; Kelsey Hutchison; Michelle Nixon; Danielle; Bourgi-Balsinde; Ana Cristina Leeson; Cher Westcott Hite; Simone Prangen; Julia Kovalchuk; H Hiebert; Lexi Sergio; Lisa June Mueller; Hannah Tabea; Autumn, mama of 7; Ripley; Jennifer S. Daley; Alison L.; Natalie Ollivier; Alexa H.; Maya Tatanka Butler; Mary-Ashley

Medeiros; Julia Stafford-West; Dr. Tyler Dierolf; Dr. Casey Baker; Laiken Kerr; Jenell Blickle; Raina Carpenter; Rachel Kirk; Laura the Wild of Dunster; Krystal; Megan Timmer; Amoraea O'Duir; Mariana; Annie Ubatuba; Madison Desjarlais; Carrie Jordan Barad; Leora Joy Perrie; Desirée Gabrielle; Lujain; Heather Sassine; Sabha; Sego, Luke & Leon; Karien; Ulrika Winbäck; Hrachouhi; Zakaryan; Anne Rowley; Renée Curry; Javiera; Kathleen Murry; Olivia O'Callaghan; Kiana Muhs; Sarah Holroyd Hill; Cadence Feeley; Tracey Creed-Crowhurst; Martina Psovska; Marilyn; Nancy A. Randazzo Abdul-Sater; Tiffany Toulouse; Rosa Makstadt; Julia Iserman; Jacklyn; Denise McCann; Cale Camuzzi; Dr. Jasmine Schaeffer; Lauren V.; Kirby-Lee Cormier; Bronagh Waters; Megan Cluff; Platypus Dreaming; Katharina Achhammer; Leland Stillman, MD; kori meloy; Rachel Crimmins; Christine Beckmann;Julia Tourianski; Ange Koutsofrigas; Vicki DiIoia; Michelle Warwick; Jess Edgar; Jess DeMaster; Priyanka V Rabadi; Deborah Graham; Simone Phippen; Sashah Abbott; Brooke Lustig; Sarah Heidvogel; Fanika Jenni-Austin; Andrea Clifford; Jacklyn Denise McCann; Katrina Holder; Brittany Rojo, DC, CACCP; Ren; Zara Domingues; Ashley Johnson; Chantal Molenaar; Nancy Guo; Taylor Adler; Hannah Barber; Vanessa Lees; Alexandra Hughes; Randi Finn; Vayla Sonderegger; Sarah Sabin-Mickelsen; Marta Villadóniga; Martín; Mina Sarenac; Jhulan Purnima; Caroline Traynor; Tara Antonakos; Louise Graham; Melissa Thielmann; Haley Wise; Renee Dresser; Erika Conrad; Lydia Harris; Katie Wilkerson; Mahalia Mermaid; Katherine Niven; Christine Milentis; Rebecca Cohen; Jenny Bredeken; Kate Schuerman; Dr Twink Lim; Victoria Brown; Malavika Kundu; Sara Cousineau; Griebel Agapi; Alliance Foundation; Jenna Doris Weaver; Carmen Moreno; Ashli Bain; Carita Kristiina Harju; Victoria J; Rachel Crimmins; Michelle Santiano; Jenny-Lee Masterson; Ieva Svētiņa; Ali Coulas; Helen; Larissa Wuollet; Katelyn Broad; Lizzie Lane; Anne Roose-van Leeuwen; Griebel Agapi Alliance Foundation; Chantal Vienna Molenaar; Eugenia C; Kendra; Moraea; Christina Armstead; Mina Milosavljević - iz srca majke Srbije, za našu decu

Svetlosti; Denise Smith, and Heather, for cheerfully loading five boxes of books into your car and sending them off that morning in Hayesville.

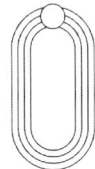

ADDITIONAL RESOURCES

For additional resources and audio meditations related to Portal (and to further integrate this material), please visit Yolande's websites at:

https://www.yolandenorris-clark.com

https://www.yncshop.com

There you will also find:

A *free* guided audio: The Breath

A hypnosis Revision meditation

A guided Pain Dissolution meditation

and

The "Freebirth in Contrast" bundle, which includes Yolande's 8th and 9th birth documentaries that she refers to in the book

PORTAL

You are warmly invited to explore Yolande's signature online program, PORTAL: The Blissful Birth Code, which is highly complementary to this book, and expands upon the central concepts shared herein.

https://www.yolandenorris-clark.com/portal-live

Stay Connected With Yolande and Check out Her Other Offerings:

Subscribe to Yolande's Email List and receive her *free* acclaimed Pregnancy Affirmations mp3: https://www.yolandenorris-clark.com/pregnancy-affirmations

Substack: https://yolandenorrisclark.substack.com/

Free Birth in Bliss Free Workshop: https://www.yolandenorris-clark.com/birth-in-bliss

The Bauhauswife Community: https://www.yolandenorris-clark.com/birthcircle

HYGEIA: https://www.yolandenorris-clark.com/hygeia

The Complete Guide to Freebirth: https://www.freebirthsocietycourses.com/cgtf

Through The Veil: https://www.freebirthsocietycourses.com/throughtheveil

The Radical Birth Keeper School: https://www.radicalbirthkeeperschool.com/

The MatriBirth Midwifery Institute: https://www.freebirthsociety.com/mmi

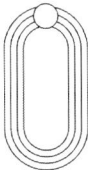

ABOUT THE AUTHOR

Yolande Norris-Clark was born in Vancouver, BC, in 1981. A leader and pioneer in the birth sovereignty and health liberation movements, Yolande is a spell-breaker, way-shower, whistle-blower, trailblazer, and beloved guide to women all over the world who are awakening to the possibility of giving birth in peace and power. For over twenty years, she has been immersed in the world of holistic, physiological, primal birth, and has supported thousands of mothers and families virtually as a birth consultant and coach, in-person as a birth-witness, and through her online programs, writing, and midwifery education. Yolande's mission is to dispel the myth that birth is an ordeal from which women must be "delivered," and to share the truth that birth as a spiritual, transformational, transcendent experience is possible for every mother and child. The mother of ten children, Yolande has given birth to all of her babies at home. She lives in Nicaragua with her husband and their eight youngest kids.

Made in United States
North Haven, CT
18 May 2025

68578969R10247